Film Cameras of the 1900s

By Gabriel F. Gargiulo

Copyright 2024 Gabriel F. Gargiulo

Table of Contents

Introduction	**5**
Agfa PD16 Clipper	**6**
Agfa Solinette	**8**
Argus 75	**10**
Argus C3	**12**
Argus C4	**14**
Canon AE-1	**16**
Canon ELPH LT 260	**18**
Ciroflex Model B	**20**
EXA	**22**
Fujica 35 FS	**24**
Keystone Model K - 8	**26**
Kodak 35	**28**
Kodak Advantix F350	**30**
Kodak Brownie 2A Model C	**32**
Kodak Brownie Reflex Synchro	**34**
Kodak # 2 Cartridge Hawk-Eye Model C	**36**
Kodak Instamatic M4	**38**
Kodak Instamatic M18	**40**
Kodak Instamatic X-35	**42**
Kodak Medalist VR35 Model K14	**44**
Kodak Pony 135 Model C	**46**
Kodak Retinette	**48**
Kodak S400SL	**50**
Kodak Signet 35	**52**
Kodak Six-16	**54**
Kodak Vigilant 6-20	**56**
Kodak 1A Pocket Kodak	**58**
Mamiya 35 S2	**60**

Table of Contents

Mamiya Ruby	62
Minolta 16 EE II	64
Minolta 16 MG-S	66
Minolta AF-Tele	68
Minolta Autopak 700	70
Minolta Maxxum 50	72
Minolta XG-A	74
Miranda DX3	76
Nikon L35 AD2	78
Nikon Light Touch Zoom 120ED	80
Nikon N6006	82
Olympus 35 SP	84
Olympus Infinity Stylus	86
Olympus Infinity Twin	88
Olympus Infinity Zoom 2000	90
Olympus OM 10	92
Olympus Trip 35	94
Pentax K1000	96
Pentax ME - Super	98
Pentax ZX-30	100
Polaroid 230	102
Polaroid Highlander, Model 80A	104
Practica FX	106
Revere Eight Model Seventy-Seven	108
Ricoh 500	110
Spartus	112
Voigtländer Brillant	114
Welmy 35	116
Yashica Mat-124G	118
Index	120

Introduction

This book contains descriptions and pictures of 57 film cameras that were made in, or were popular in the 1900s. I own all the cameras, and I took all the pictures.

I wrote this book to preserve the memories of these cameras. I went digital in 2001, and fully digital in 2016. I collect and keep my film cameras to keep my memories alive, and for future generations, specifically, my sons and grandsons.

I have tried to include accurate information for these cameras, however it's possible that some of the information is not right. cameras

There is a renewal of interest in film photography. I'm sure some of it is nostalgia, but a large part of this interest must be because film photography is fun. There is a challenge in taking a photo and having to wait one or two weeks to see how it comes out. You need to take control of the exposure and other aspects of the process. You understand better what goes on in a camera, digital or otherwise.

One of my first jobs was at a photo processing lab. Perhaps I was the one who developed and printed your vacation photos! I used to develop, print and enlarge photos at home. I stopped many decades ago, but remember every aspect of the process, especially the fascination at the image appearing on film or paper under the safelight. I just might get back into it if I find a camera club in the area with an interest in all aspects of film photography, and a suitable darkroom with a sink, and temperature-controlled water.

One of the questions many people have is "How much is my camera worth?" It is worth the amount that someone is willing to pay you for it. Condition and rarity are the major factors here! Check on Ebay. Follow a few sales. Check out the price of a mint condition Leica I! Then check the price of an Argus C3.

Thank you Ellen Wilde for reminding me and nudging me to write this book. I wouldn't have written it without your encouragement.

Thanks to my dad for introducing me to photography, and to my mom for putting up with the smelly chemicals in her baking pans.

I hope you enjoy the book. It was a pleasure writing it.

Gabe Gargiulo
Hartford CT

Agfa PD16 Clipper

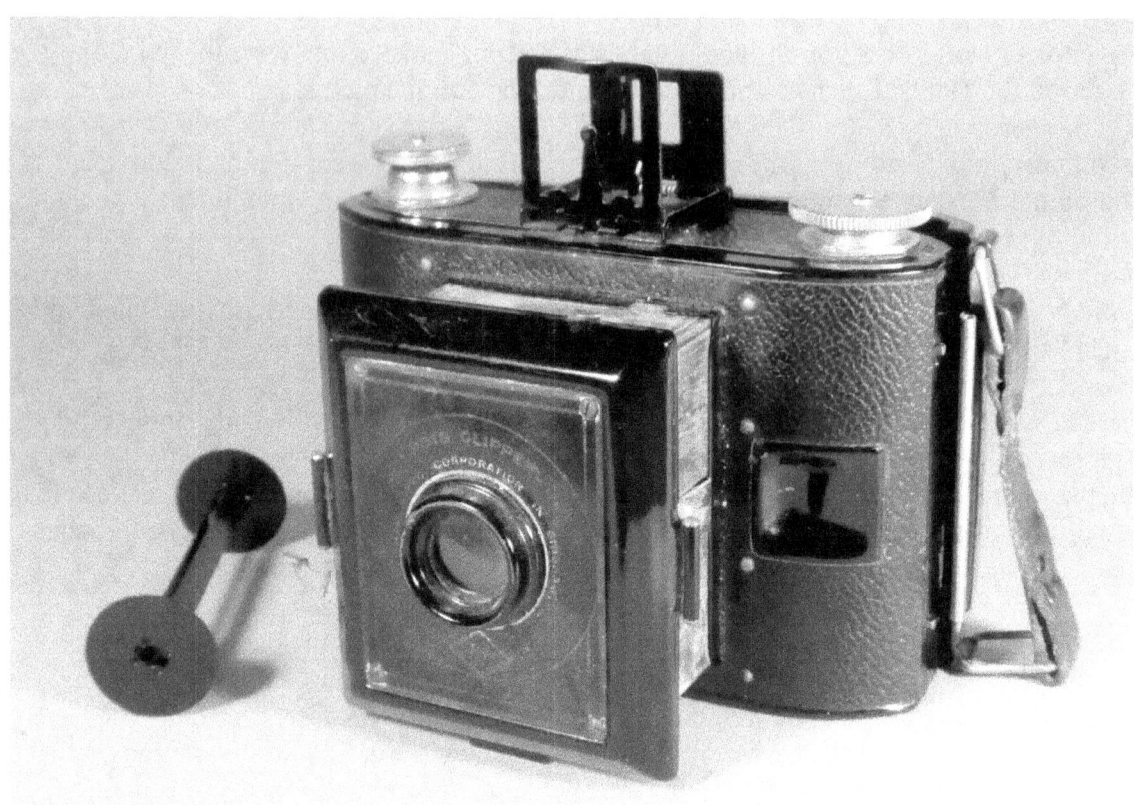

Name: Agfa PD16 Clipper.
Type: Rollfilm.
Film Size: 616.
Year of manufacture: 1928.
Manufacturer: Agfa Ansco Corp.
Country: USA
Shutter settings: B and fixed shutter speed (1/60). Pull out small tab over lens for B. (On right side of lens mount in above picture.)
Aperture settings: Fixed aperture.
Exposure setting: Manual.
Lens:
Interchangeable lenses? No.
How do you focus? Fixed focus.
Viewfinder: Eye level.
Loading film: Open back, insert full roll, thread paper leader onto takeup spool.
Automatic film advance? No (manual).
Automatic film rewind? N/A.
Cable release socket: No.
Tripod socket: No.
Battery type: None.
Unique features: To extend lens, pull lens mount.

Agfa PD16 Clipper

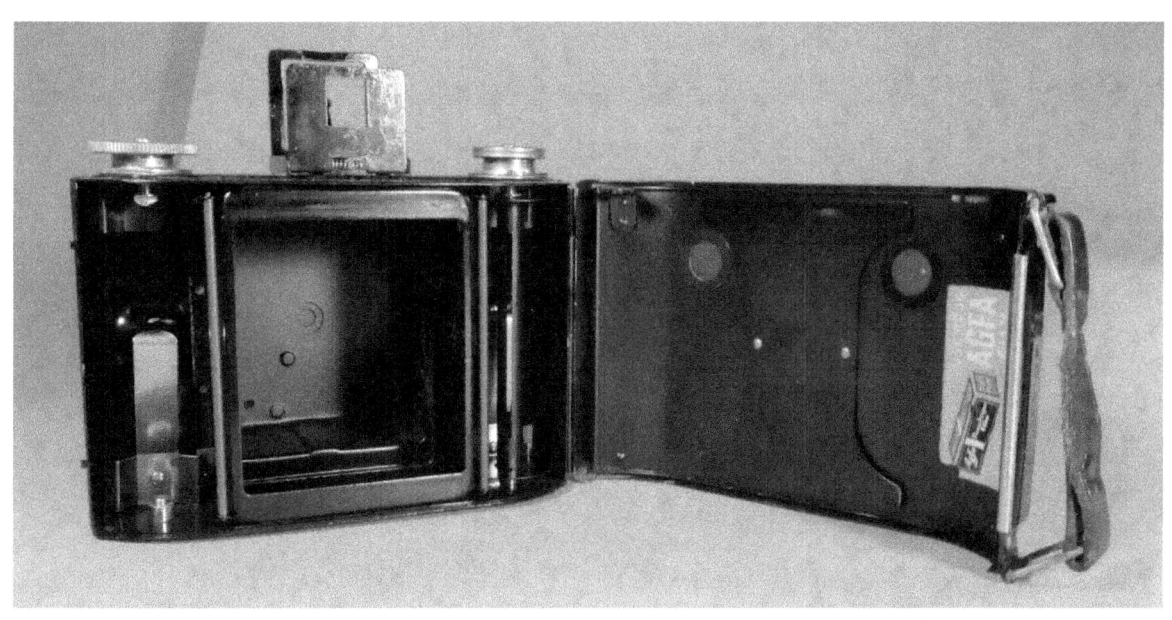

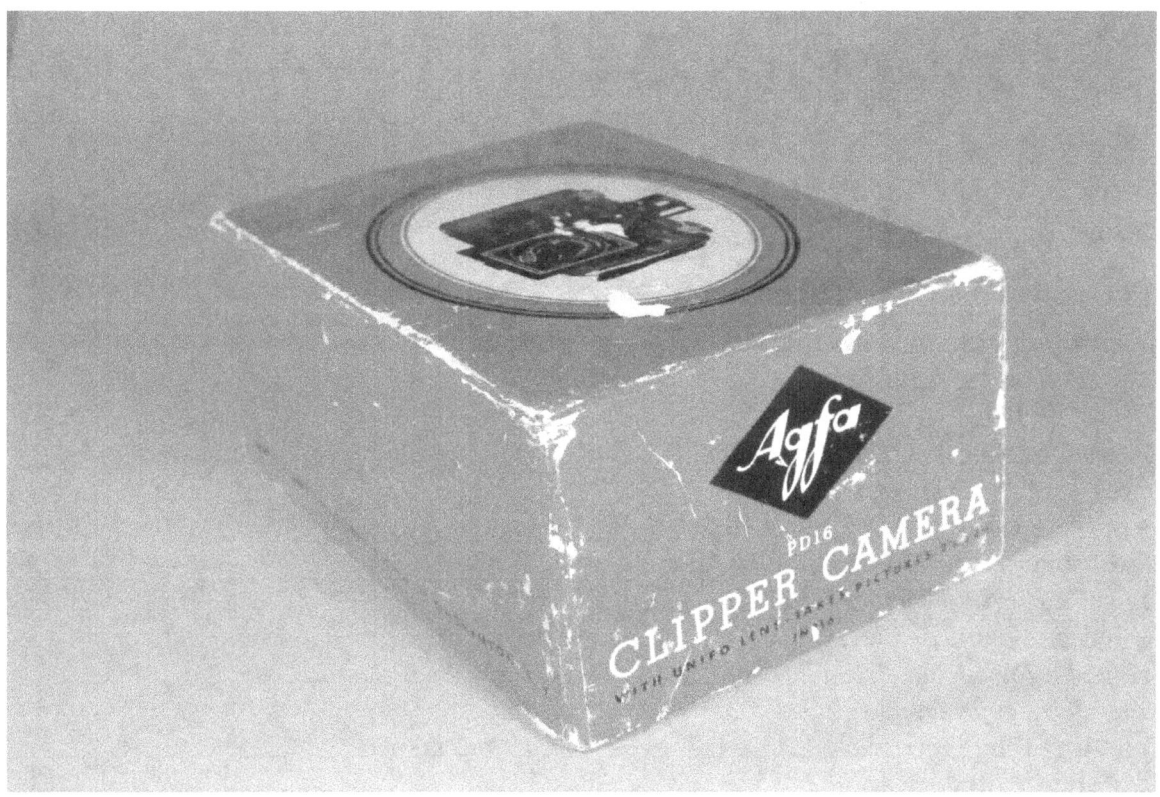

Agfa Solinette

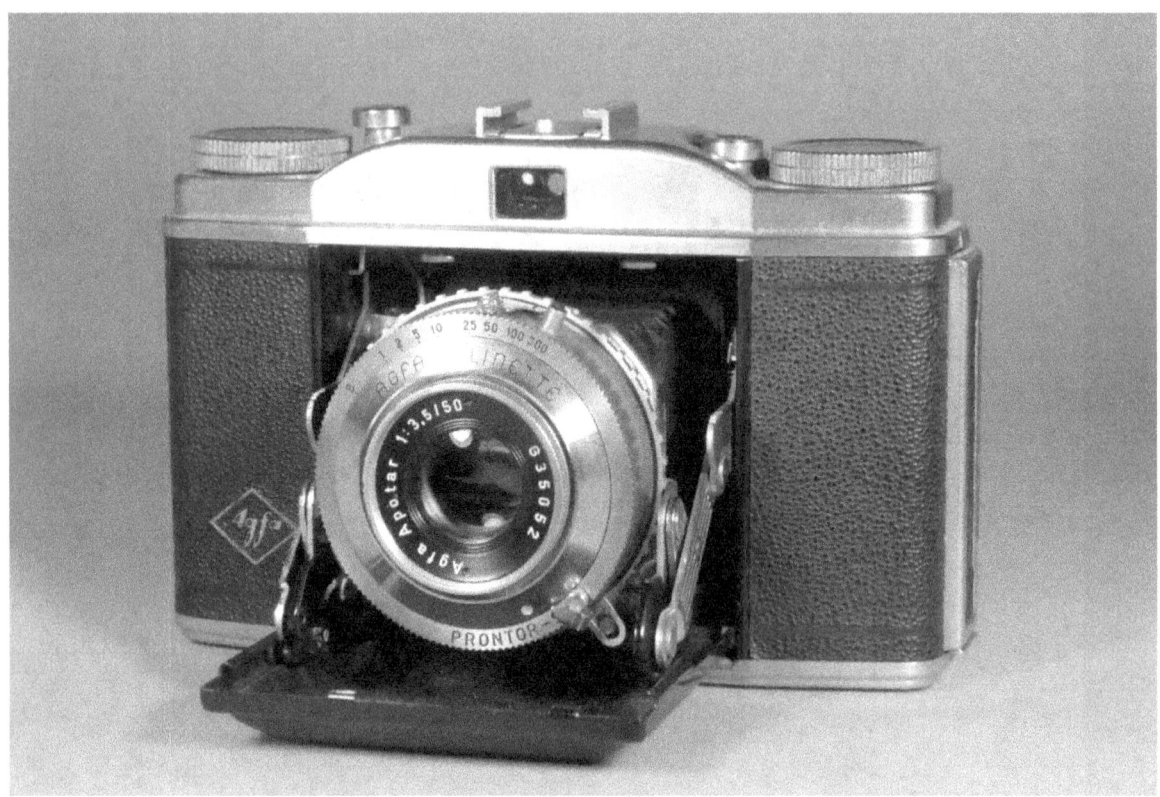

Name: Agfa Solinette.
Type: Folding 35MM.
Film Size: 35MM.
Year of manufacture: 1954.
Manufacturer: Agfa/Ansco.
Country: USA.
Shutter settings: B, 1 second - 1/300.
Cock shutter before each shot.
Aperture settings: F/3.5 - F/22.
Exposure setting: Manual.
Lens: Agfa Apotar F/3.5 50MM.
Interchangeable lenses? No.
How do you focus? Estimate distance, turn lens element.
Viewfinder: Eyelevel.
Loading film: Open back, load full cassette, thread into takeup reel.
Automatic film advance? No.
Automatic film rewind? No.
Cable release socket: Yes.
Tripod socket: Yes.
Battery type: None.
Unique features:
Double exposure prevention.

Agfa Solinette

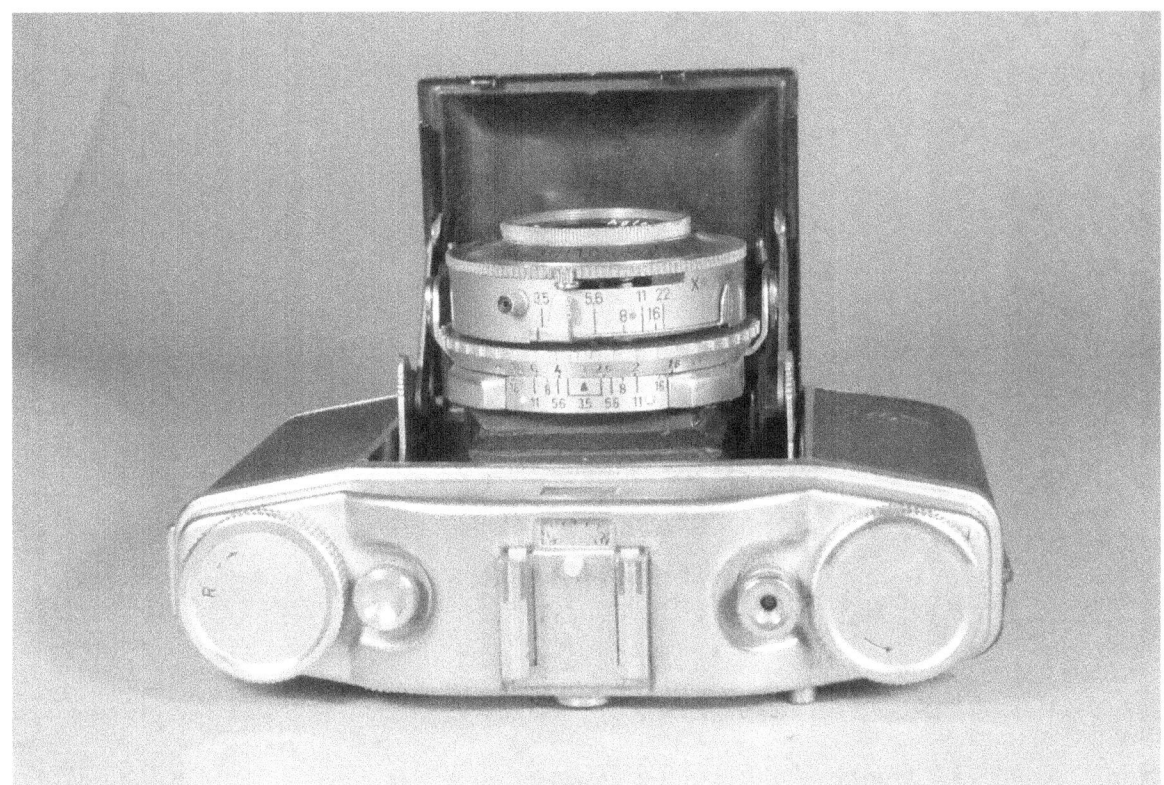

Shutter cocking lever on lens, top, front. X/M flash sync lever on lens, top, right. Exposure counter on top of camera, center.

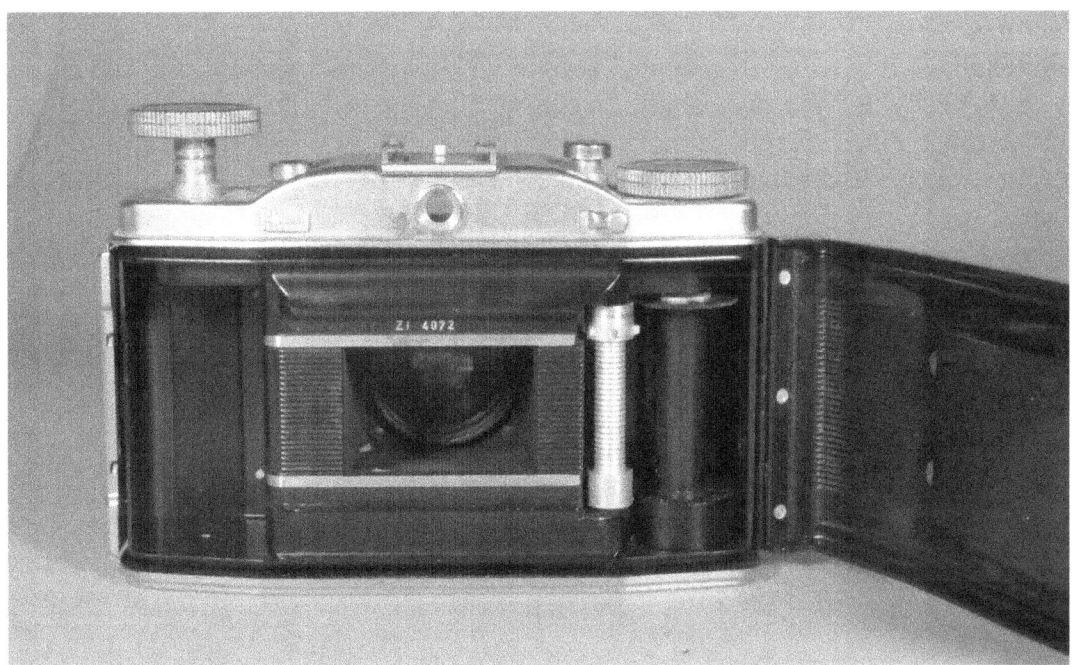

Locking button, with arrow, on back, top left. Allows changing exposure counter. Rewind lever on back, top right. Push left to allow rewinding.

Argus 75

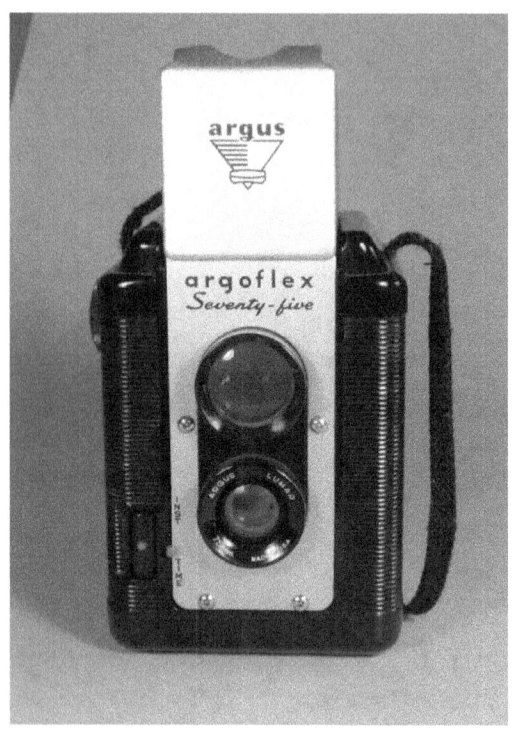

Name: Argus 75. (Argoflex 75).
Type: Twin lens reflex. Rollfilm.
Film Size: 620.
Year of manufacture: Around 1960.
Manufacturer: Argus.
Country: USA.
Shutter settings: T and I – instantaneous. Fixed shutter speed.
Aperture settings: Fixed aperture, around F/11.
Exposure setting: No user control over exposure.
Lens: Lumar 75MM.
Interchangeable lenses? No.
How do you focus? Fixed focus.
Viewfinder: Waist level.
Loading film: Open back, insert full roll, thread paper leader onto takeup spool.
Automatic film advance? No (manual).
Automatic film rewind? N/A.
Cable release socket: No.
Tripod socket: Yes.
Battery type: None.
Unique features: Double exposure prevention.

Argus 75

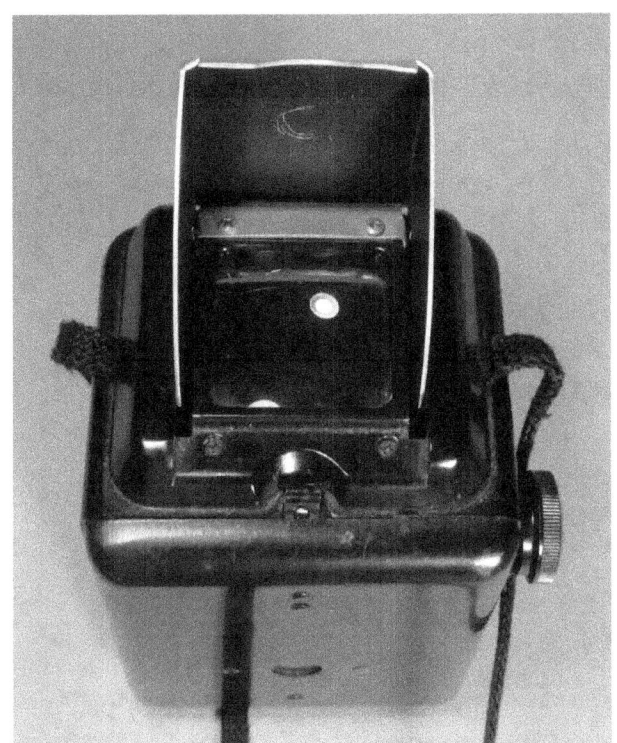

Argus C3

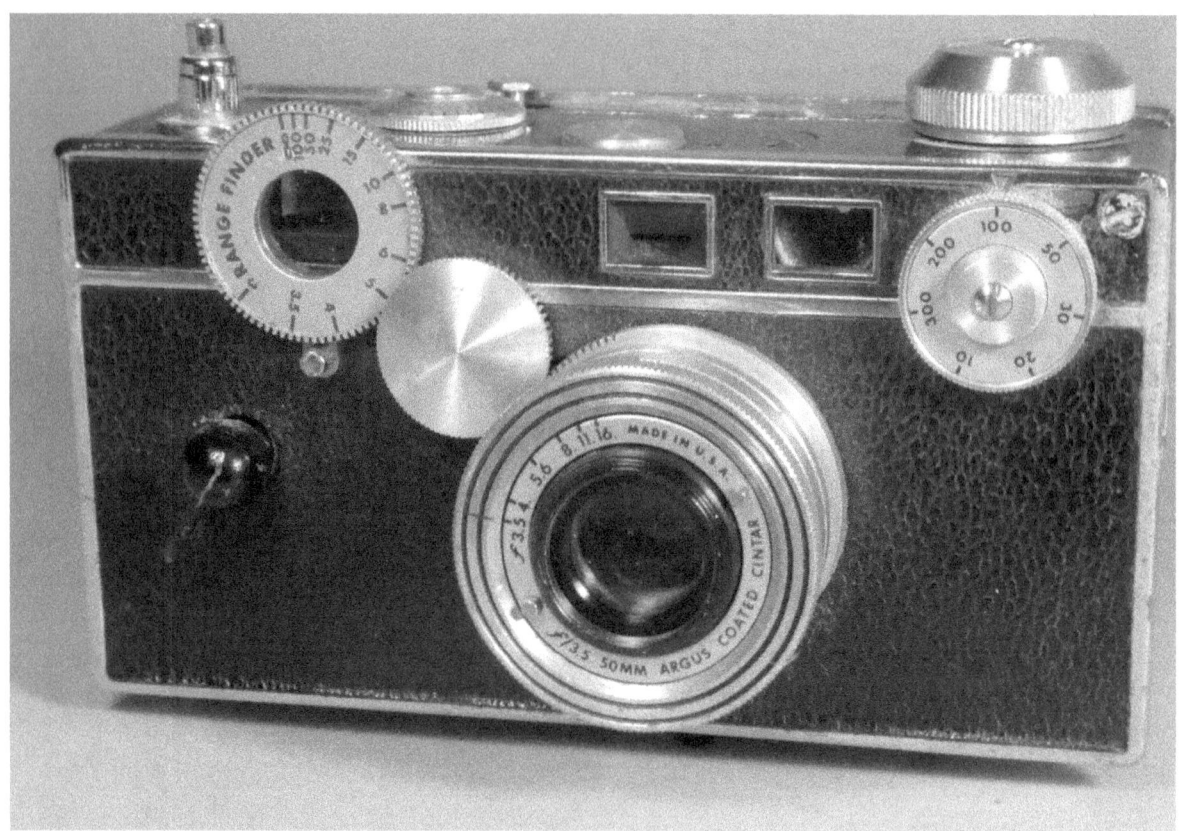

Name: Argus C3.
Type: Rangefinder 35MM.
Film Size: 35MM.
Year of manufacture: 1939 - 1956.
Manufacturer: Argus.
Country: USA.
Shutter settings: 1/10 – 1/300.
Cock shutter before each shot.
Aperture settings: F/3.5 – F/16.
Exposure setting: Manual.
Lens: Cintar 50MM F/3.5.
Interchangeable lenses? Yes.
How do you focus? Coupled rangefinder.
Viewfinder: Eye level.
Loading film: Open back, load full cassette, thread into takeup reel.
Automatic film advance? No (manual).
Automatic film rewind? No (manual).
Cable release socket: Yes.
Tripod socket: Yes.
Battery type: None.
Unique features:

Argus C3

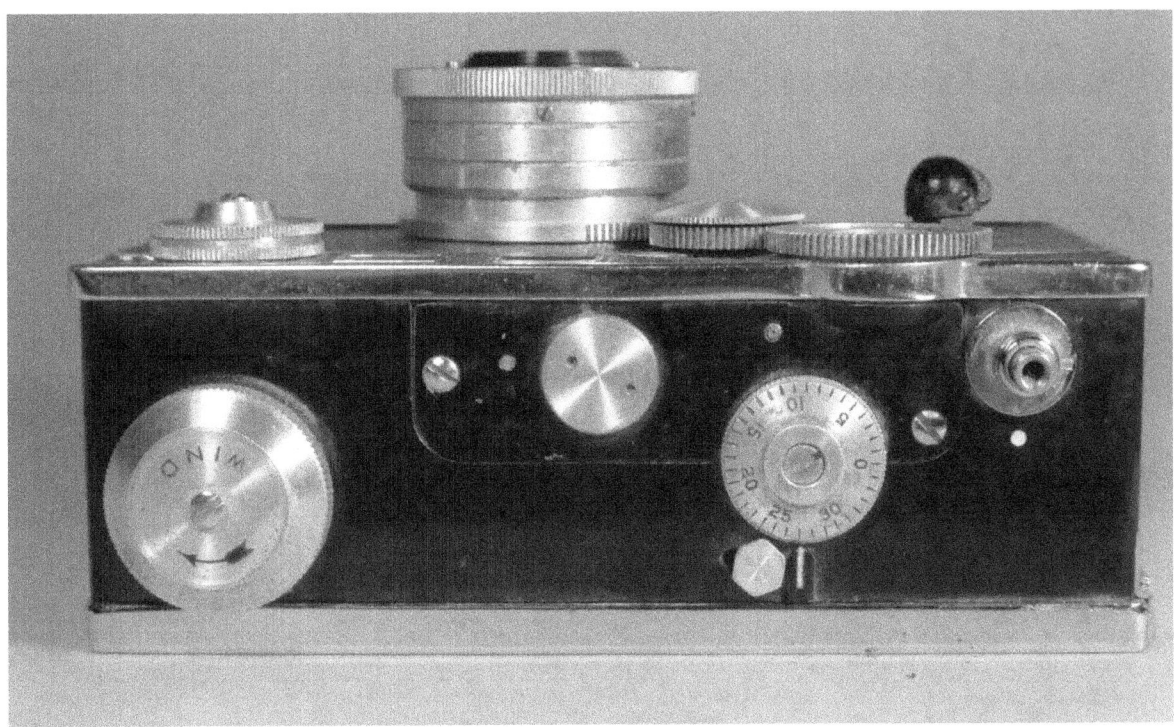

Shutter cocking lever is on right, at top of picture. Film catch lever is under exposure counter. You hold it down, for a quarter of a turn, to wind the film for the next exposure.

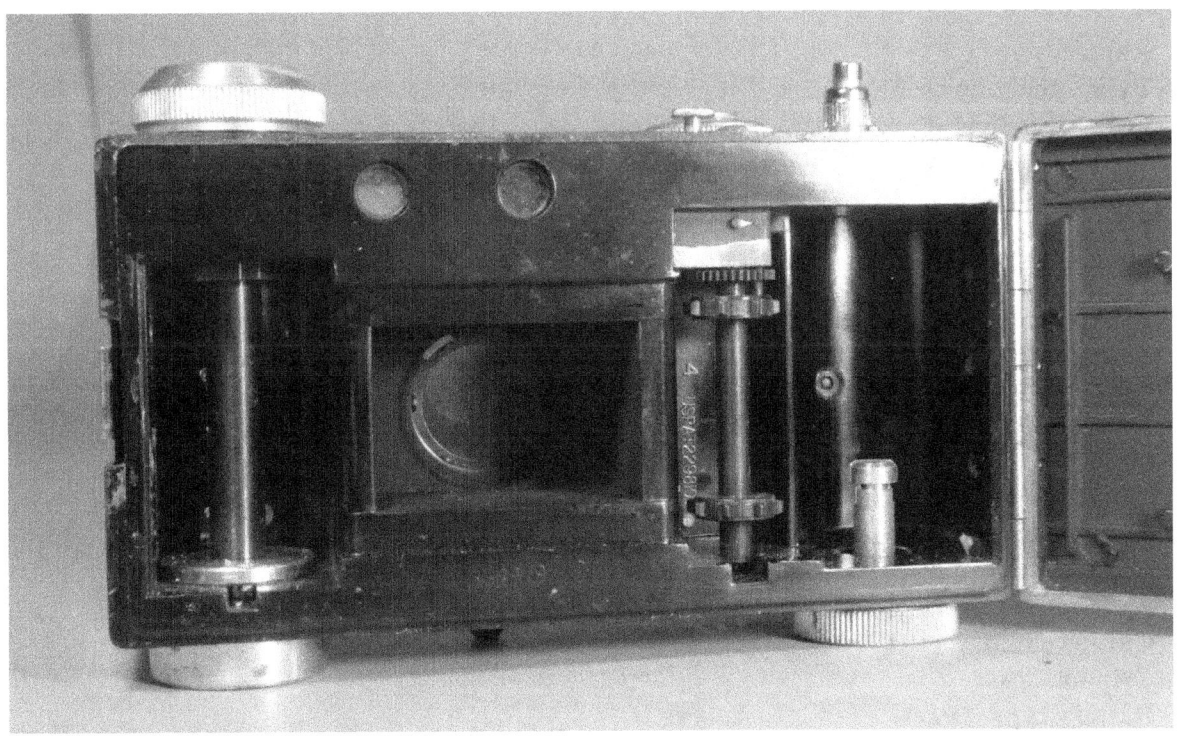

Argus C4

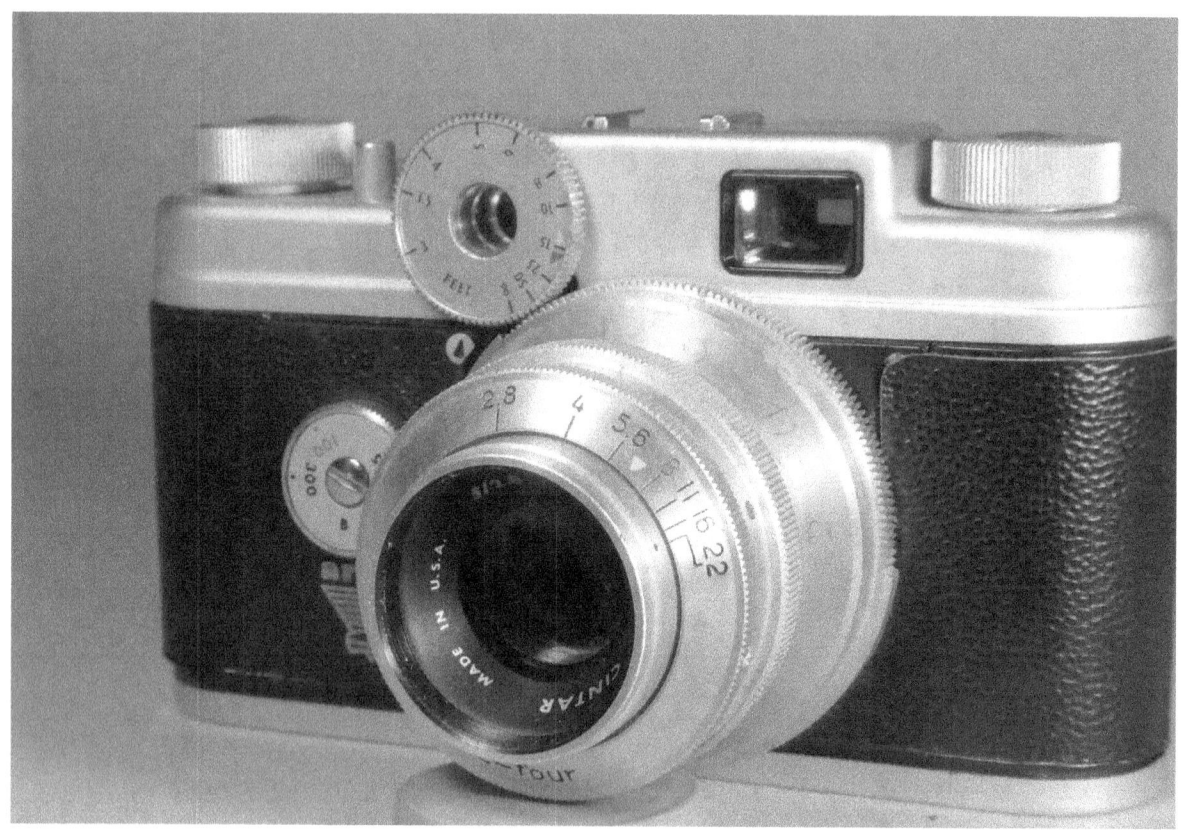

Name: Argus C4.
Type: Rangefinder 35MM.
Film Size: 35MM.
Year of manufacture: 1951 - 1958.
Manufacturer: Argus.
Country: USA.
Shutter settings: B, 1/10 – 1/300.
Aperture settings: F/2.8 – F/22.
Exposure setting: Manual.
Lens: Cintar 50MM F/2.8.
Interchangeable lenses? No.
How do you focus? Coupled rangefinder.
Viewfinder: Eye level.
Loading film: Open back, load full cassette, thread into takeup reel.
Automatic film advance? No (manual).
Automatic film rewind? No (manual).
Cable release socket: Yes.
Tripod socket: Yes.
Battery type: None.
Unique features:

Argus C4

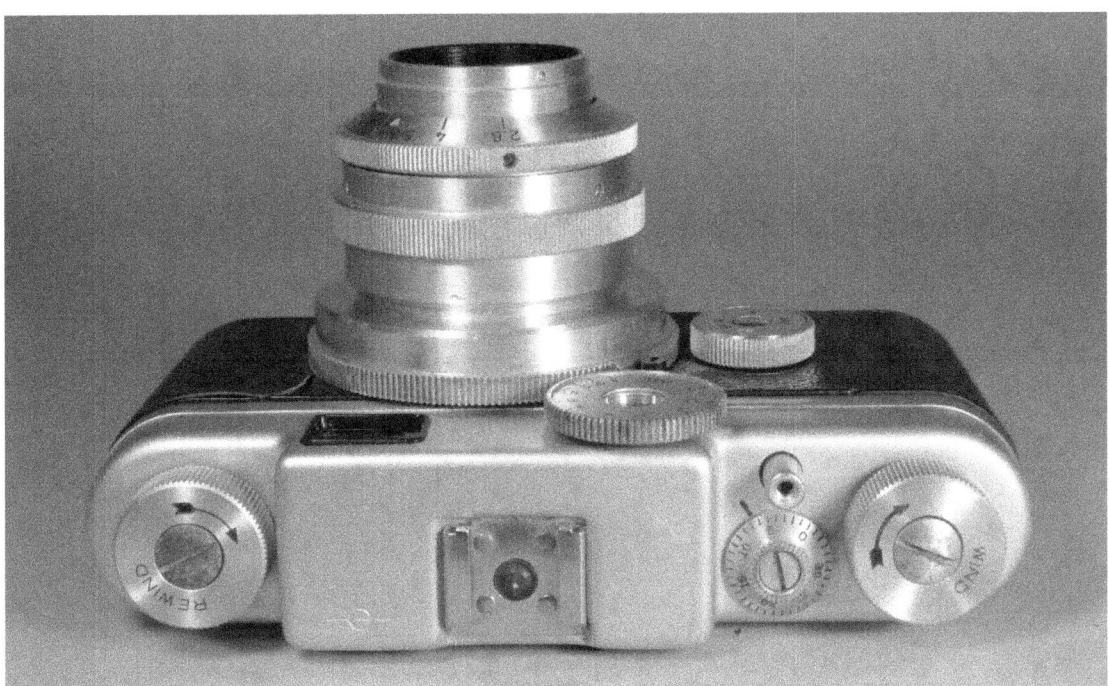

The film plane marker is shown between the rewind knob and the accessory shoe.

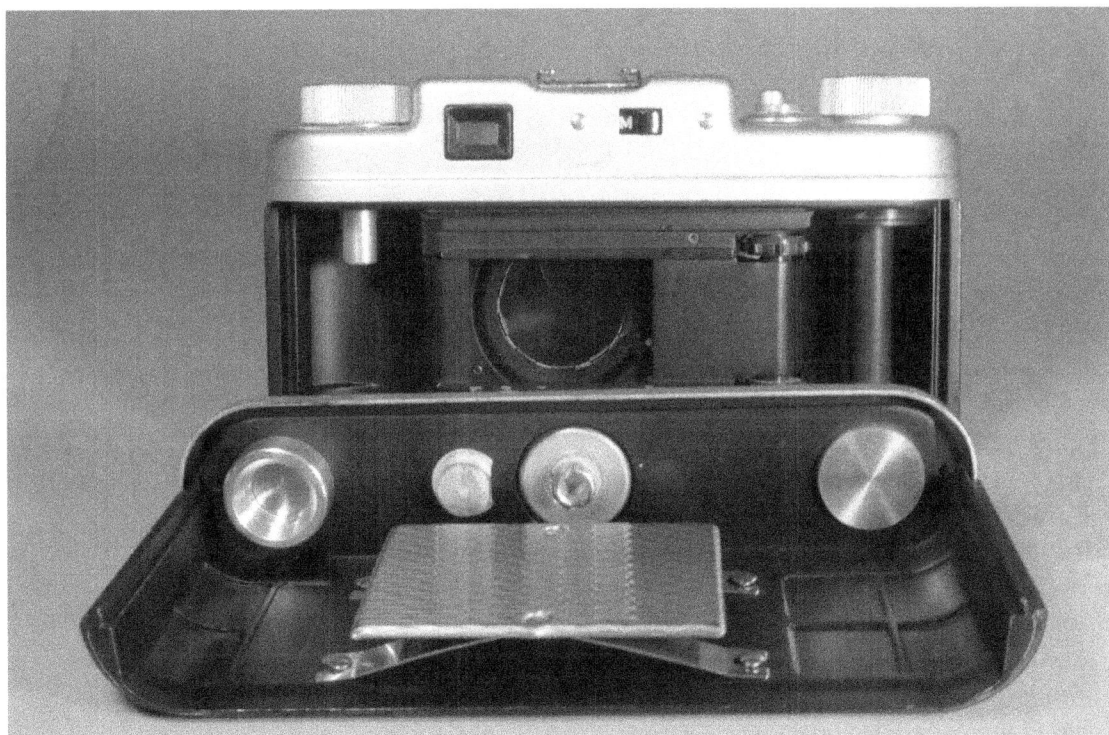

The flash sync lever is on the back of the camera, top, center. You choose M or X sync for flash. M for flashbulbs, X for electronic flash.

Canon AE-1

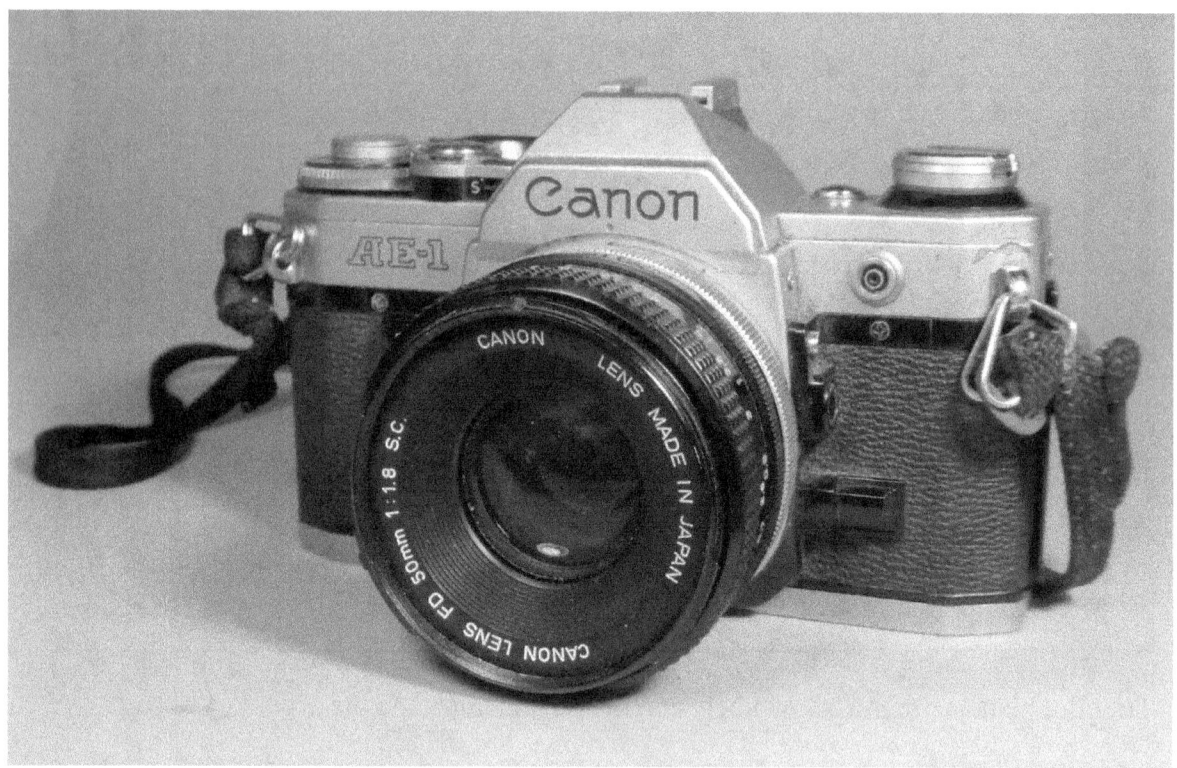

Name: Canon AE-1
Type: SLR 35MM.
Film Size: 35MM.
Year of manufacture: Around 1980.
Manufacturer: Canon.
Country: Japan
Shutter settings: B, 1/10 – 1/300.
Aperture settings: B, 2 seconds – 1/1000.
Exposure setting: Manual or shutter priority automatic metered exposure.
Lens: Canon 50MM F/1.8.
Interchangeable lenses? Yes.
How do you focus? Ground glass, split image.
Viewfinder: Eye level.
Loading film: Open back, load full cassette, thread into takeup reel.
Automatic film advance? No (manual). Power winder available.
Automatic film rewind? No (manual).
Cable release socket: Yes.
Tripod socket: Yes.
Battery type: 6V silver oxide. Eveready 544, Mallory PX28,
    Eveready 537, Mallory 7K34. Shutter does not function without battery.
Unique features:

Canon AE-1

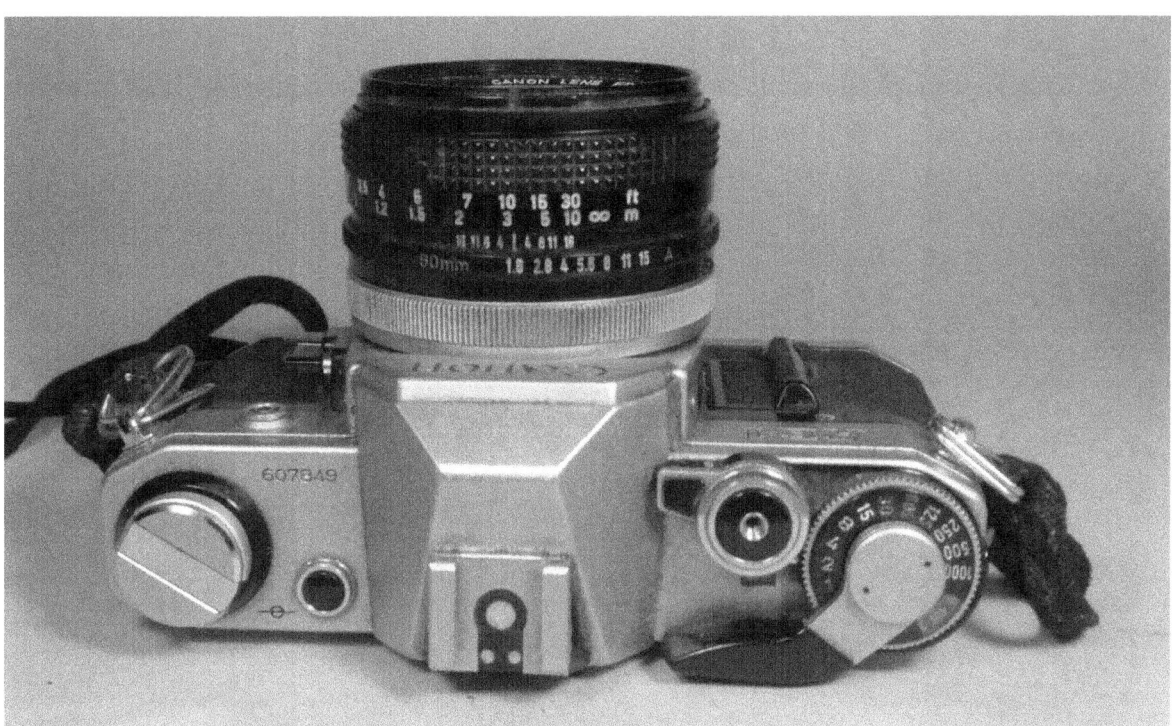

The film plane marker is shown between the rewind knob and the accessory shoe. The battery check button is next to that. Shutter release is on right, next to film rewind lever. The self-timer lever is right next to shutter release.

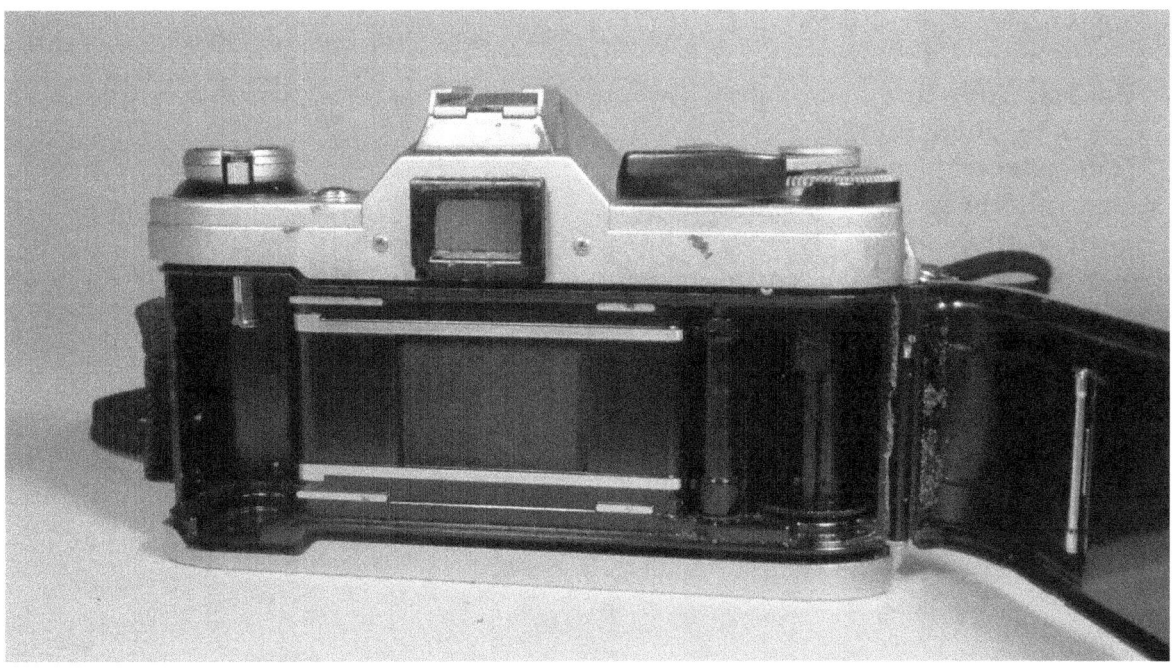

Canon ELPH LT 260

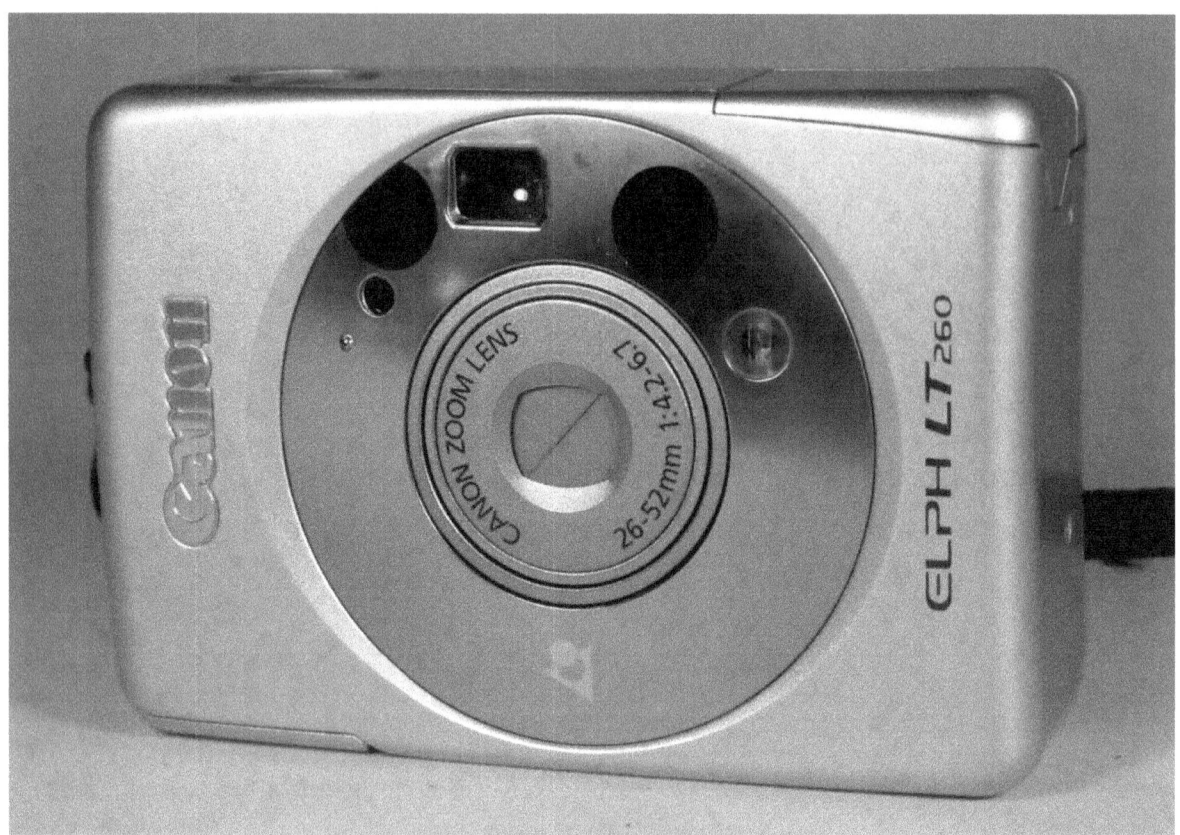

Name: Canon ELPH LT 260.
Type: Advanced Photo System.
Film Size: APS.
Year of manufacture: 2000.
Manufacturer: Canon.
Country: Taiwan.
Shutter settings: No user control.
Aperture settings: No user control.
Exposure setting: Automatic.
Lens: 26 - 52MM, F/1.4-F/6.7.
Interchangeable lenses? No.
How do you focus? Autofocus.
Viewfinder: Eyelevel.
Loading film: APS film cartridge. Open cover, insert film cartridge.
Automatic film advance? Yes.
Automatic film rewind? N/A.
Cable release socket: No.
Tripod socket: Yes.
Battery type: CR2.
Unique features: 2X zoom and retractable flash. Date and print info can be recorded on film.

Canon ELPH LT 260

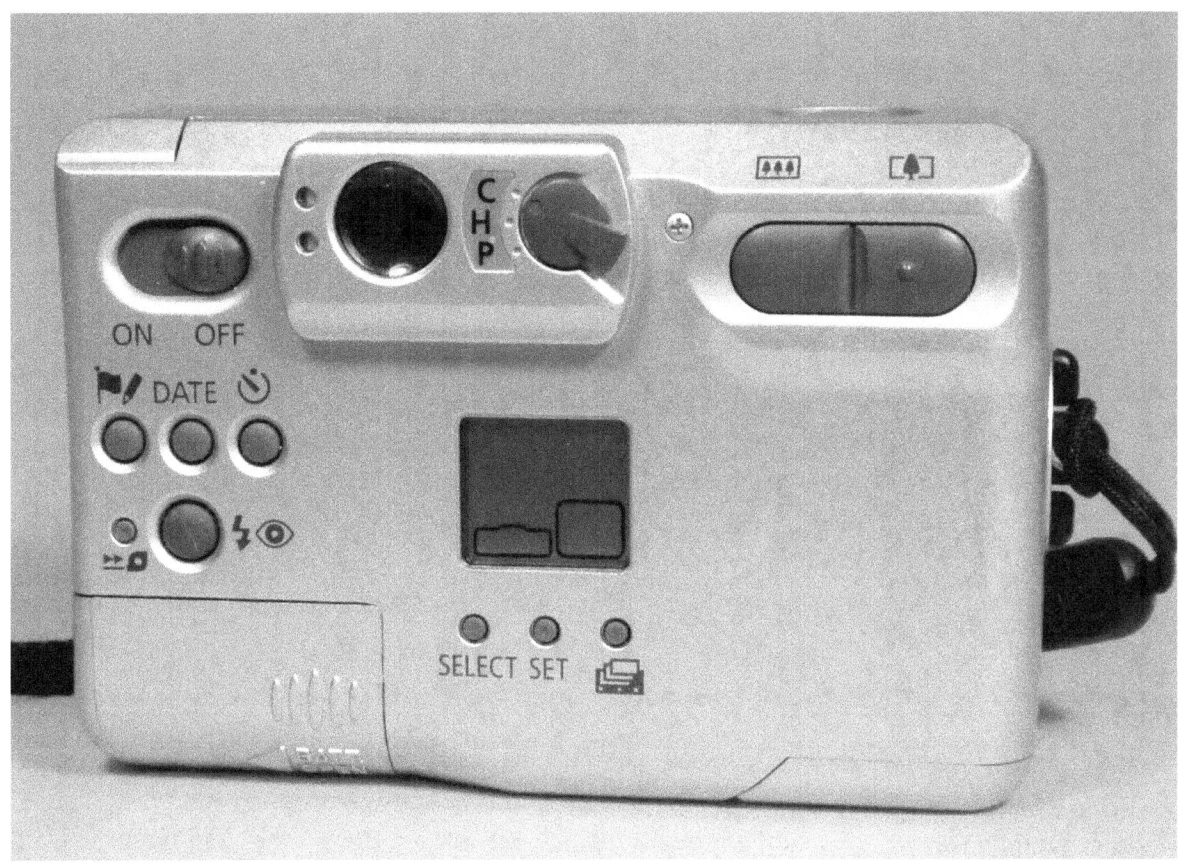

CHP lever is for print type selection. C = 24/36. H=24/42, P = panoramic 24/72.
Control with flag is for imprinting titles on film.
Controls in center of camera are for setting print quantity.

Ciroflex Model B

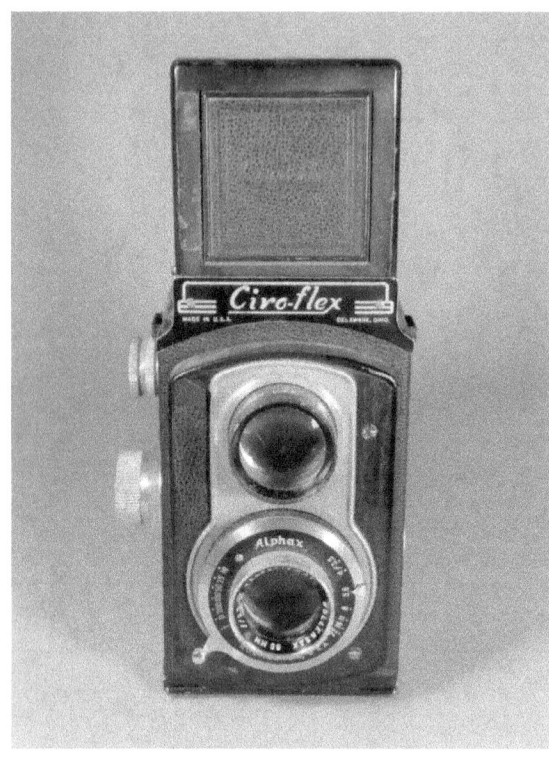

Name: Ciroflex. Probably Model B.
Type: Twin lens reflex, rollfilm.
Film Size: 120.
Year of manufacture:
Manufacturer: Ciroflex.
Country: USA.
Shutter settings: T, B, 1/10 - 1/200.
Aperture settings: F/3.5 – F/22.
Exposure setting: Manual.
Lens: Velostigmat, 85MM.
Interchangeable lenses? No.
How do you focus? Knob on right with distance scale. Ground glass with magnifier.
Viewfinder: Waist level.
Loading film: Open back, insert full roll, thread paper leader onto takeup spool.
Automatic film advance? No (manual).
Automatic film rewind? N/A.
Cable release socket: Yes.
Tripod socket: Yes.
Battery type: None.
Unique features:

Ciroflex Model B

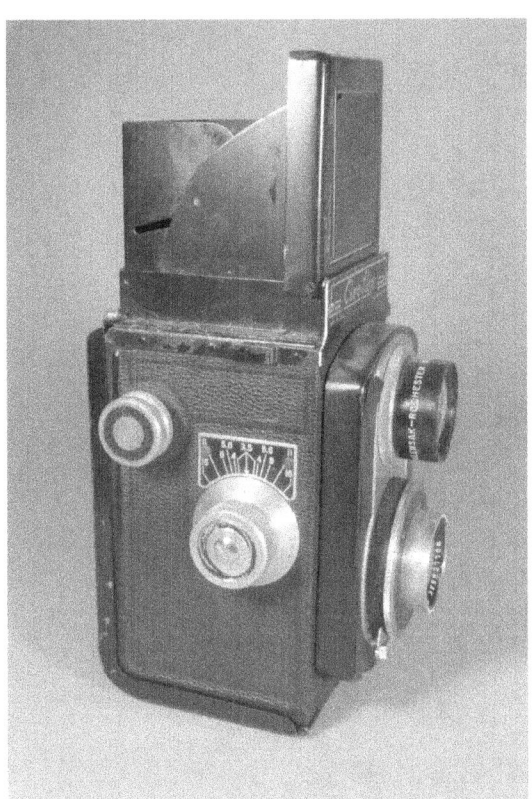

Distance scale on focusing knob. Depth of focus scale over it.

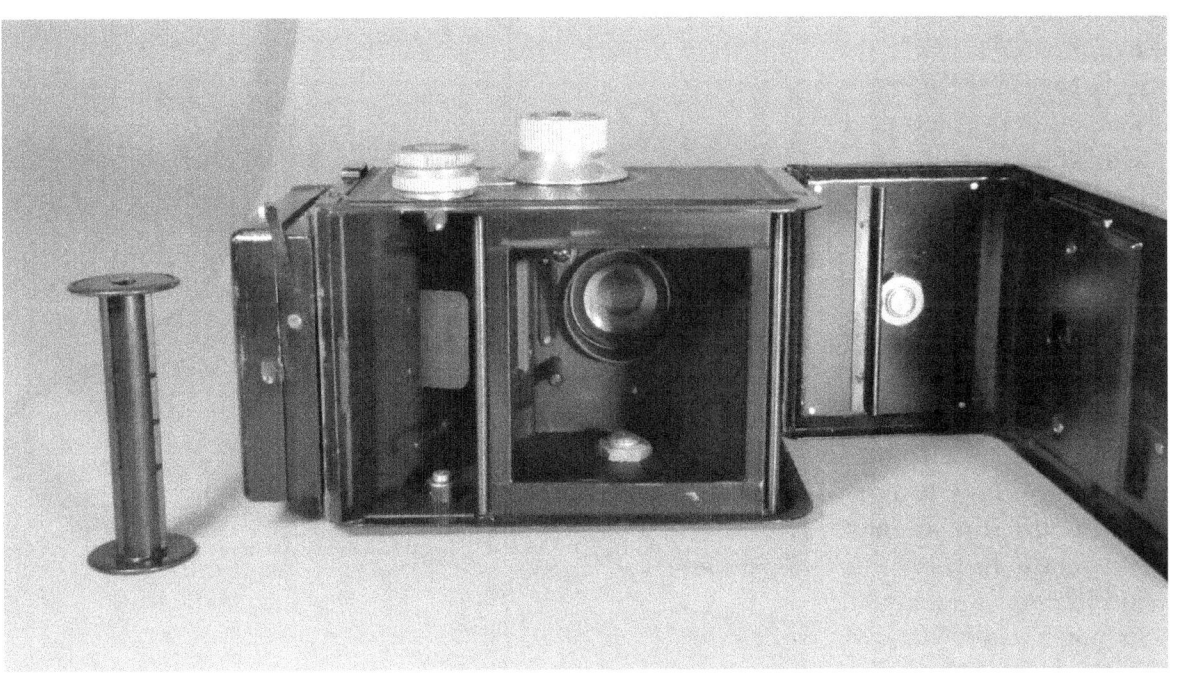

EXA

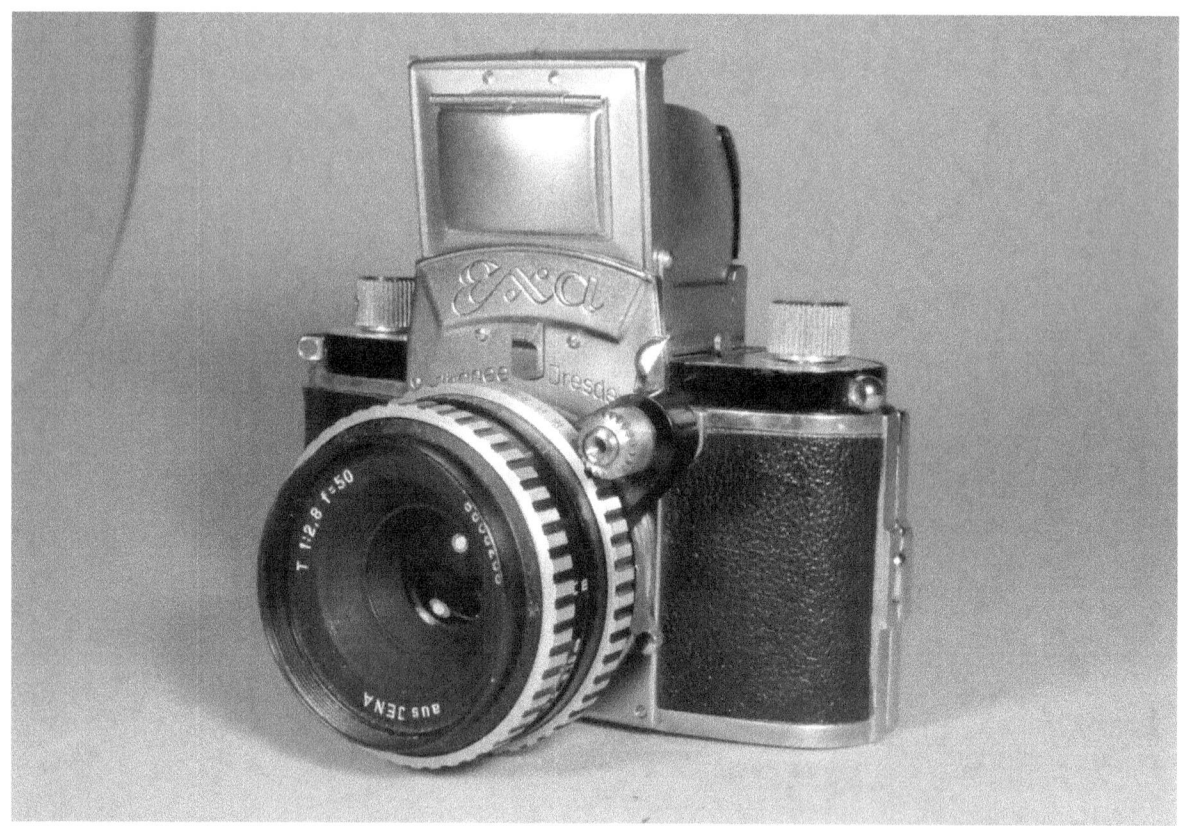

Name: EXA.
Type: 35MM SLR.
Film Size: 35MM.
Year of manufacture: 1951.
Manufacturer: Ihagee.
Country: Germany.
Shutter settings: B, 1/25, 1/50, 1/100, 1/150.
Aperture settings: This lens, F/2.8 – F/22.
Exposure setting: Manual.
Lens: The lens on this camera is Carl Zeiss Jena F/2.8, 50MM.
Interchangeable lenses? Yes. All Exakta lenses.
How do you focus? Ground glass, turn lens element.
Viewfinder: Waistlevel, eyelevel. Magnifier available in viewfinder.
Loading film: Open back, load full cassette, thread into takeup reel.
Automatic film advance? No.
Automatic film rewind? No.
Cable release socket: Yes.
Tripod socket: Yes.
Battery type: None.
Unique features: Uses all Exakta lenses and accessories.
    Interchangeable viewfinders.
        Advancing film returns mirror to viewing position.

EXA

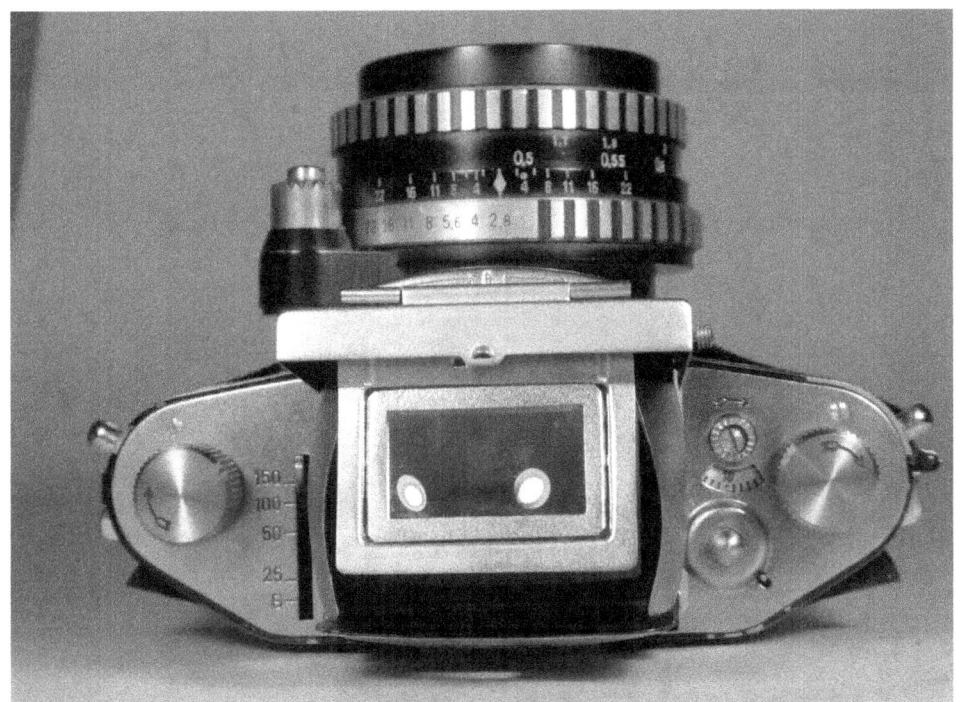

Small lever on top, right, near winding knob is to be pushed after unloading film. Button near winding knob is to enable rewind.

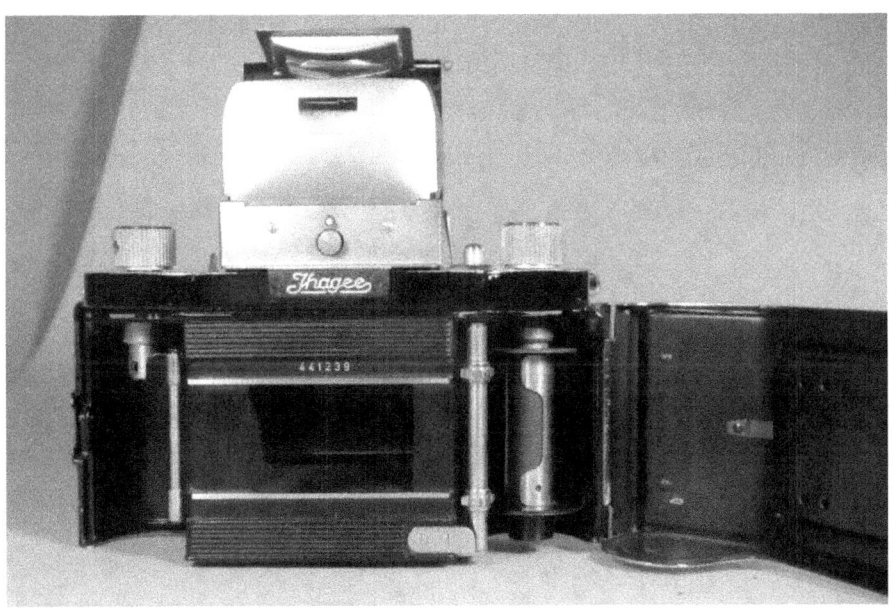

Fujica 35 FS

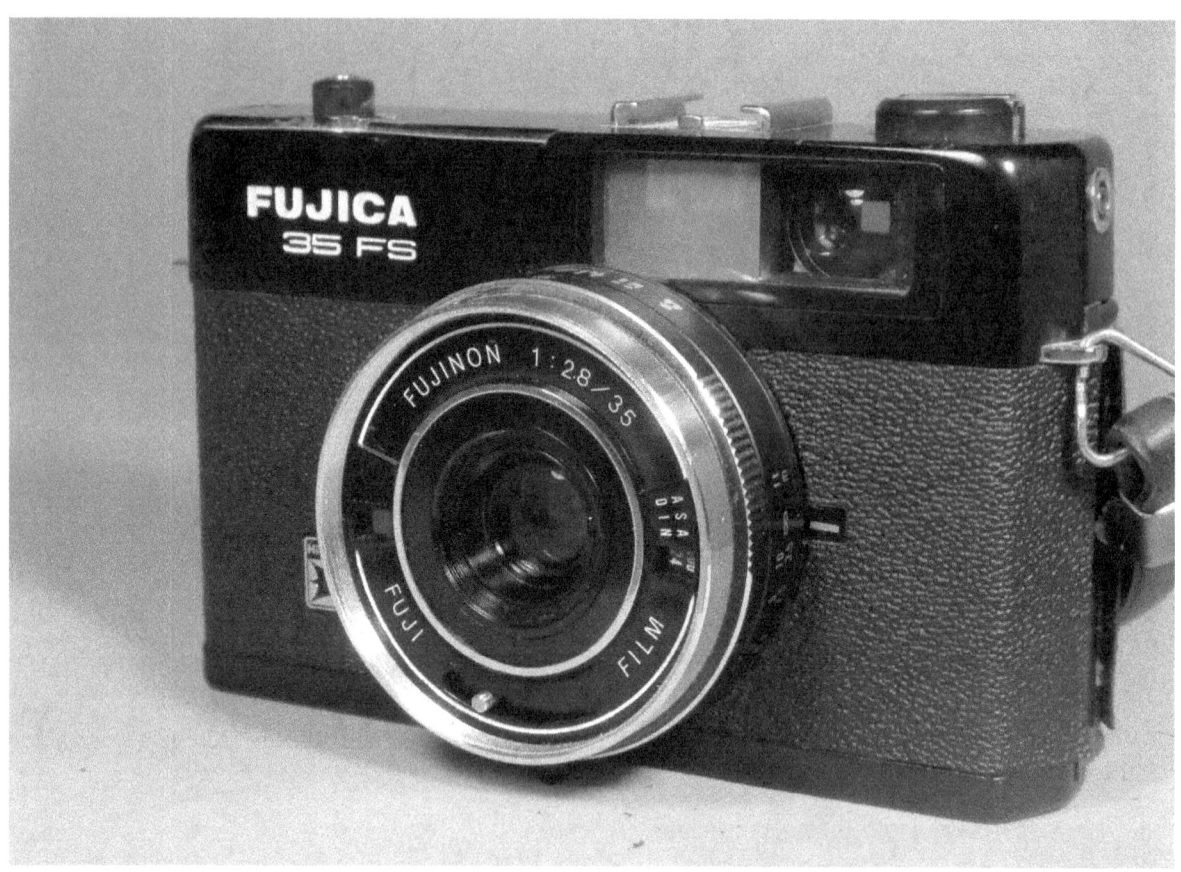

Name: Fujica 35 FS.
Type: 35MM, zone focusing, autoexposure.
Film Size: 35MM.
Year of manufacture: 1971.
Manufacturer: Fuji.
Country: Japan.
Shutter settings: B, 1/30 - 1/250.
Aperture settings: F/2.8 – F/22. Set automatically. No user control.
Exposure setting: Manual or shutter priority automatic metered exposure.
Lens: Fujinon F/2.8, 35MM.
Interchangeable lenses? No.
How do you focus? Estimate distance by zones. Turn distance scale on lens.
Viewfinder: Eye level.
Loading film: Open back, load full cassette, thread into takeup reel.
Automatic film advance? No (manual).
Automatic film rewind? No (manual).
Cable release socket: Yes.
Tripod socket: Yes.
Battery type: 1.3V Mercury. Eveready EPX-13, Mallory PX13.
Unique features:

Fujica 35 FS

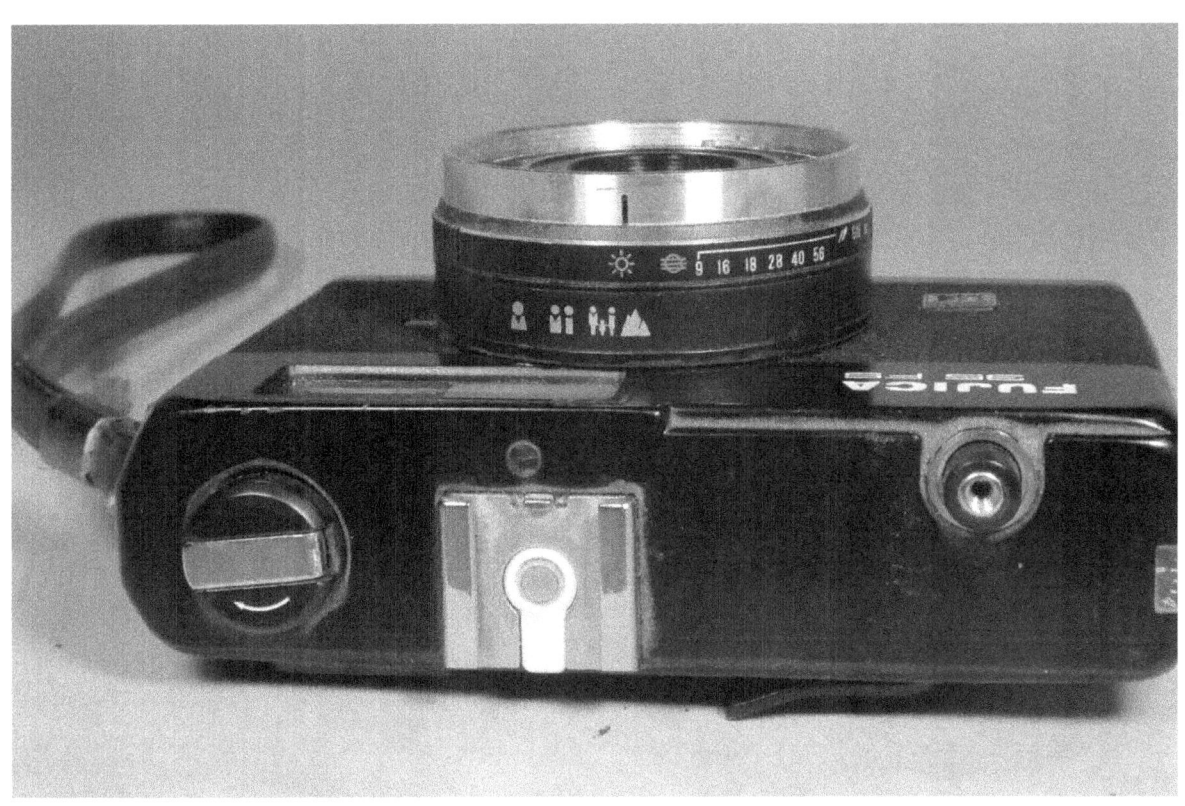

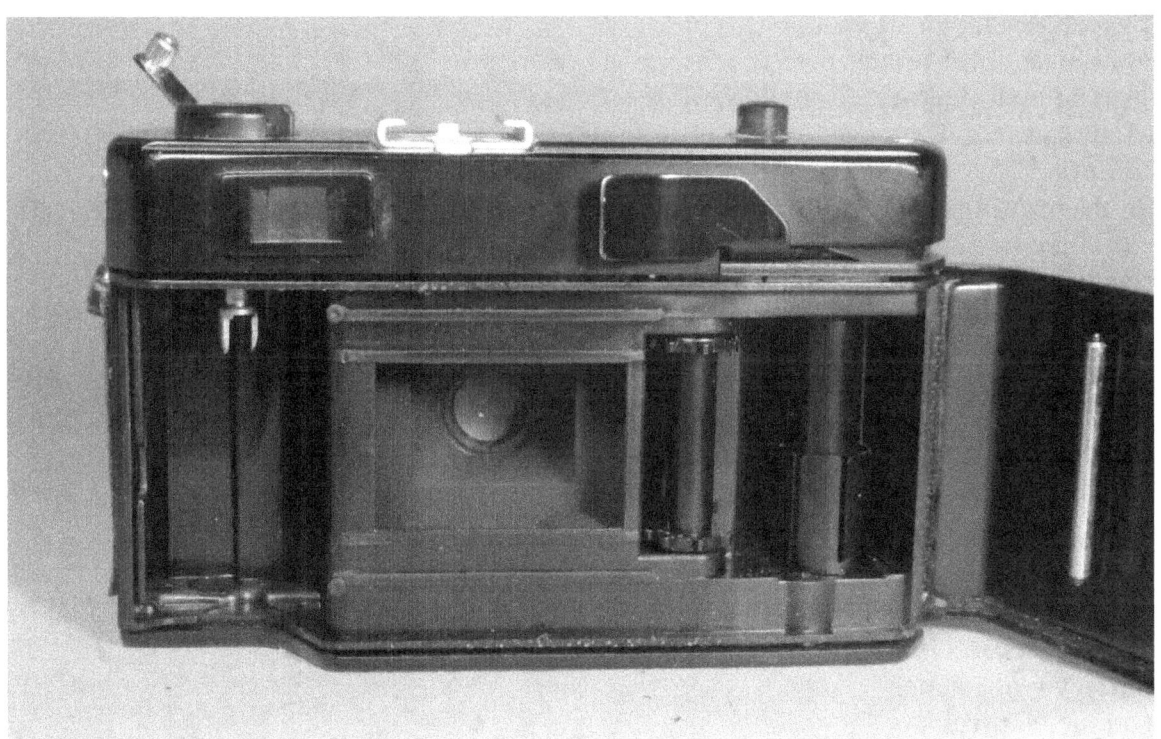

Keystone Model K - 8

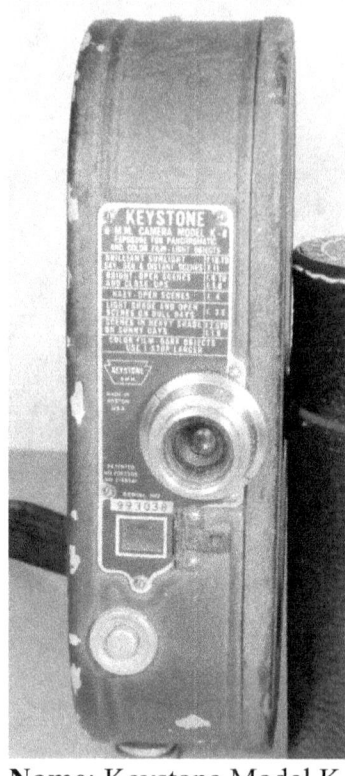

Name: Keystone Model K - 8
Type: 8MM movie camera.
Film Size: 8MM Double 8.
Year of manufacture: Around 1936.
Manufacturer: Keystone.
Country: USA.
Shutter settings: None, but you can control the speed and create slow motion movies.
Aperture settings: F/2.5 – F/16.
Exposure setting: Set aperture. Can use handy chart printed on camera body.
Lens: Wollensak Velostigmat F/2.5, 13MM.
Interchangeable lenses? No.
How do you focus? Fixed focus.
Viewfinder: Eye level.
Loading film: Open camera back, thread film into takeup spool. Flip when one side exposed.
Automatic film advance? N/A.
Automatic film rewind? N/A.
Cable release socket: No.
Tripod socket: No.
Battery type: None.
Unique features:
    Wind spring, which drives motor.

Keystone Model K - 8

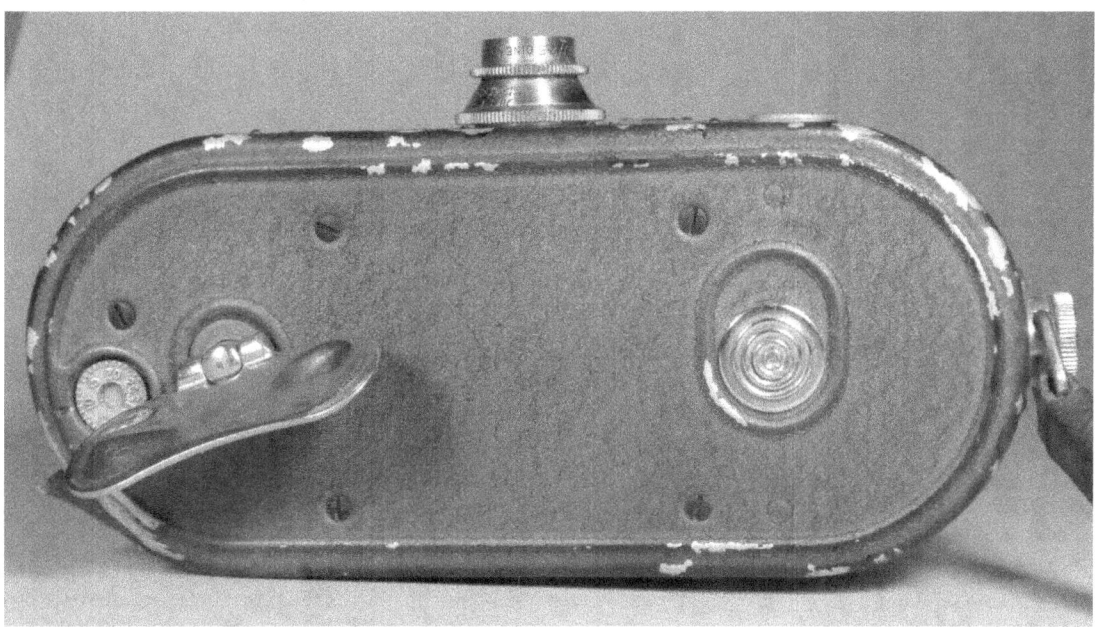

Motor winding lever on left. Wind before taking pictures.

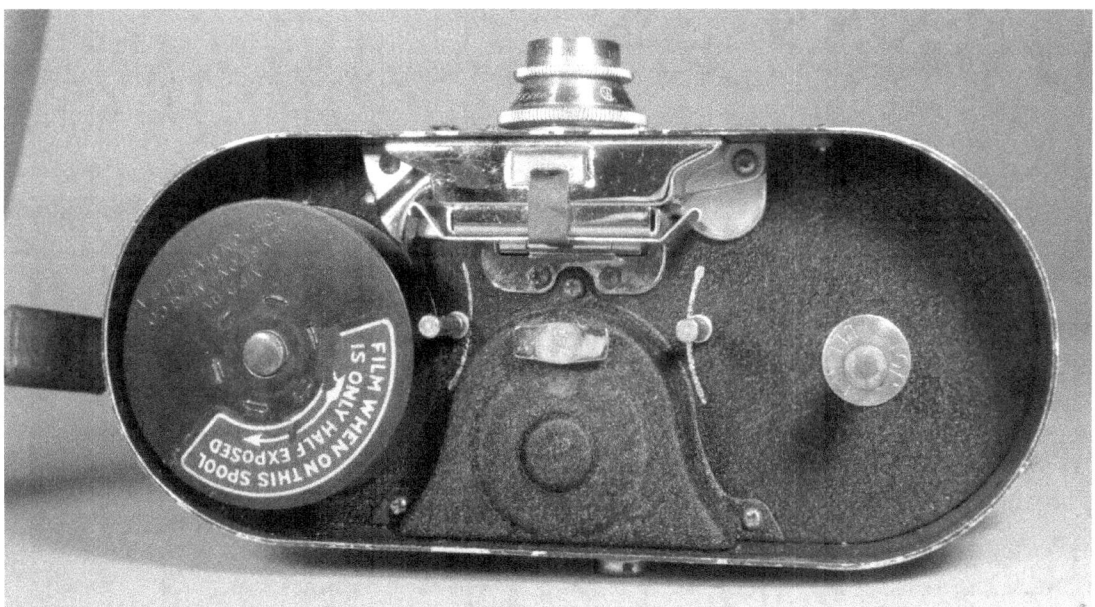

Double 8 requires you to turn the film spool around when it is halfway exposed. You are exposing both sides, lengthwise, of the film. During processing, the two halves are separated and spliced end to end.

Kodak 35

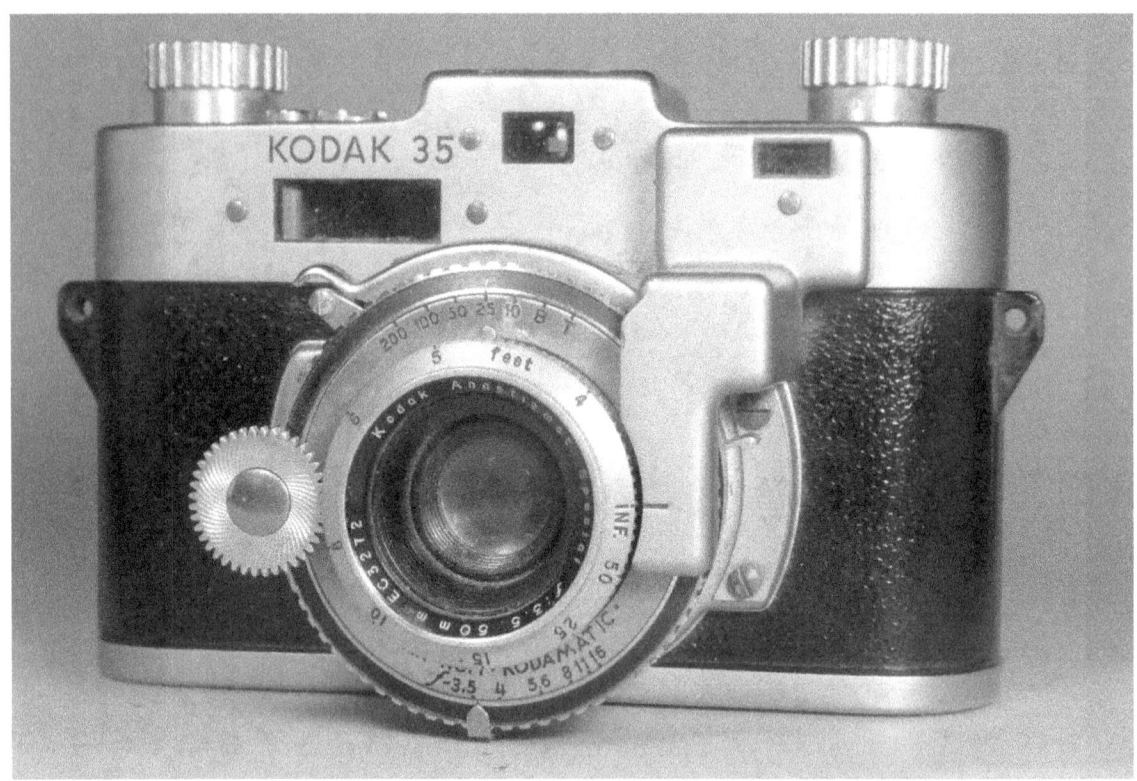

Name: Kodak 35.
Type: 35MM rangefinder.
Film Size: 35MM.
Year of manufacture: 1929.
Manufacturer: Eastman Kodak Company.
Country: USA.
Shutter settings: T, B, 1/10 – 1/200.
Aperture settings: F/3.5 – F/16.
Exposure setting: Manual.
Lens: Kodak anastigmat special, 50MM, F/3.5.
Interchangeable lenses? No.
How do you focus? Coupled rangefinder. Turn front lens element.
Viewfinder: Two viewfinders: one for rangefinder, other for picture. Eye level.
Loading film: Open back, load full cassette, thread into takeup reel.
Automatic film advance? No (manual)
Automatic film rewind? No (manual).
Cable release socket: Yes, but you must remove a screw first.
Tripod socket: Yes.
Battery type: None.
Unique features:
    Shutter release lever is on lens, right near the "200" shutter mark.

Kodak 35

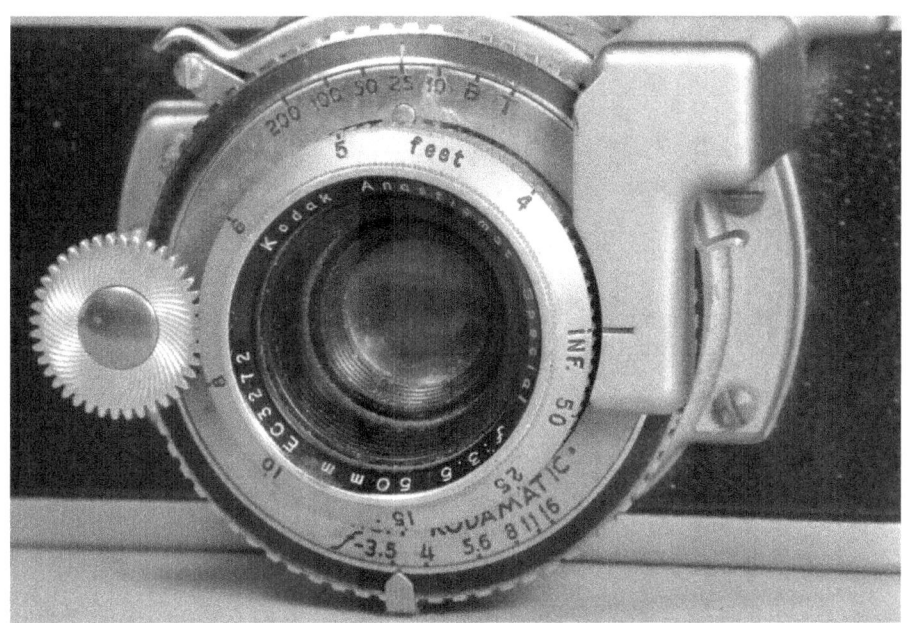

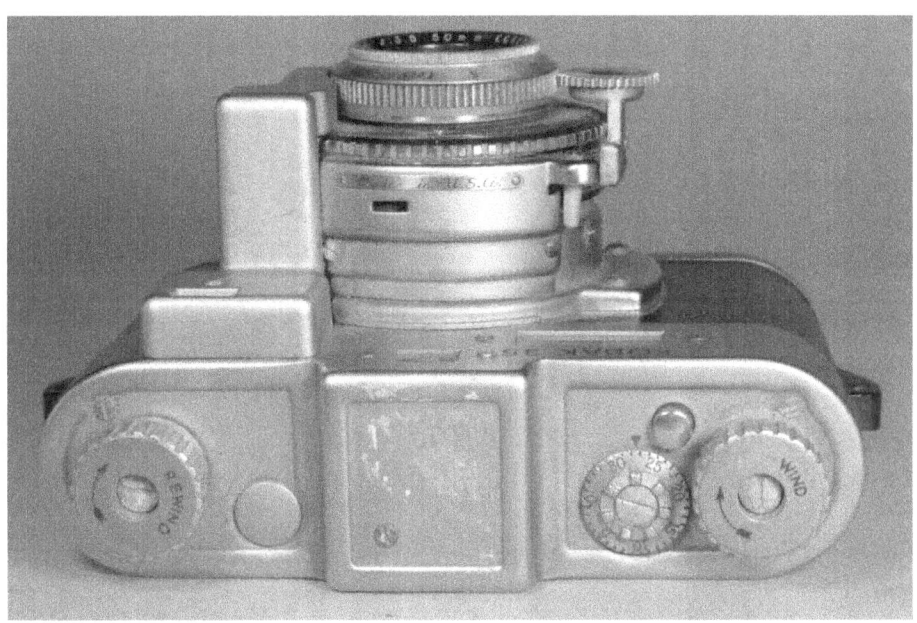

Kodak Advantix F350

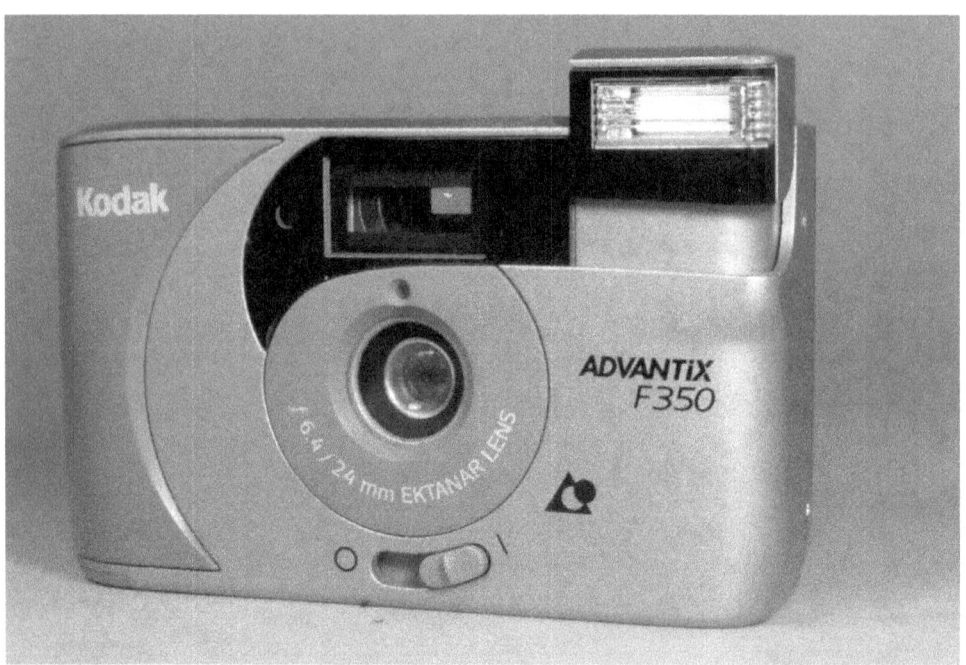

Name: Kodak Advantix F350.
Type: Advanced Photo System.
Film Size: APS.
Year of manufacture: late 1990s.
Manufacturer: Kodak.
Country: China.
Shutter settings: Not under user control.
Aperture settings: Not under user control.
Exposure setting: Automatic.
Lens: Kodak Ektanar F/6.4 24MM.
Interchangeable lenses? No.
How do you focus? Fixed focus.
Viewfinder: Eyelevel.
Loading film: Open compartment, insert film cartridge.
Automatic film advance? Yes.
Automatic film rewind? N/A.
Cable release socket: No.
Tripod socket: Yes.
Battery type: CR2, 3V.
Unique features:

Kodak Advantix F350

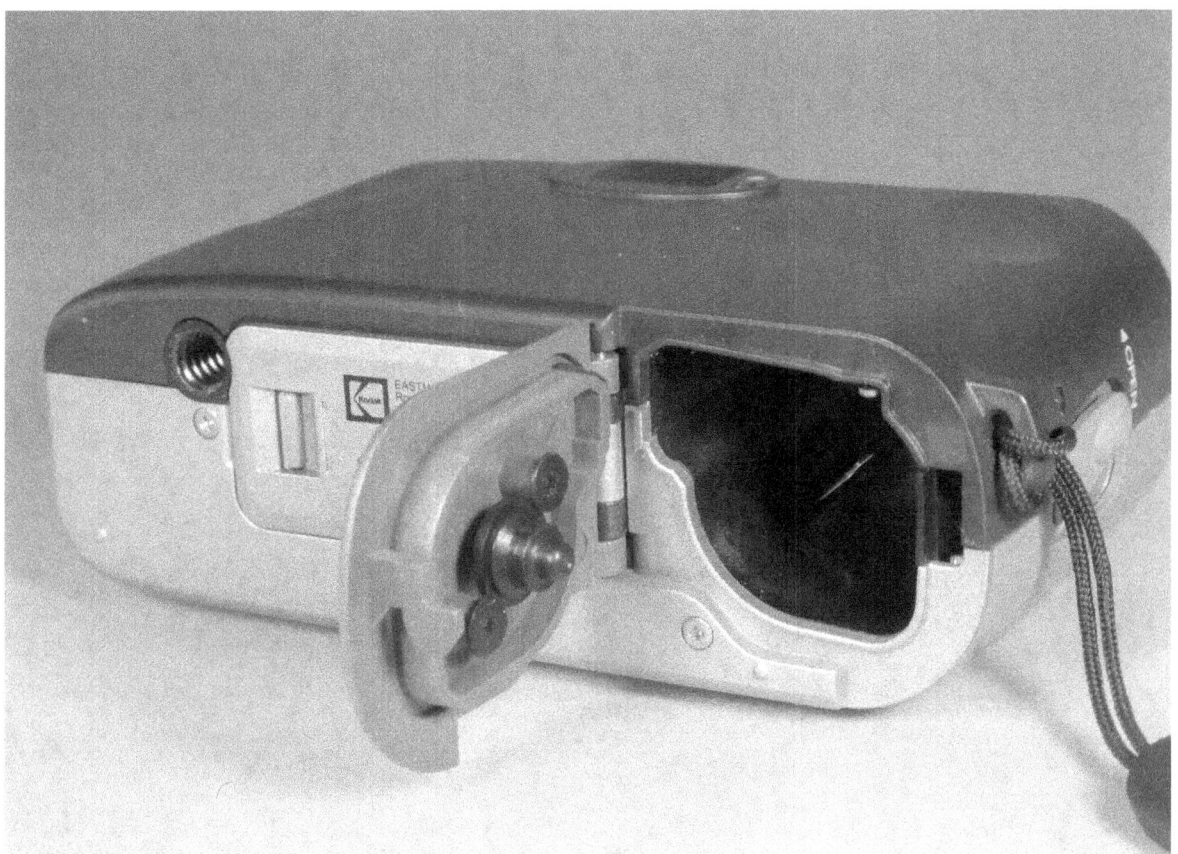

Lever to open film compartment (shown open here) is at extreme right of photo.

The Advanced Photo System (APS) is from the late 1990s.
Film came in cartridges. Information about the photo was recorded on the film on a magnetic strip.
The image area on the film is smaller than that of 35mm. Although no more film has been produced since 2011, the film is still available at Amazon.com. At least one photo lab can still process APS: Process One photo lab.

Kodak Brownie 2A Model C

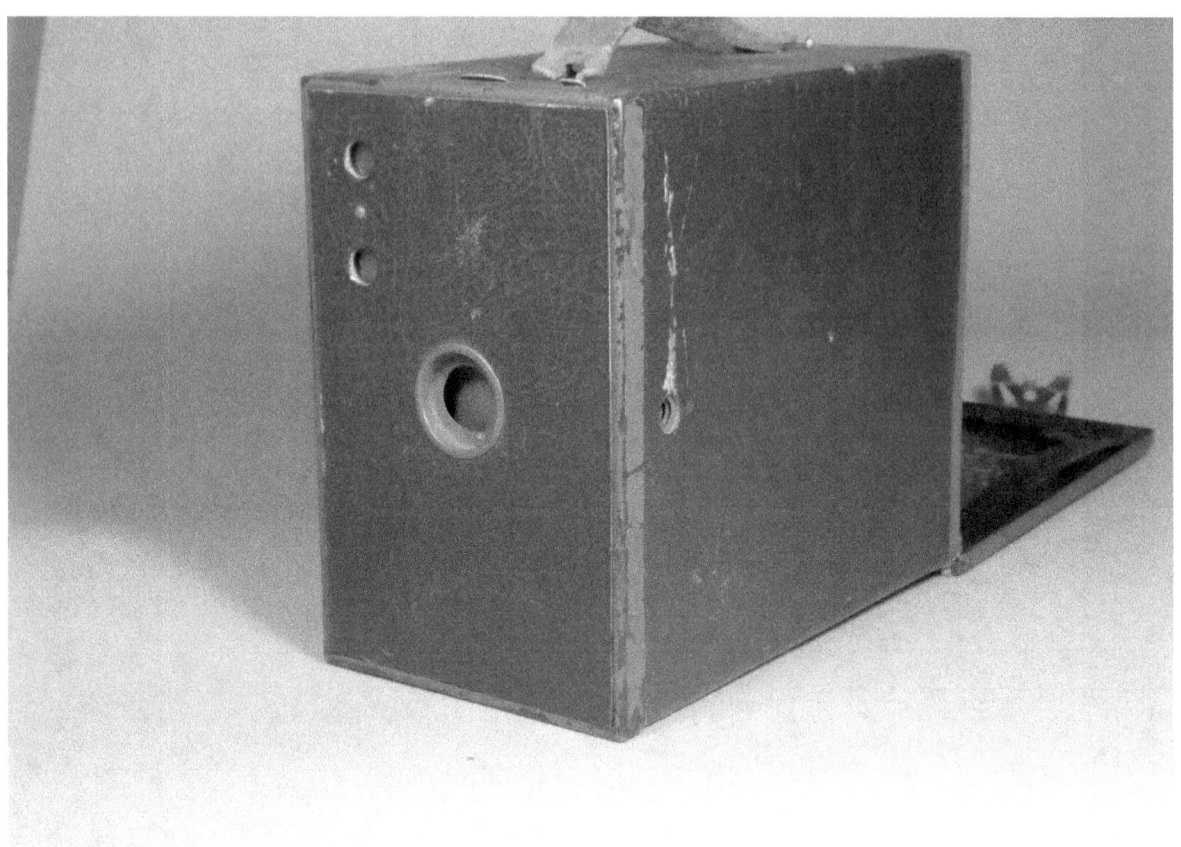

Name: Kodak Brownie 2A Model C.
Type: Rollfilm, box.
Film Size: 116.
Year of manufacture: 1907.
Manufacturer: Eastman Kodak Company.
Country: USA.
Shutter settings: No settings.
Aperture settings: No settings.
Exposure setting: Fixed settings.
Lens:
Interchangeable lenses? No.
How do you focus? Fixed focus.
Viewfinder: Waist level.
Loading film: Open back, insert full roll, thread paper leader onto takeup spool.
Automatic film advance? No (manual)
Automatic film rewind? No (manual).
Cable release socket: No.
Tripod socket: No.
Battery type: None.
Unique features:
    This camera belonged to my father.

Kodak Brownie 2A Model C

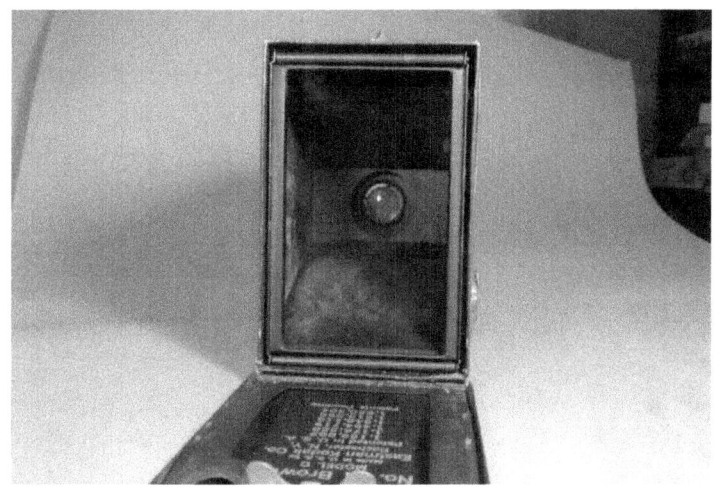

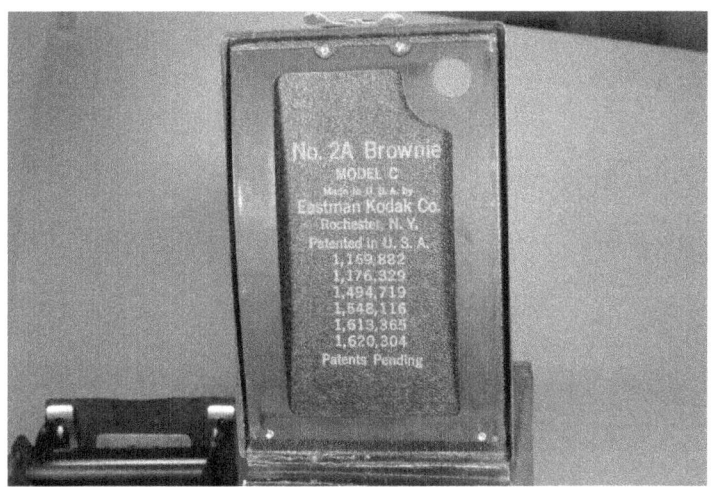

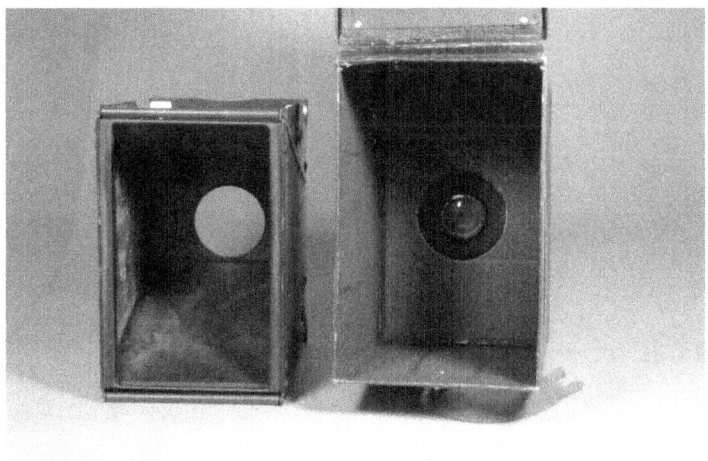

Kodak Brownie Reflex Synchro

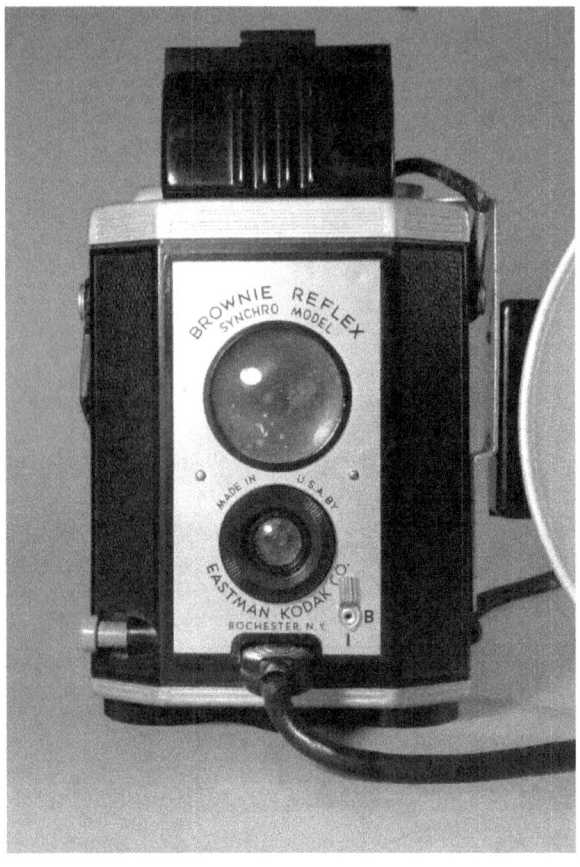

Name: Kodak Brownie Reflex Synchro.
Type: Twin lens reflex.
Film Size: 127.
Year of manufacture: 1940.
Manufacturer: Kodak.
Country: USA.
Shutter settings: B, I.
Aperture settings: Fixed aperture.
Exposure setting: B, I.
Lens:
Interchangeable lenses? No.
How do you focus? Fixed focus.
Viewfinder: Waist level.
Loading film: Open back, insert full roll, thread paper leader onto takeup spool.
Automatic film advance? No (manual).
Automatic film rewind? No (manual).
Cable release socket: No.
Tripod socket: Yes.
Battery type: None.
Unique features:

Kodak Brownie Reflex Synchro

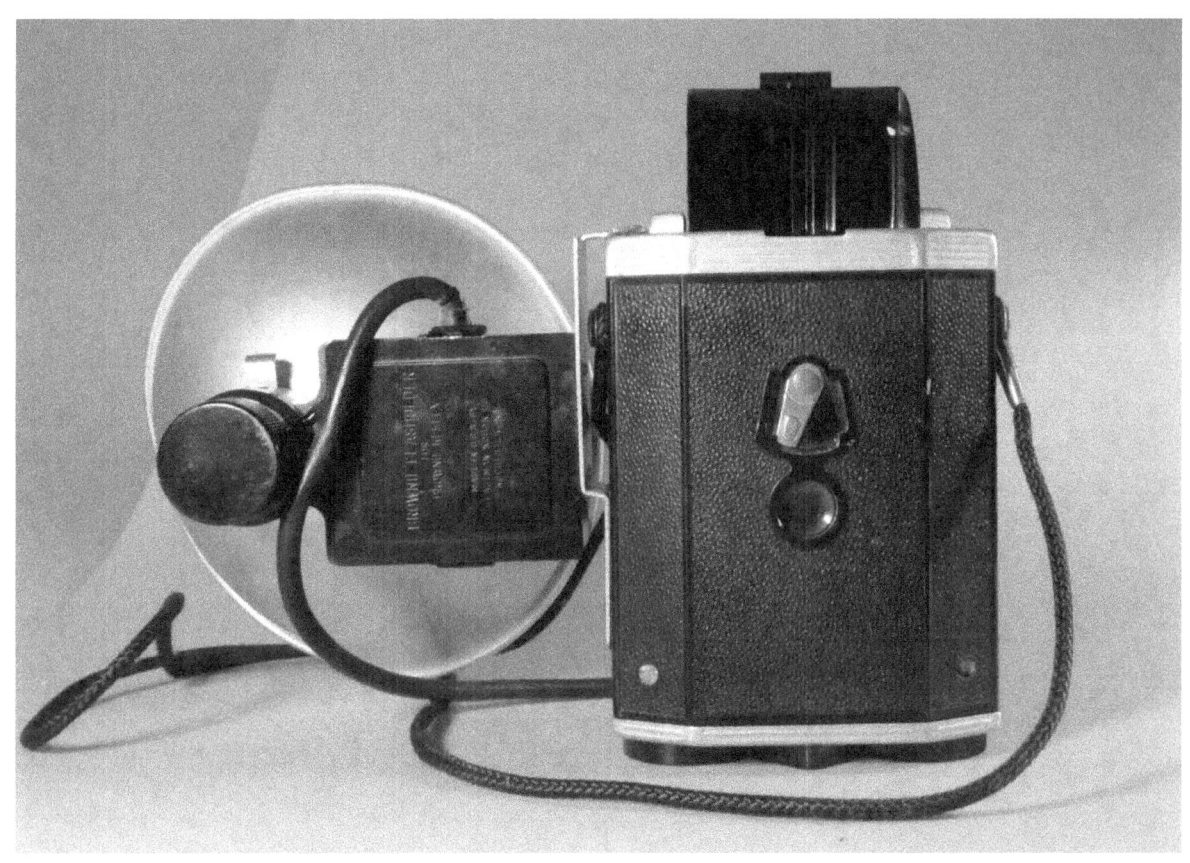

Kodak # 2 Cartridge Hawk-Eye Model C

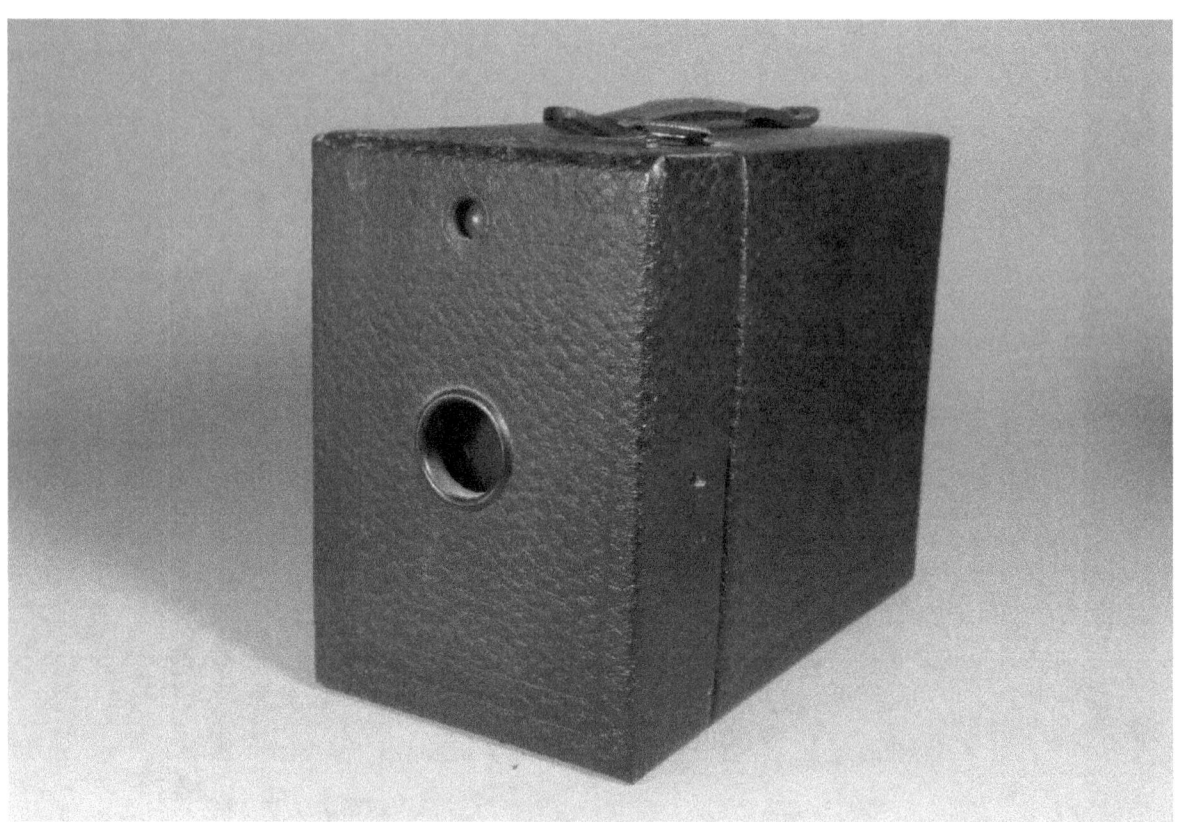

Name: Kodak Cartridge #2 Hawk-Eye Model C.
Type: Rollfilm box.
Film Size: 120.
Year of manufacture: 1926.
Manufacturer: Eastman Kodak Company.
Country: USA.
Shutter settings: No settings.
Aperture settings: No settings.
Exposure setting: Fixed settings.
Lens:
Interchangeable lenses? No.
How do you focus? Fixed focus.
Viewfinder: Waist level.
Loading film: Open back, insert full roll, thread paper leader onto takeup spool.
Automatic film advance? No (manual)
Automatic film rewind? No (manual).
Cable release socket: No.
Tripod socket: No.
Battery type: None.
Unique features:

Kodak # 2 Cartridge Hawk-Eye Model C

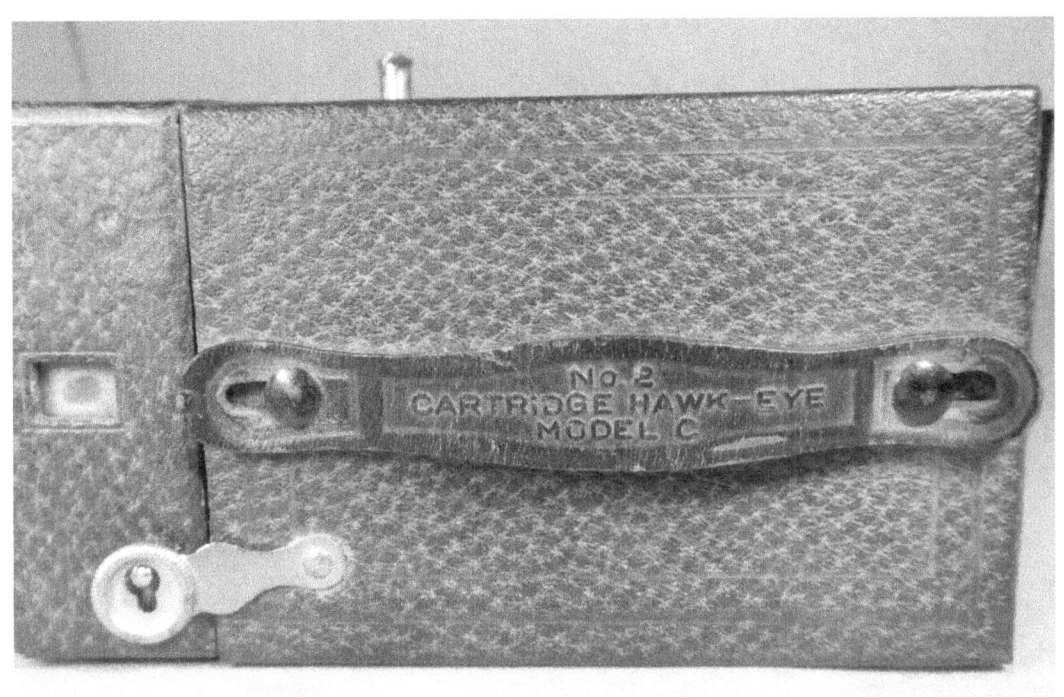

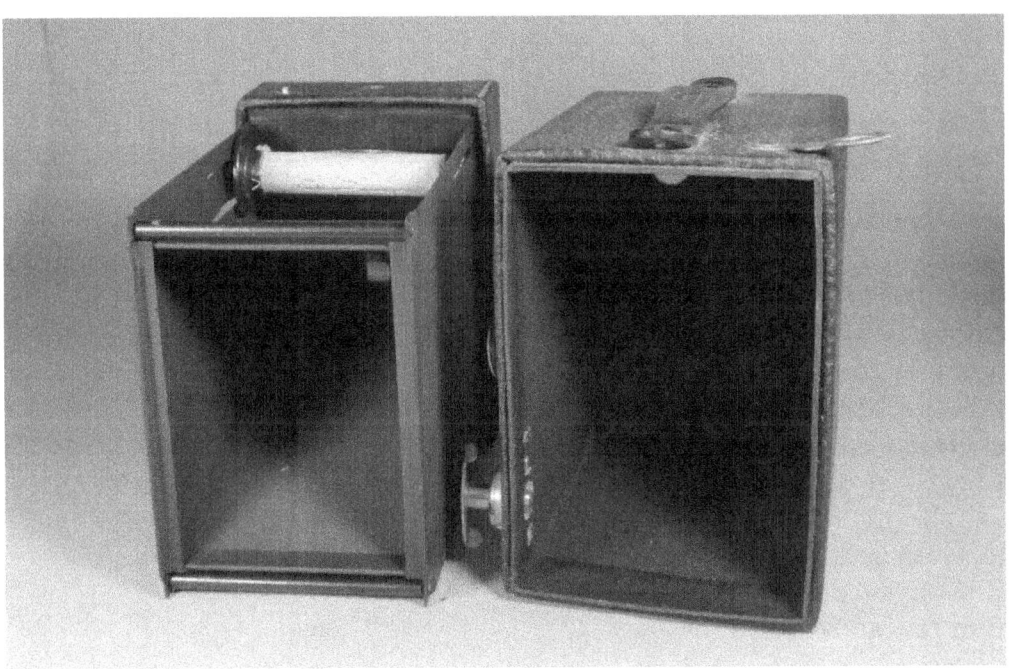

Kodak Instamatic M4

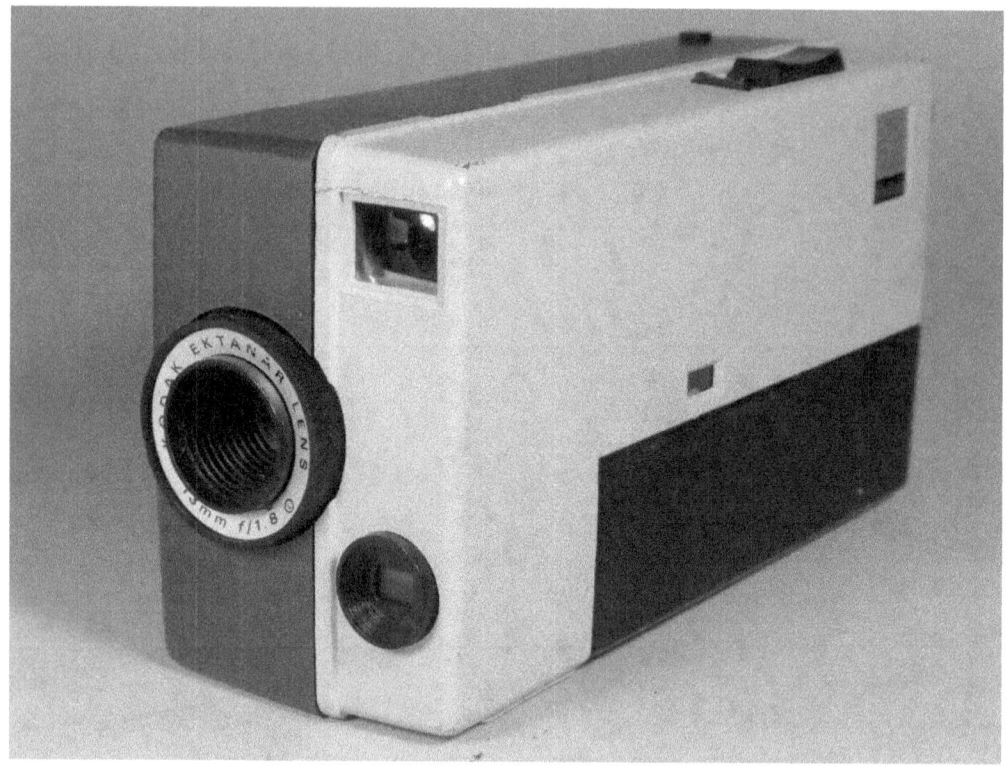

Name: Kodak Instamatic M4.
Type: 8MM movie camera.
Film Size: Super 8MM.
Year of manufacture: Around 1965.
Manufacturer: Eastman Kodak Company.
Country: USA.
Shutter settings: Not under user control.
Aperture settings: Not under user control.
Exposure setting: Automatic.
Lens: Kodak Ektanar. 13MM, F/1.8.
Interchangeable lenses? No.
How do you focus? Fixed focus.
Viewfinder: Eye level.
Loading film: Open back, load full cassette.
Automatic film advance? N/A.
Automatic film rewind? N/A.
Cable release socket: No.
Tripod socket: Yes.
Battery type: AA, quantity 4. For meter: PX-13, 1.35 Volt.
Unique features:
Super 8 does not require you to turn the film spool around, as does Double 8.

Kodak Instamatic M4

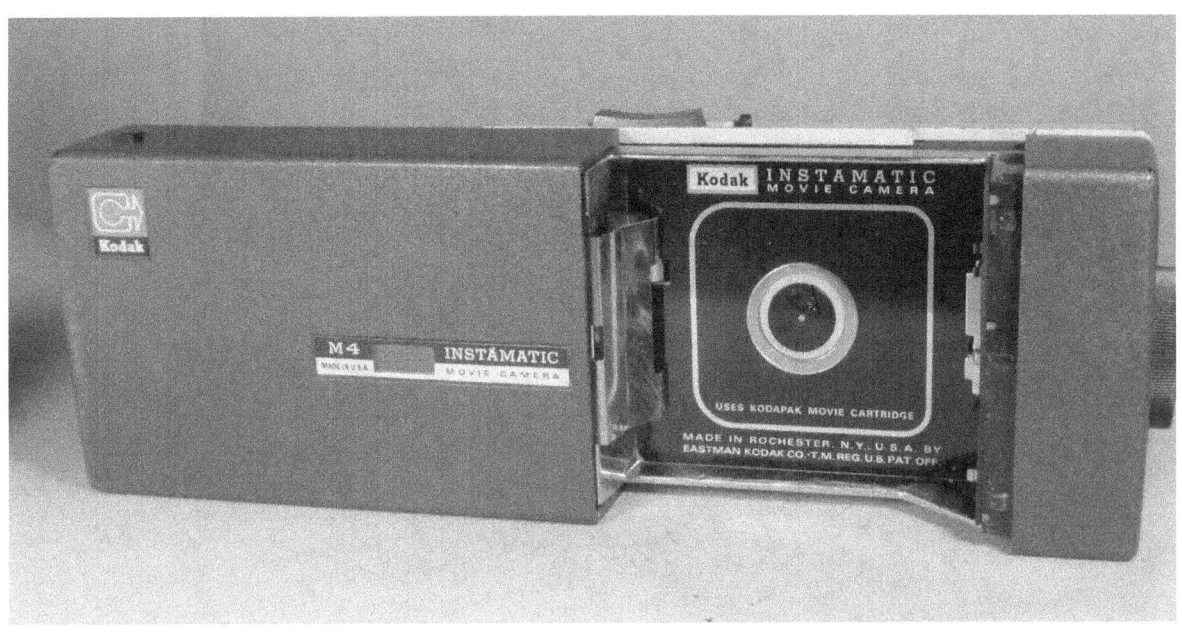

Kodak Instamatic M18

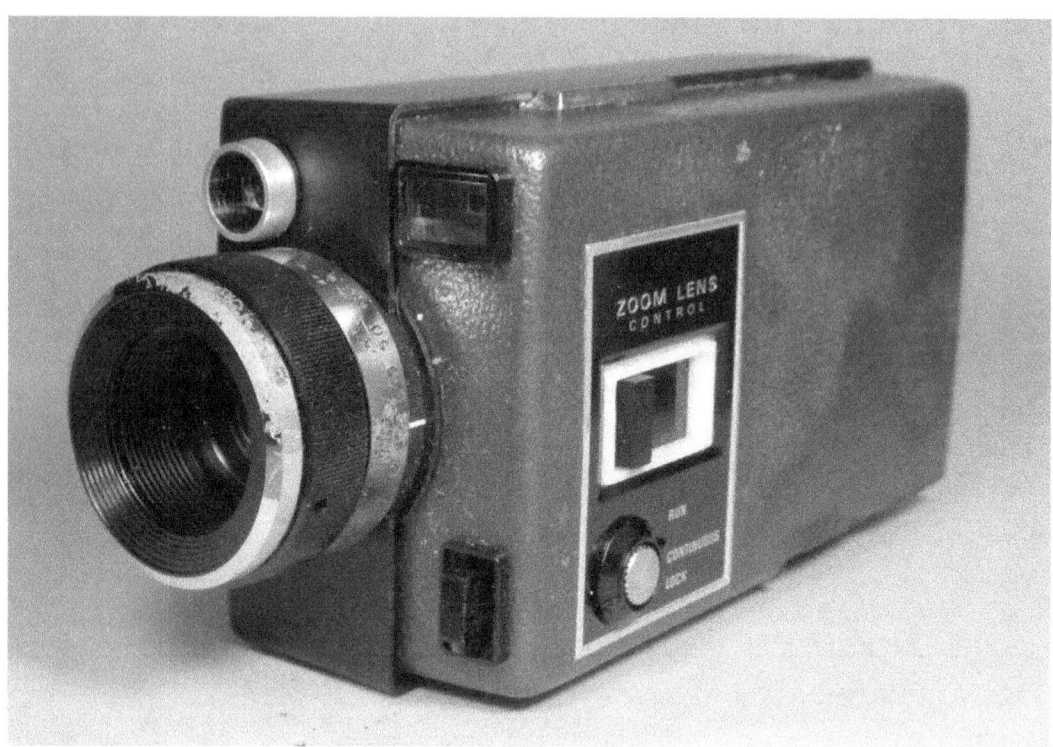

Name: Kodak Instamatic M18.
Type: 8MM movie camera.
Film Size: Super 8MM.
Year of manufacture: Around 1965.
Manufacturer: Eastman Kodak Company.
Country: USA.
Shutter settings: Not under user control.
Aperture settings: Not under user control.
Exposure setting: Automatic.
Lens: Kodak zoom, 13MM, F/2.7.
Interchangeable lenses? No.
How do you focus? Estimate distance, turn ring on lens.
Viewfinder: Eye level.
Loading film: Open back, load full cassette.
Automatic film advance? N/A.
Automatic film rewind? N/A.
Cable release socket: No
Tripod socket: Yes.
Battery type: AA, quantity 4.
Unique features:
Super 8 does not require you to turn the film spool around, as does Double 8.

Kodak Instamatic M18

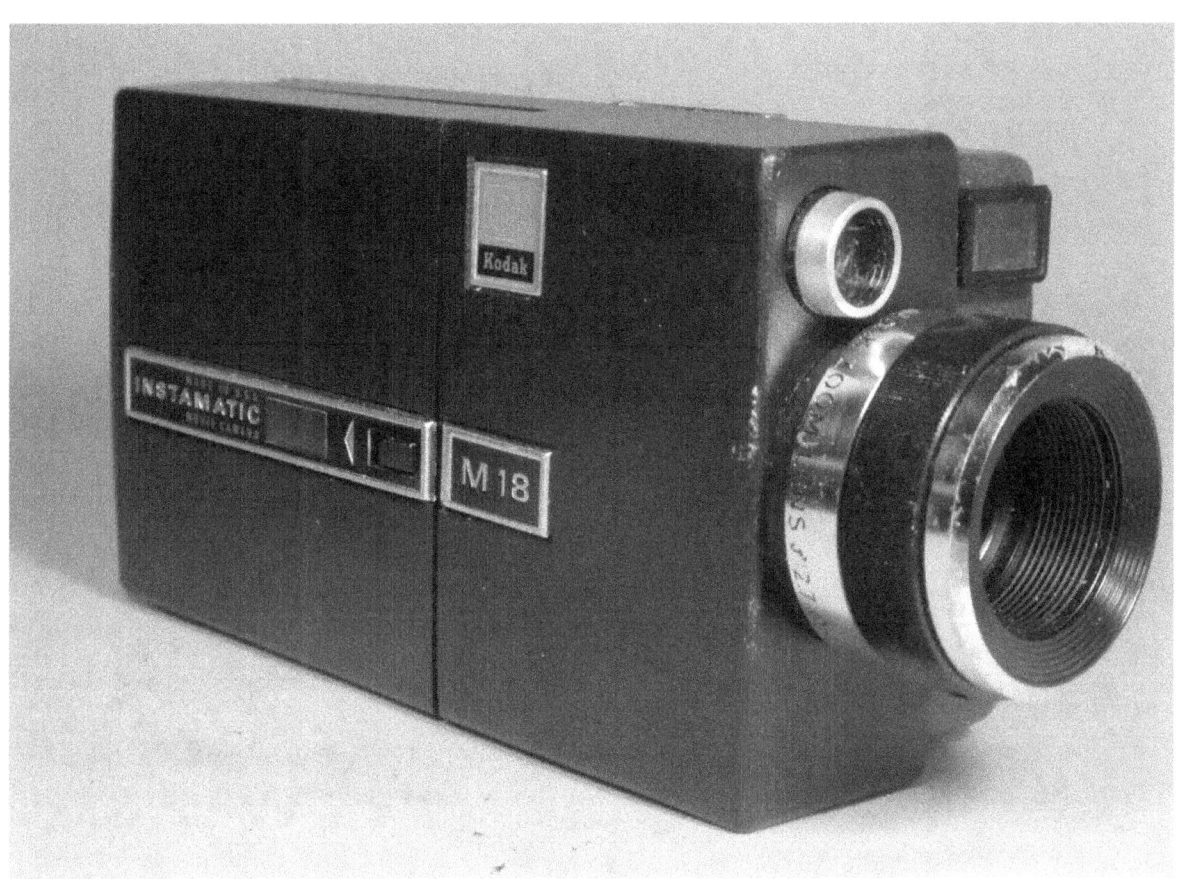

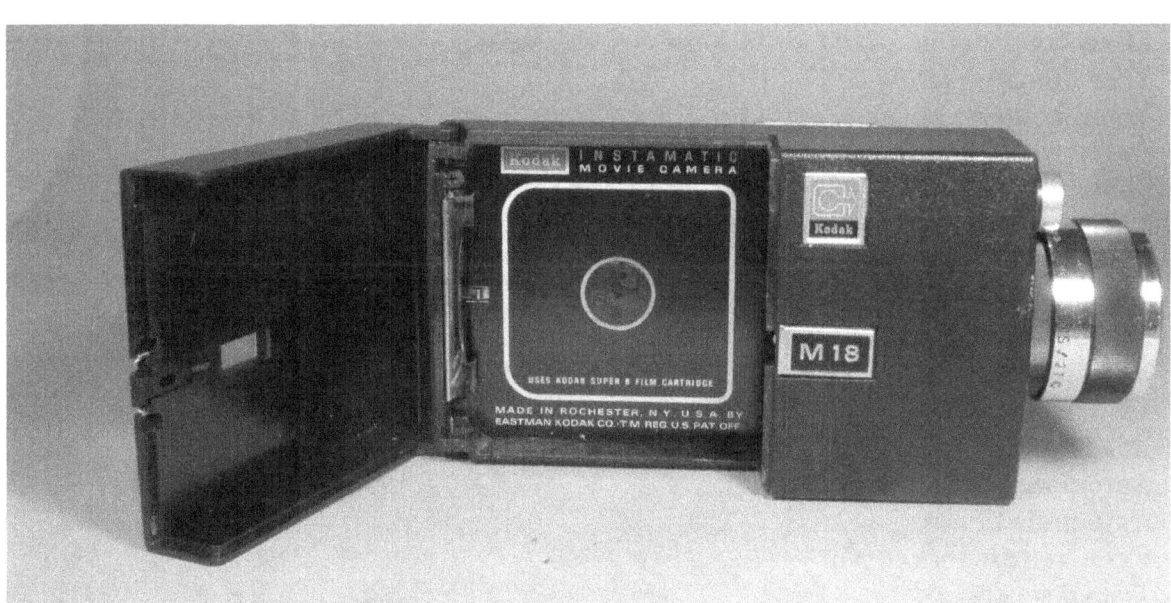

Kodak Instamatic X-35

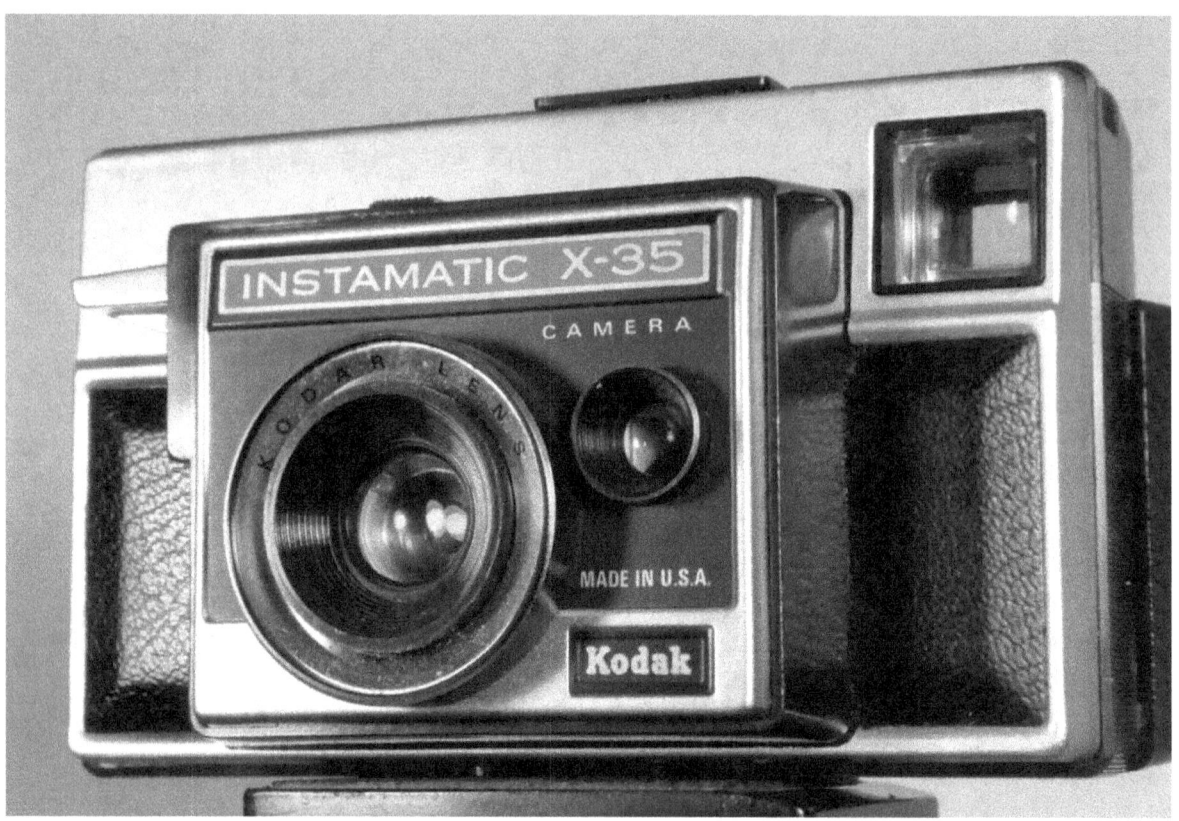

Name: Kodak Instamatic X-35.
Type: Point and Shoot.
Film Size: 126 film cartridge. No longer manufactured.
Year of manufacture: 1970.
Manufacturer: Kodak.
Country: USA.
Shutter settings: Not under user control.
Aperture settings: Not under user control.
Exposure setting: Automatic.
Lens: Kodak Ektanar F/8 41MM.
Interchangeable lenses? No.
How do you focus? Zone focus. Estimate distance, choose zone.
Viewfinder: Eyelevel.
Loading film: Open compartment, insert 126 film cartridge.
Automatic film advance? No.
Automatic film rewind? N/A.
Cable release socket: No.
Tripod socket: Yes.
Battery type: PX30, 3 volts.
Unique features:
Uses Magicube flash cubes.

Kodak Instamatic X-35

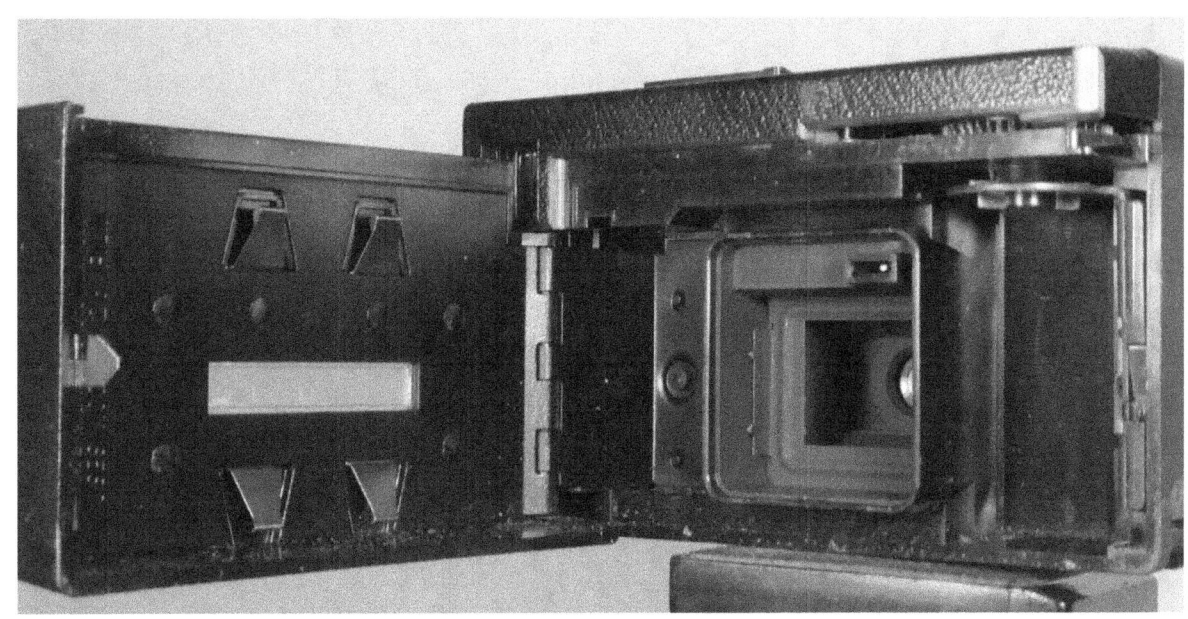

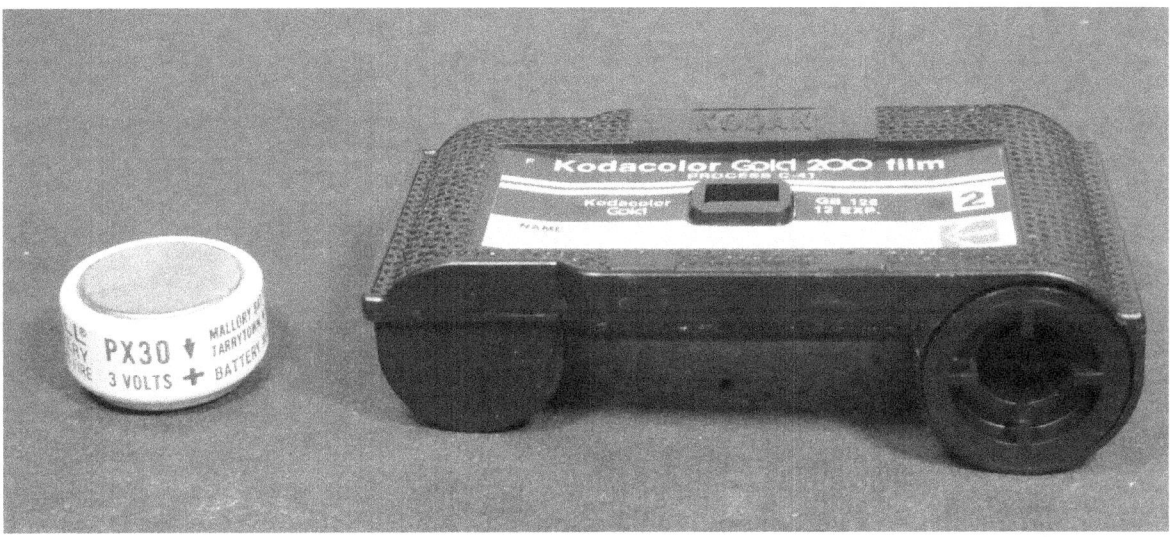

Kodak Medalist VR35 Model K14

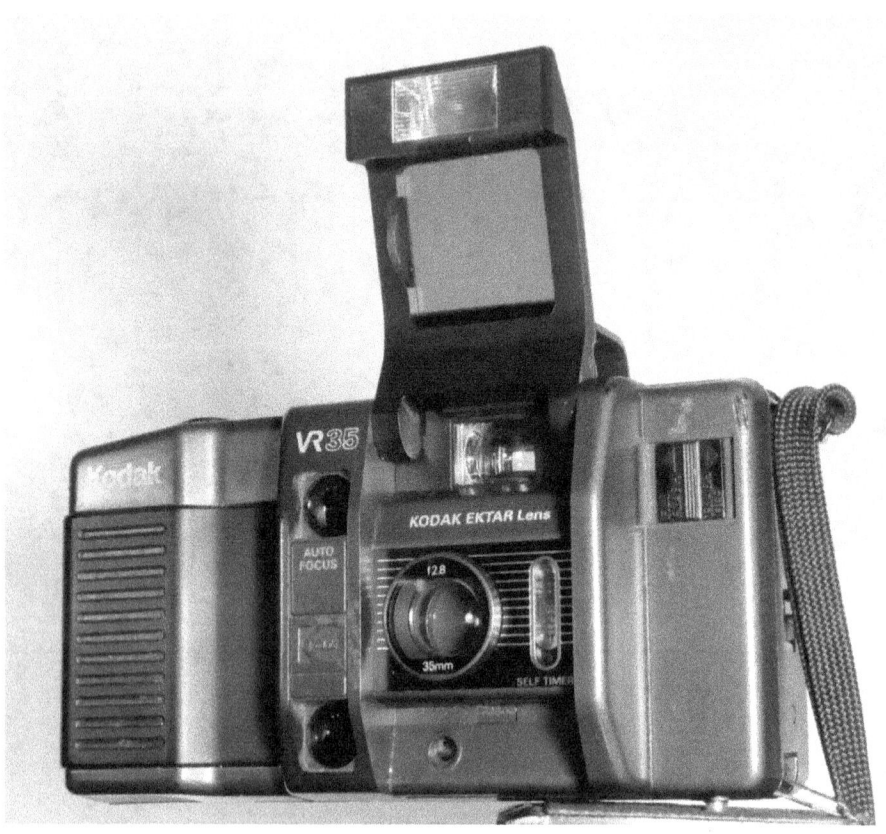

Name: Kodak Medalist VR35 Model K14.
Type: 35MM Point and Shoot.
Film Size: 35MM.
Year of manufacture: 1986.
Manufacturer: Eastman Kodak Company.
Country: Made in Japan.
Shutter settings: Not under user control.
Aperture settings: Not under user control.
Exposure setting: Automatic.
Lens: Kodak Ektar, 35MM, F/2.8.
Interchangeable lenses? No.
How do you focus? Fixed focus.
Viewfinder: Eye level.
Loading film: Open back, load full cassette, automatic threading into takeup reel.
Automatic film advance? Yes.
Automatic film rewind? Yes.
Cable release socket: No.
Tripod socket: Yes.
Battery type: 9 V lithium ultralife powerpack, or 9 V alkaline. 3 V CR2025 for clock.
Unique features: Can set date, on back.

Kodak Medalist VR35 Model K14

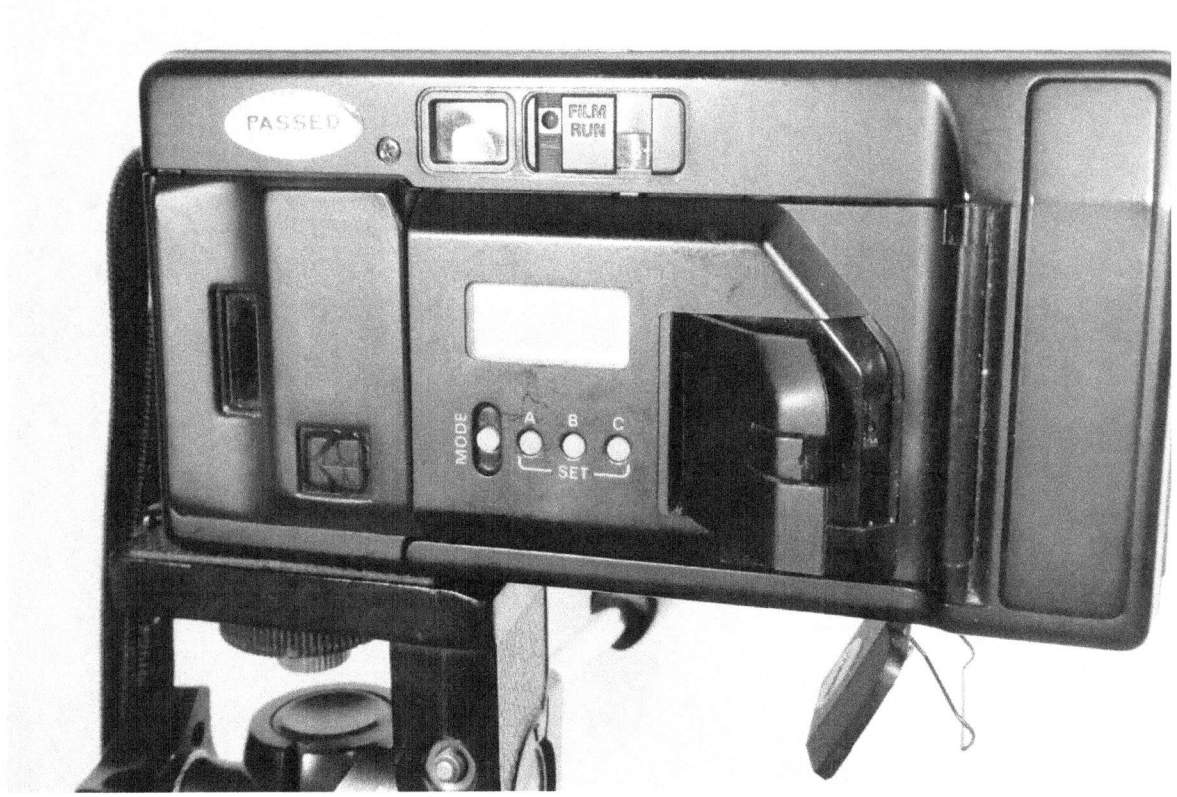

Controls for setting date in lower center.
Compartment for date battery on lower right, shown open.

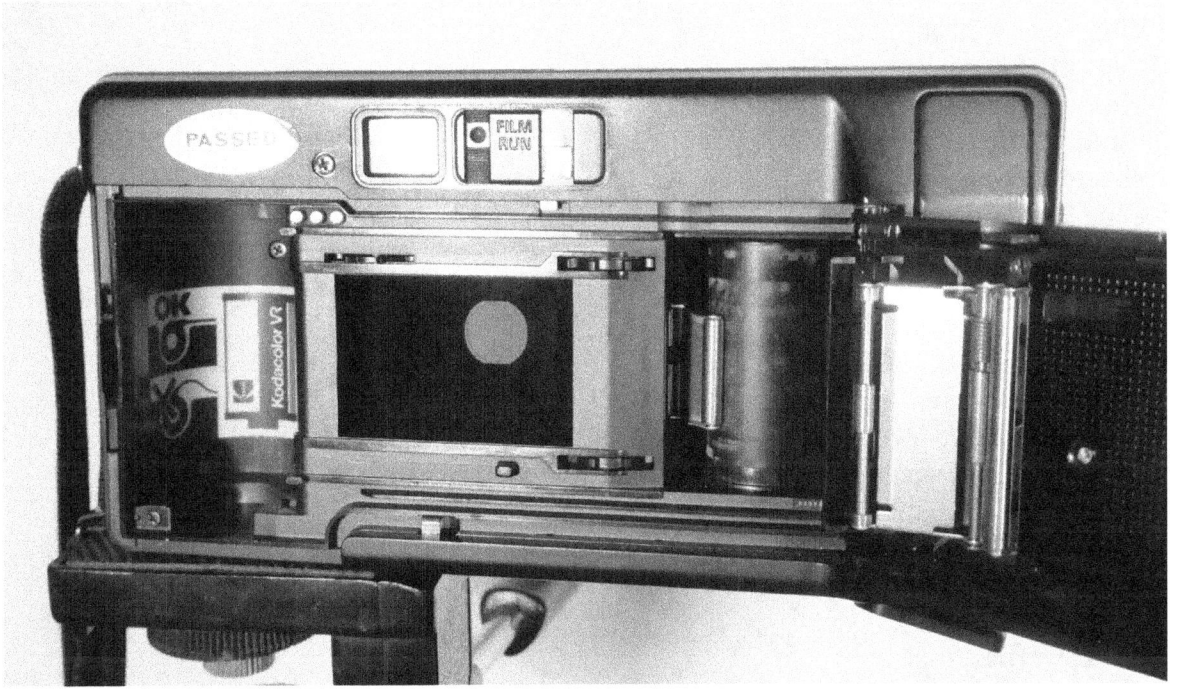

Kodak Pony 135 Model C

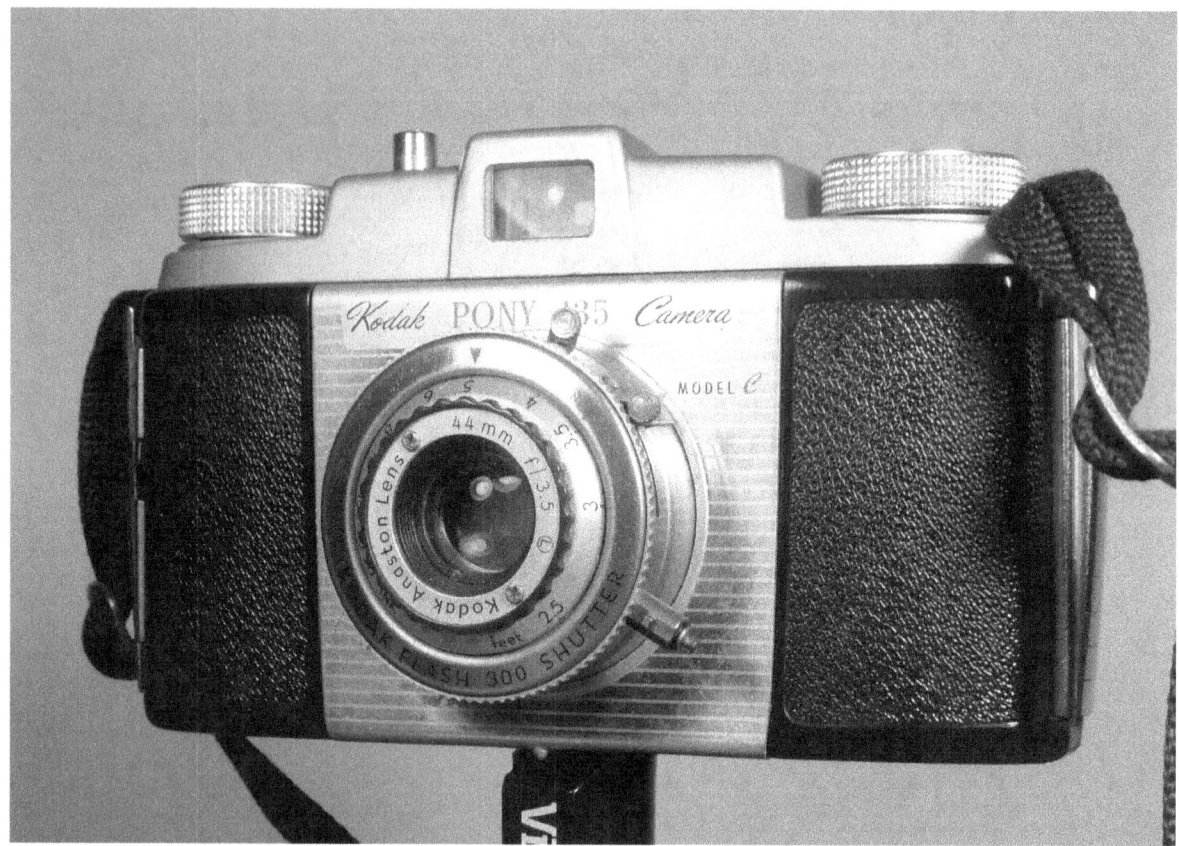

Name: Kodak Pony 135 Model C.
Type: 35MM rangefinder.
Film Size: 35MM.
Year of manufacture: 1950s.
Manufacturer: Eastman Kodak Company.
Country: USA.
Shutter settings: B, 1/25 – 1/300.
Cock shutter before taking picture.
Aperture settings: F/3.5 – F/22.
Exposure setting: Manual.
Lens: Kodak Anaston, 44MM, F/3.5.
Interchangeable lenses? No.
How do you focus? Estimate distance, turn front lens element.
Viewfinder: Eye level.
Loading film: Open back, load full cassette, thread into takeup reel.
Automatic film advance? No (manual).
Automatic film rewind? No (manual).
Cable release socket: Yes.
Tripod socket: Yes.
Battery type: None.
Unique features:

Kodak Pony 135 Model C

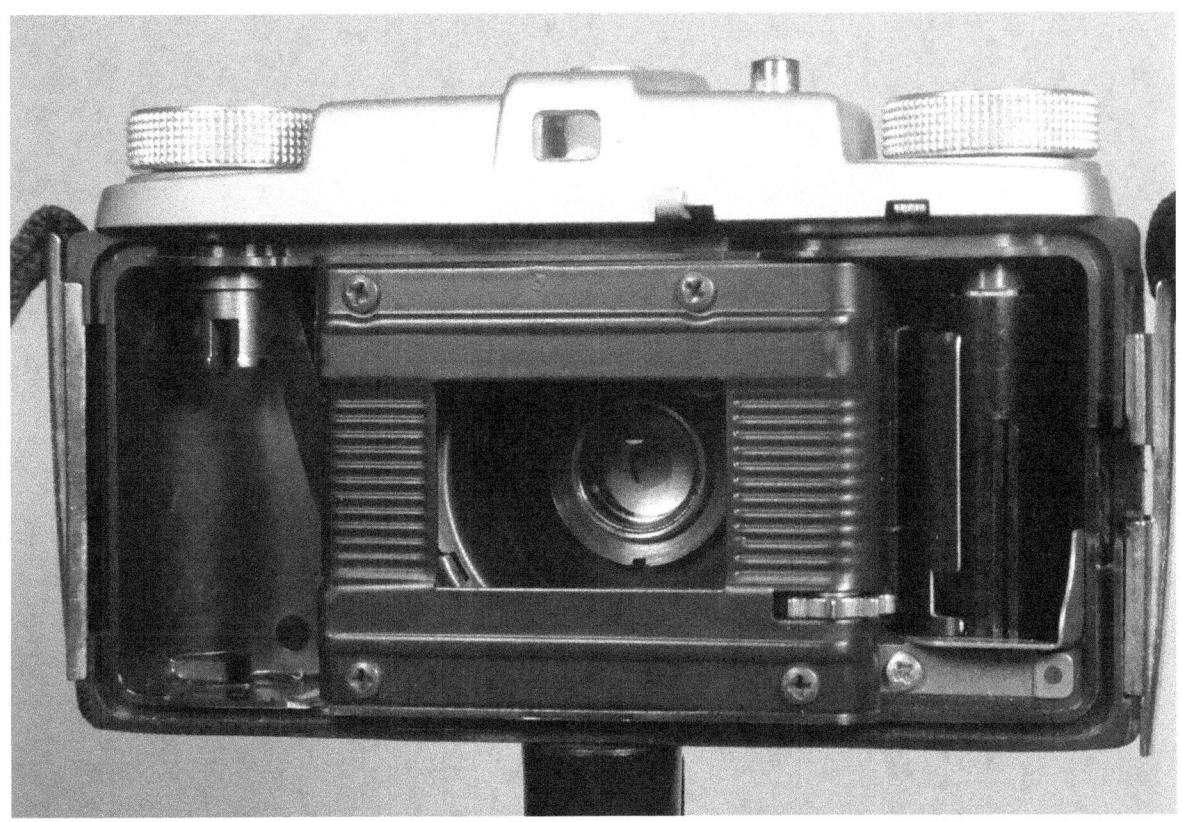

The small lever on the back, top right, is the rewind lever. Push it and hold it to rewind film at the end of roll. The lever next to it is the film release lever. You push it to the right when loading film. It allows you to advance the film with the "wind" knob so as to bring unexposed film into the film plane, ready for taking pictures.

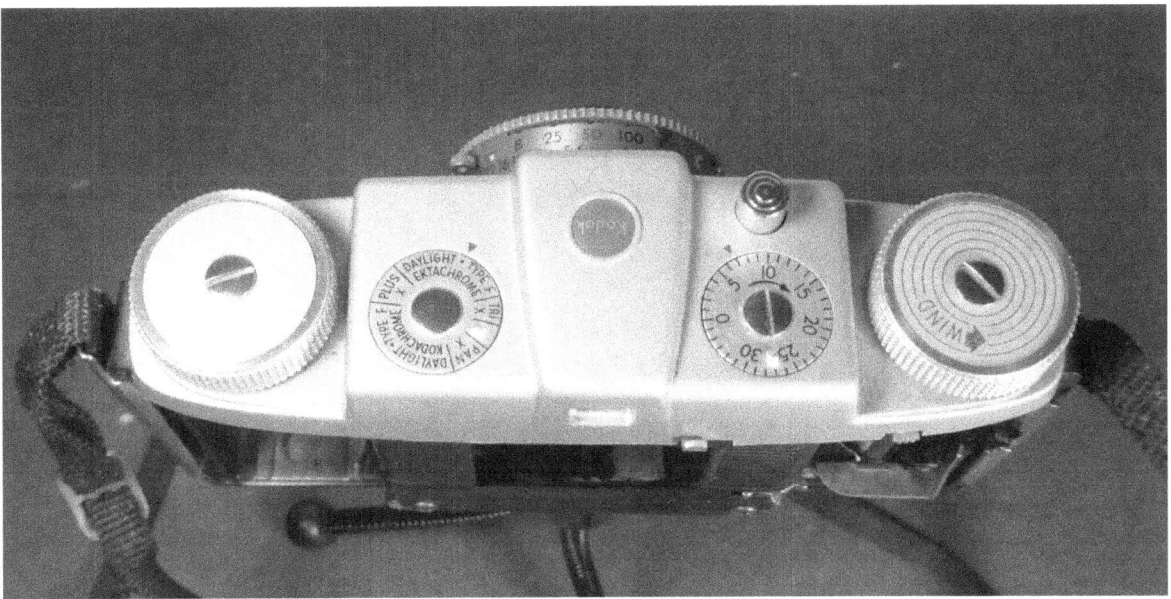

Kodak Retinette

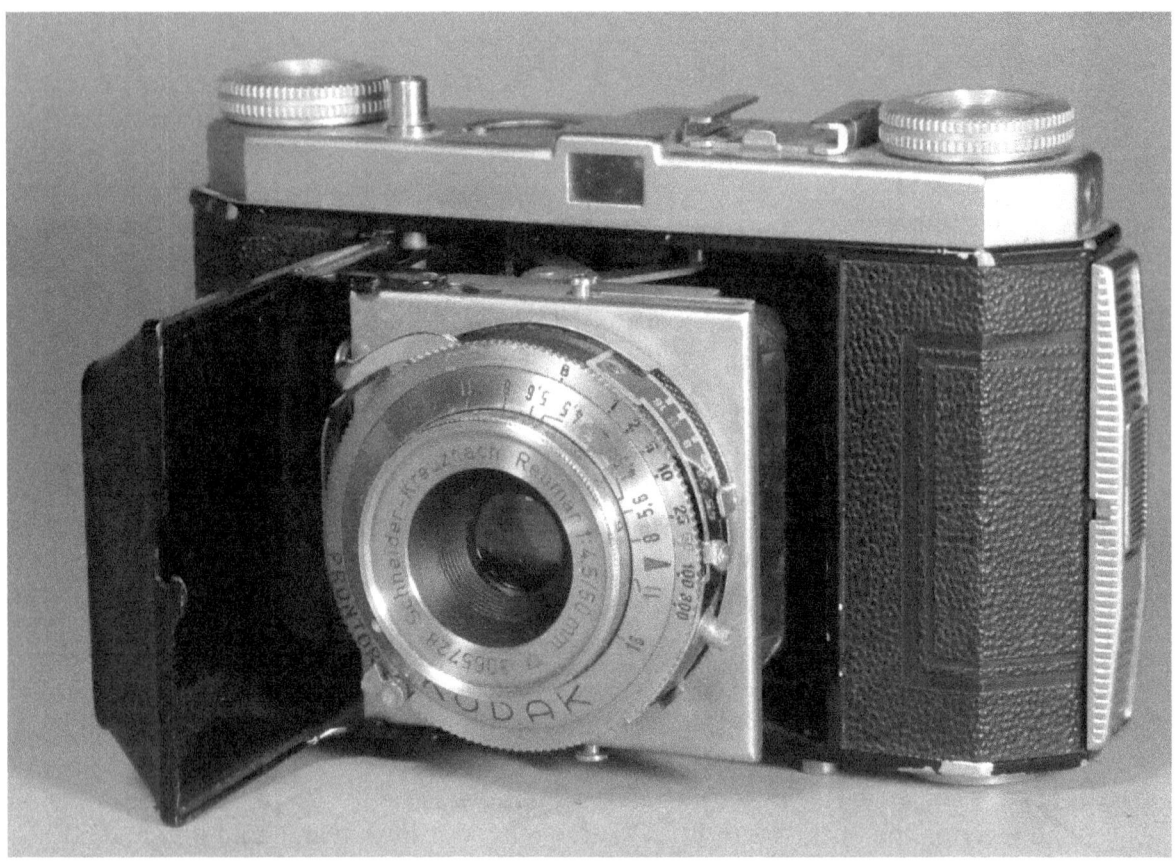

Name: Kodak Retinette.
Type: 35MM, folding.
Film Size: 35MM.
Year of manufacture: 1950s.
Manufacturer: Eastman Kodak Company.
Country: USA.
Shutter settings: B, 1 second - 1/300.
Aperture settings: F/4.5, 8, 11, 16
Exposure setting: Manual.
Lens: Schneider-Kreuznach Reomar, 50MM.
Interchangeable lenses? No.
How do you focus? Estimate distance, set distance scale on front lens element. No rangefinder.
Viewfinder: Eye level.
Loading film: Open back, load full cassette, thread into takeup reel.
Automatic film advance? No (manual).
Automatic film rewind? N/A.
Cable release socket: Yes.
Tripod socket: Yes.
Battery type: None.
Unique features:

Kodak Retinette

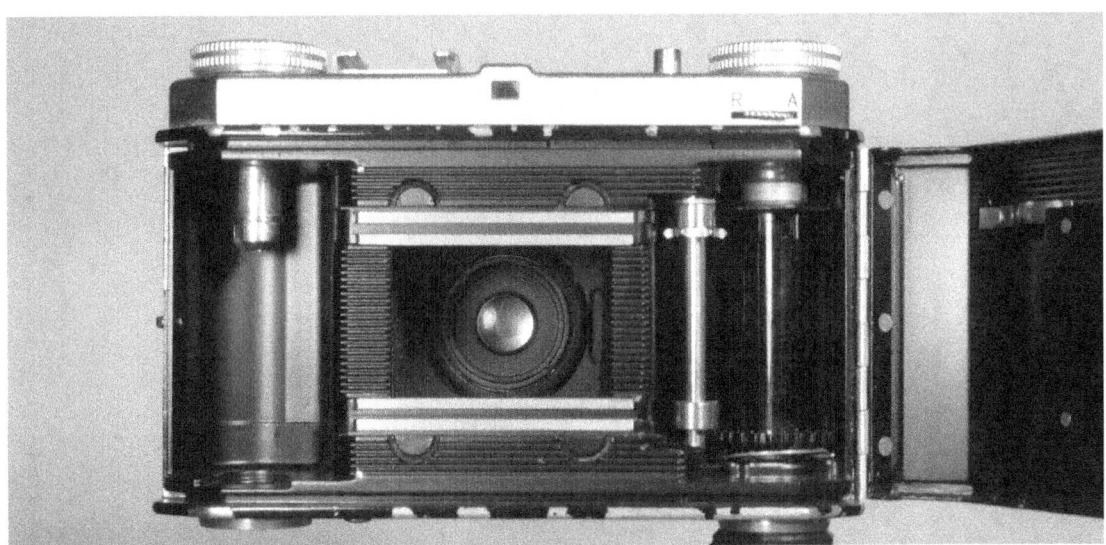

The R/A lever enables rewinding. Push towards R and hold while turning rewind dial on top left of camera.

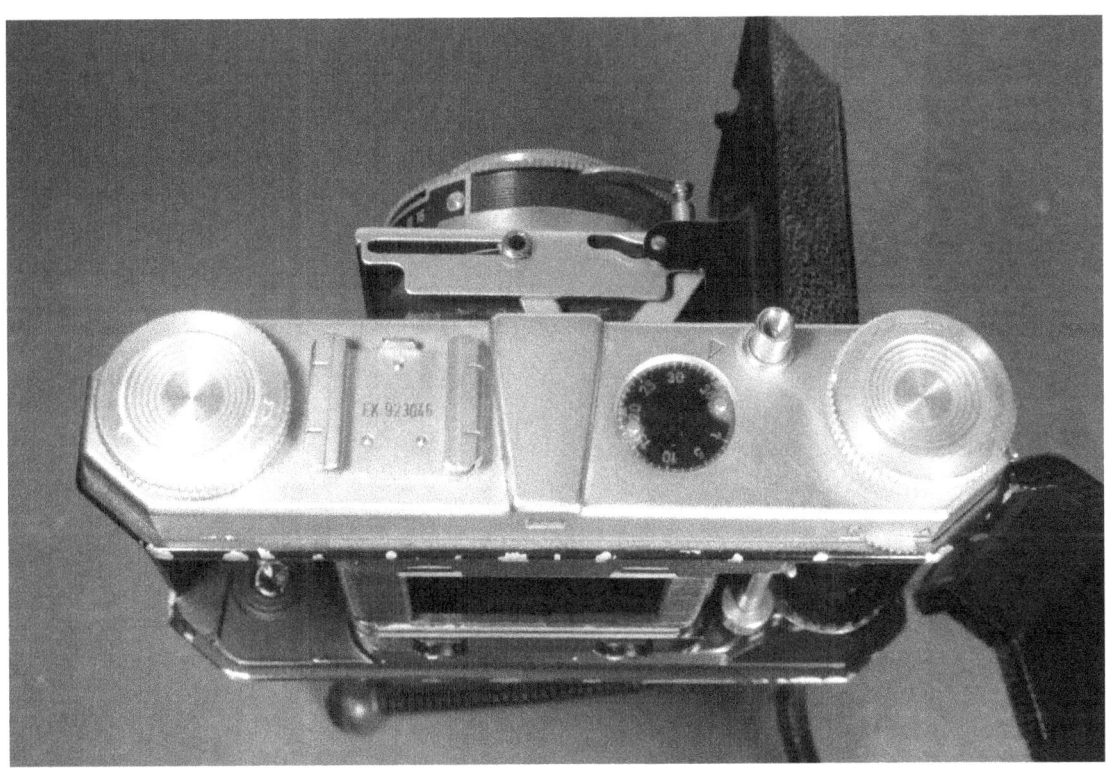

Kodak S400SL

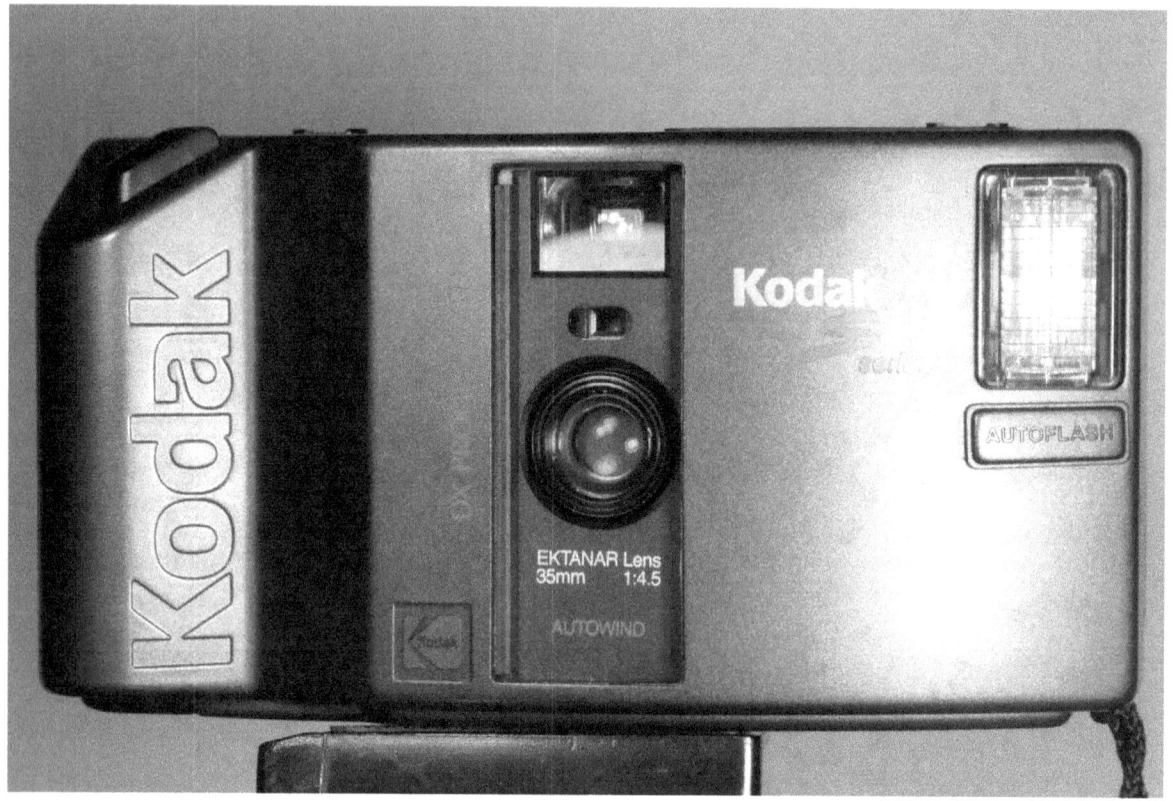

Name: Kodak S400SL.
Type: 35MM Point and Shoot.
Film Size: 35MM.
Year of manufacture: late 1980s.
Manufacturer: Eastman Kodak Company.
Country: USA.
Shutter settings: None.
Aperture settings: None.
Exposure setting: Automatic.
Lens: Kodak Ektanar 35MM, F/4.5.
Interchangeable lenses? No.
How do you focus? Fixed focus.
Viewfinder: Eye level.
Loading film: Open back, load full cassette, extend film to mark.
Automatic film advance? Yes.
Automatic film rewind? Yes.
Cable release socket: No.
Tripod socket: No.
Battery type: AA, quantity 2.
Unique features:
> Detects the ISO (ASA) speed of the film with DX sensing. While common now, it was relatively new at the time.

Kodak S400SL

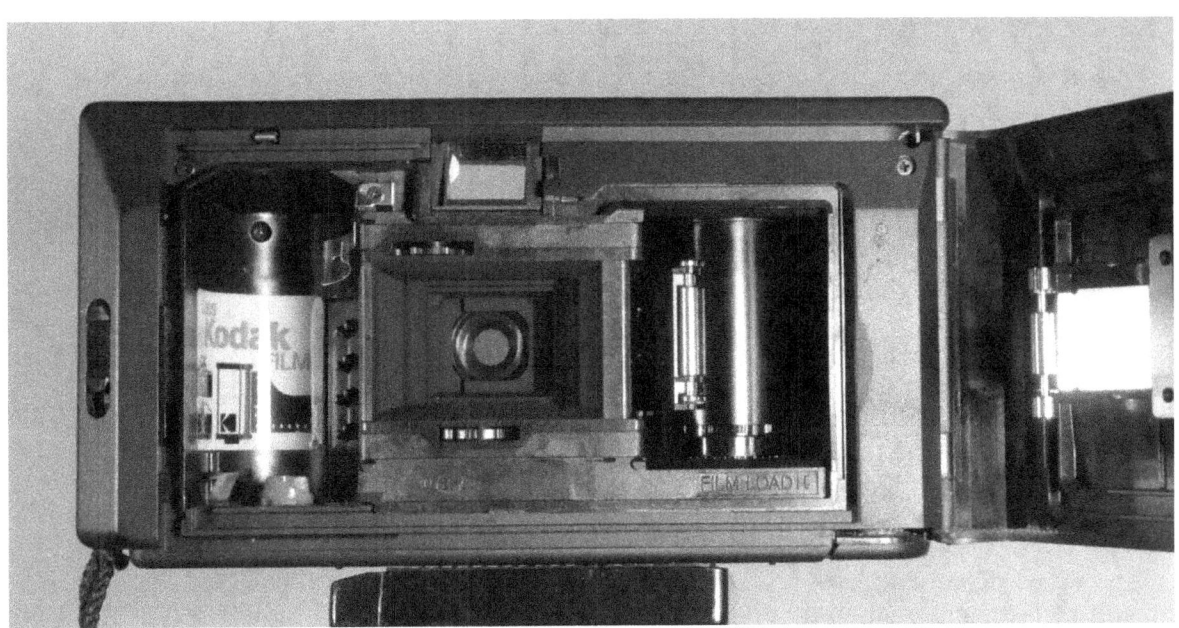

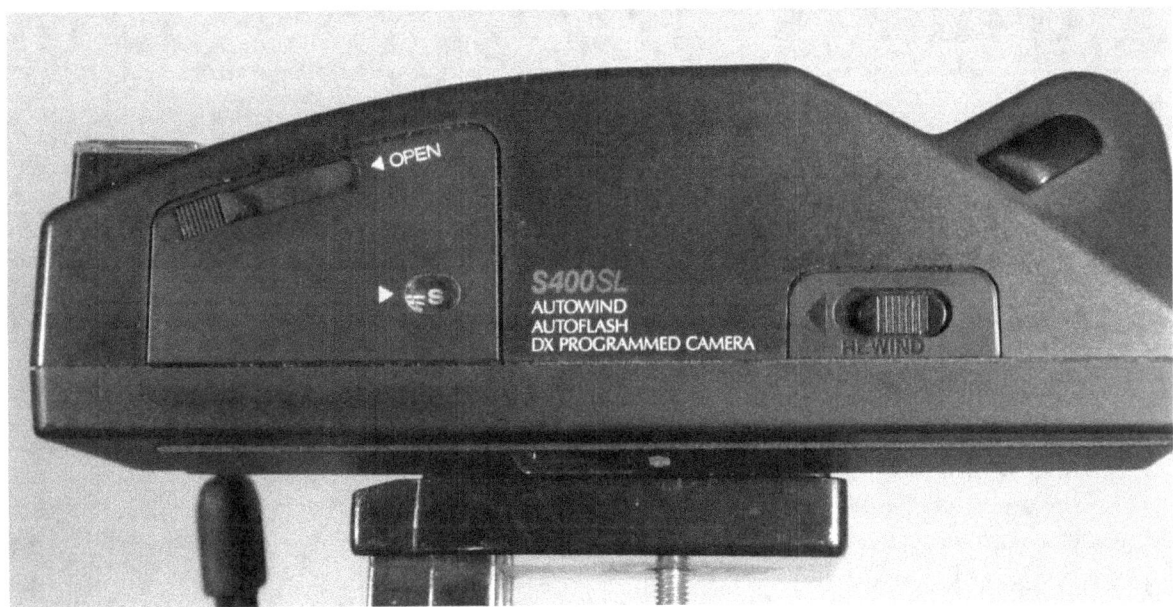

Kodak Signet 35

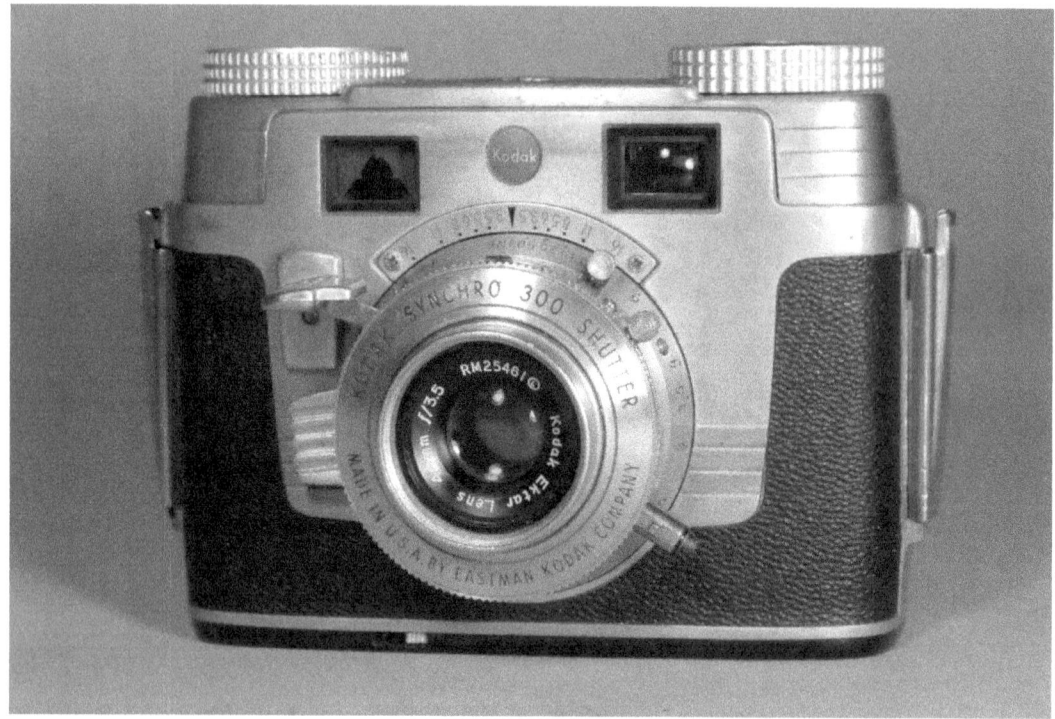

Name: Kodak Signet 35.
Type: 35MM, rangefinder.
Film Size: 35MM.
Year of manufacture: 1950s.
Manufacturer: Eastman Kodak Company.
Country: USA.
Shutter settings: B, 1/25, 1/50, 1/100, 1/300.
Cock shutter before taking picture.
Aperture settings: F/3.5, 4, 5.6, 8, 11, 16, 22.
Exposure setting: Manual.
   Manual exposure guide on back.
Lens: Kodak Ektar, 44MM.
Interchangeable lenses? No.
How do you focus? Coupled rangefinder, distance scale on lens, turn lever around lens.
Viewfinder: Eye level.
Loading film: Open back, load full cassette, thread into takeup reel.
Automatic film advance? No (manual).
Automatic film rewind? No (manual).
Cable release socket: Yes.
Tripod socket: Yes.
Battery type: None.
Unique features: Flash synchronization up to 1/300. Handy exposure guide on back of camera. Small lever on camera front, bottom, allows intentional double exposures.

Kodak Signet 35

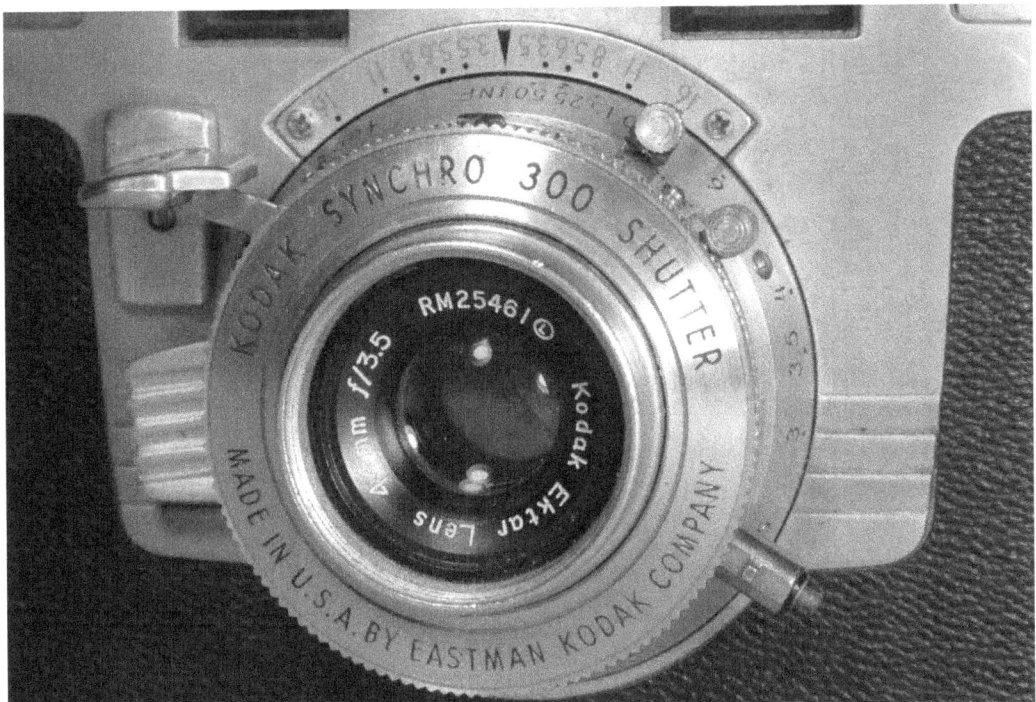

There are two round levers on the lens ring. The one shown here at "one o'clock" is the aperture setting lever. The one at "two o'clock" is the shutter cocking lever.

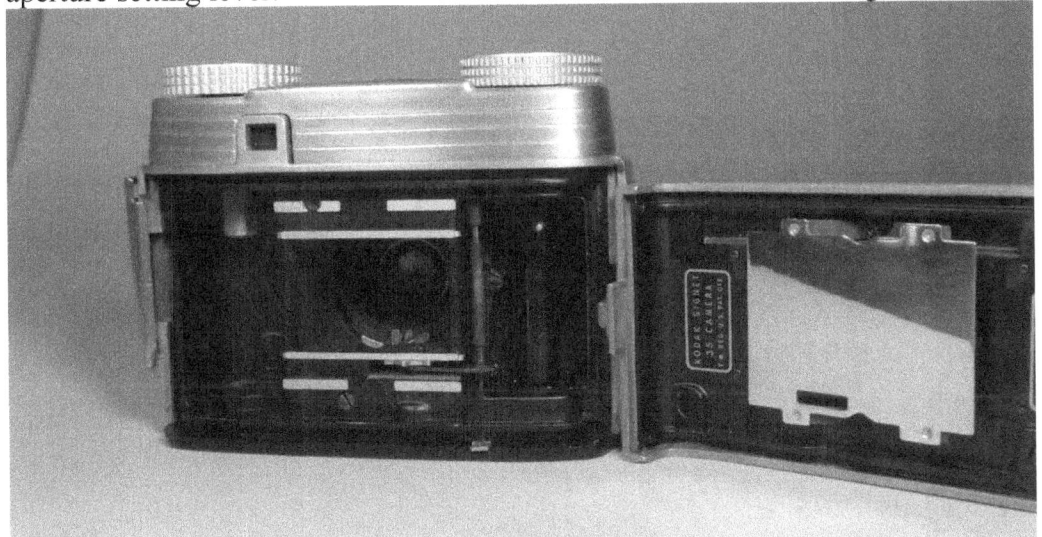

At the end of the roll, press the rewind lever, shown on the back of the camera, bottom right, to the left, and turn the rewind knob, upper left in this picture.

Kodak Six-16

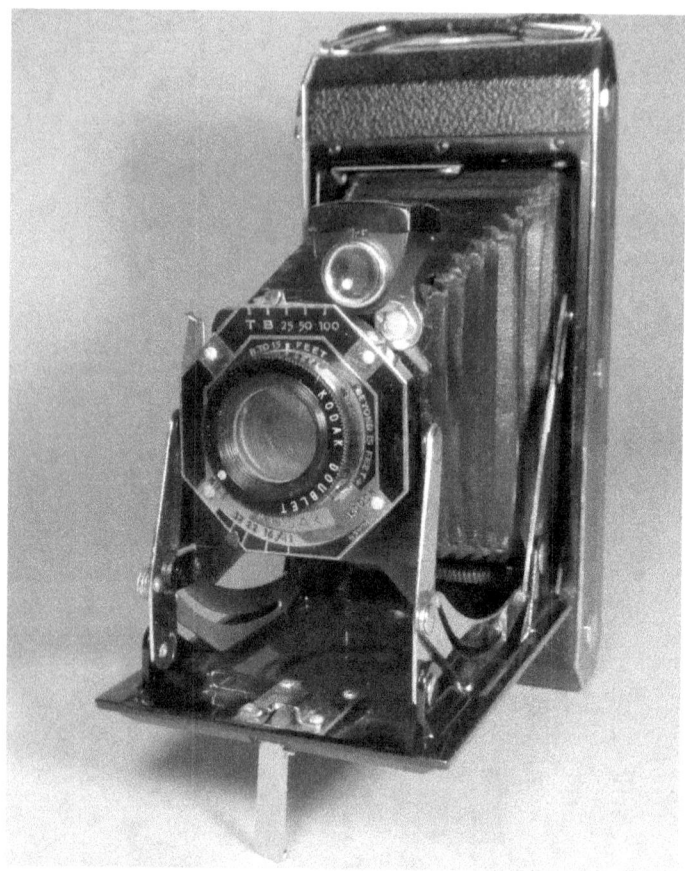

Name: Kodak Six-16.
Type: Folding bellows rollfilm.
Film Size: 616.
Year of manufacture: 1930s.
Manufacturer: Eastman Kodak Company.
Country: USA.
Shutter settings: T, B, 1/25, 1/50, 1/100.
Aperture settings: F/11, 16, 22, 32.
Exposure setting: Manual.
Lens: Kodak Doublet, about 125MM focal length.
Interchangeable lenses? No.
How do you focus? Estimate distance, turn front lens element.
Viewfinder: Waist level.
Loading film: Open back, insert full roll, thread paper leader onto takeup spool.
Automatic film advance? No (manual).
Automatic film rewind? N/A.
Cable release socket: No.
Tripod socket: Yes.
Battery type: None.
Unique features:

Kodak Six-16

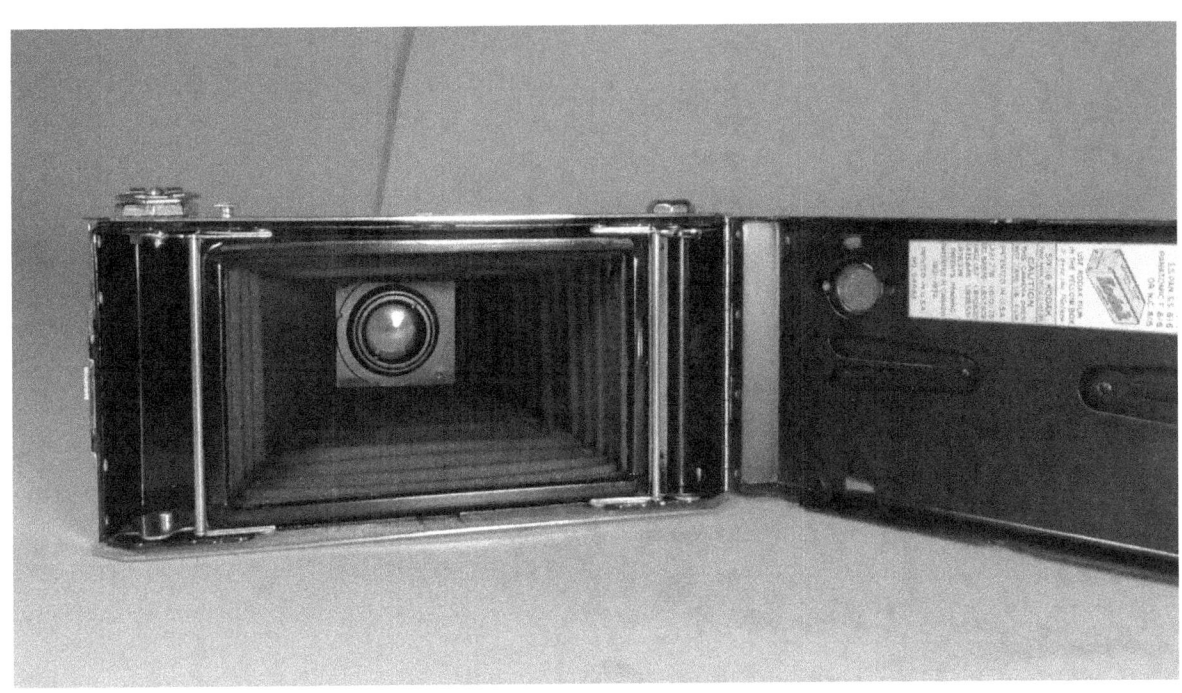

Kodak Vigilant 6-20

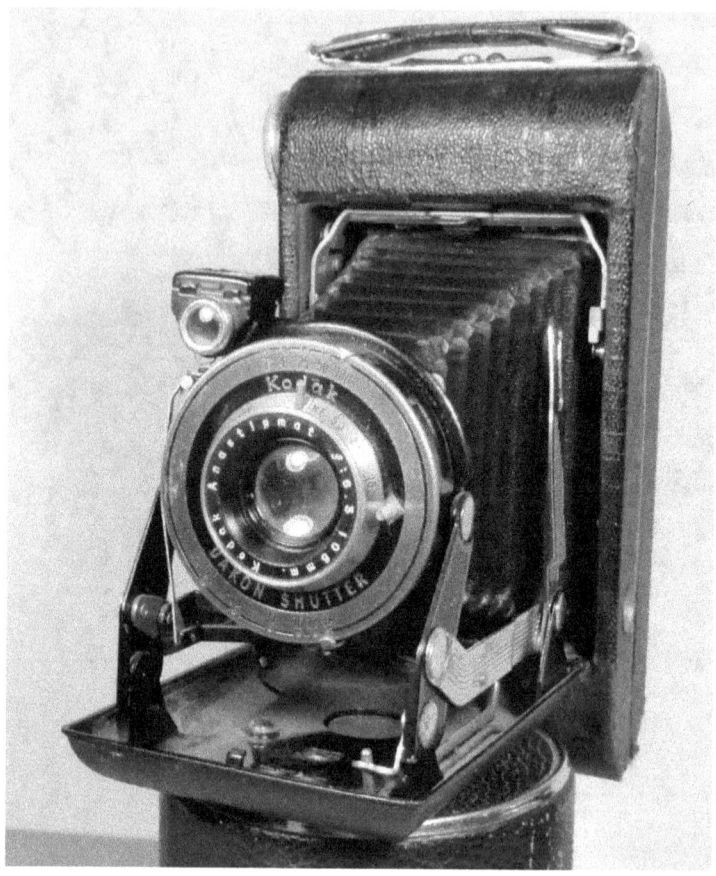

Name: Kodak Vigilant 6-20.
Type: Folding bellows, rollfilm.
Film Size: 620.
Year of manufacture: Early 1940s.
Manufacturer: Eastman Kodak Company.
Country: USA.
Shutter settings: T, B, 1/25, 1/50, 1/100.
Aperture settings: F/6.3, 8, 11, 16, 22, 32. (Other models had different lens openings.)
Exposure setting: Manual.
Lens: Kodak Anastigmat, 105MM.
Interchangeable lenses? No.
How do you focus? Front lens element.
Viewfinder: Waist level, eye level.
Loading film: Open back, insert full roll, thread paper leader onto takeup spool.
Automatic film advance? No (manual).
Automatic film rewind? N/A.
Cable release socket: Yes.
Tripod socket: Yes.
Battery type: None.
Unique features:

Kodak Vigilant 6-20

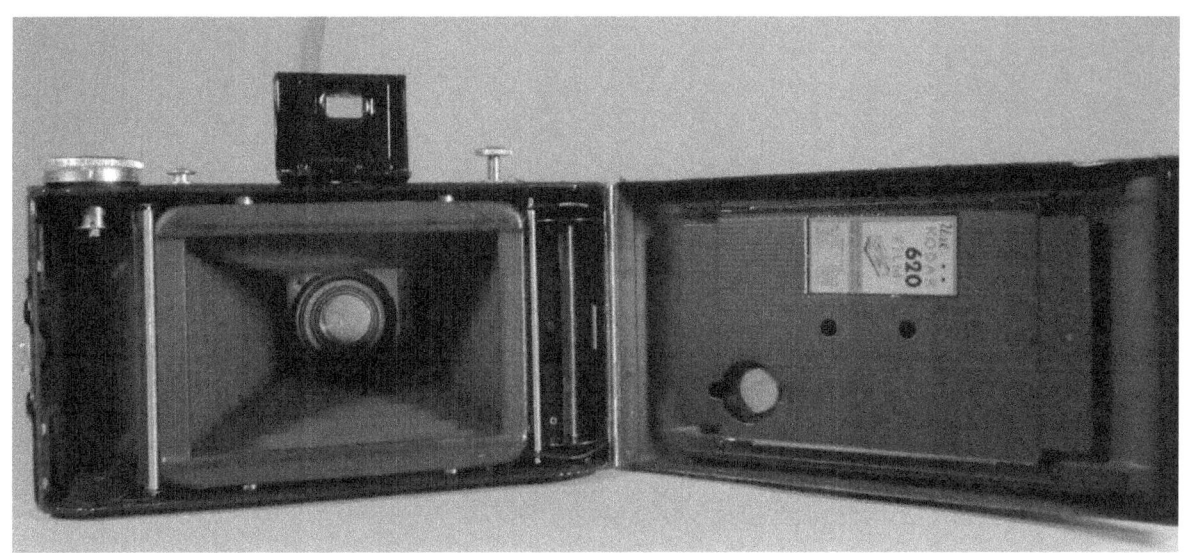

Kodak 1A Pocket Kodak

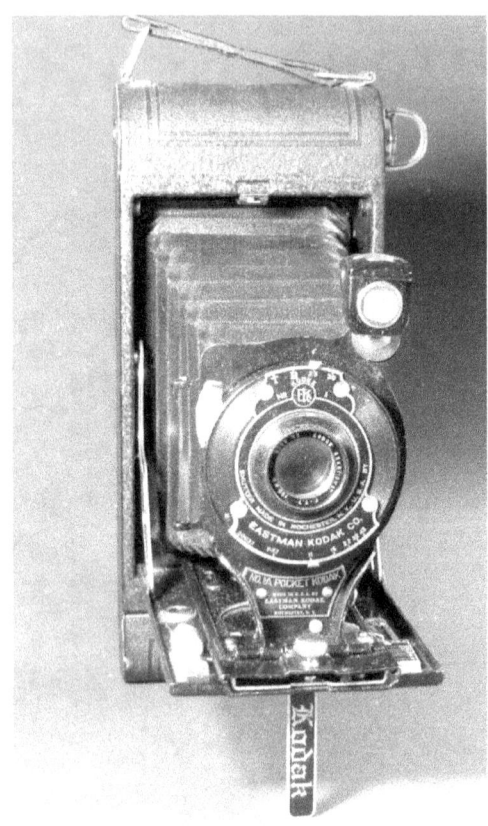

Name: No 1A Pocket Kodak.
Type: Folding bellows, rollfilm.
Film Size: A-116.
Year of manufacture: Around 1930.
Manufacturer: Eastman Kodak Company.
Country: USA.
Shutter settings: T, B, 1/25, 1/50.
Aperture settings: F/7.7 to F/45.
Exposure setting: Manual.
Lens: Kodak Anastigmat, 130MM.
Interchangeable lenses? No.
How do you focus? Distance Scale, front element.
Viewfinder: Reflecting waist level, frame.
Loading film: Open back, insert full roll, thread paper leader onto takeup spool.
Automatic film advance? No (manual).
Automatic film rewind? No (manual).
Cable release socket: Yes.
Tripod socket: Yes.
Battery type:None.
Unique features: Uses autographic film. You were able to write notes which would appear on the developed film.

Kodak 1A Pocket Kodak

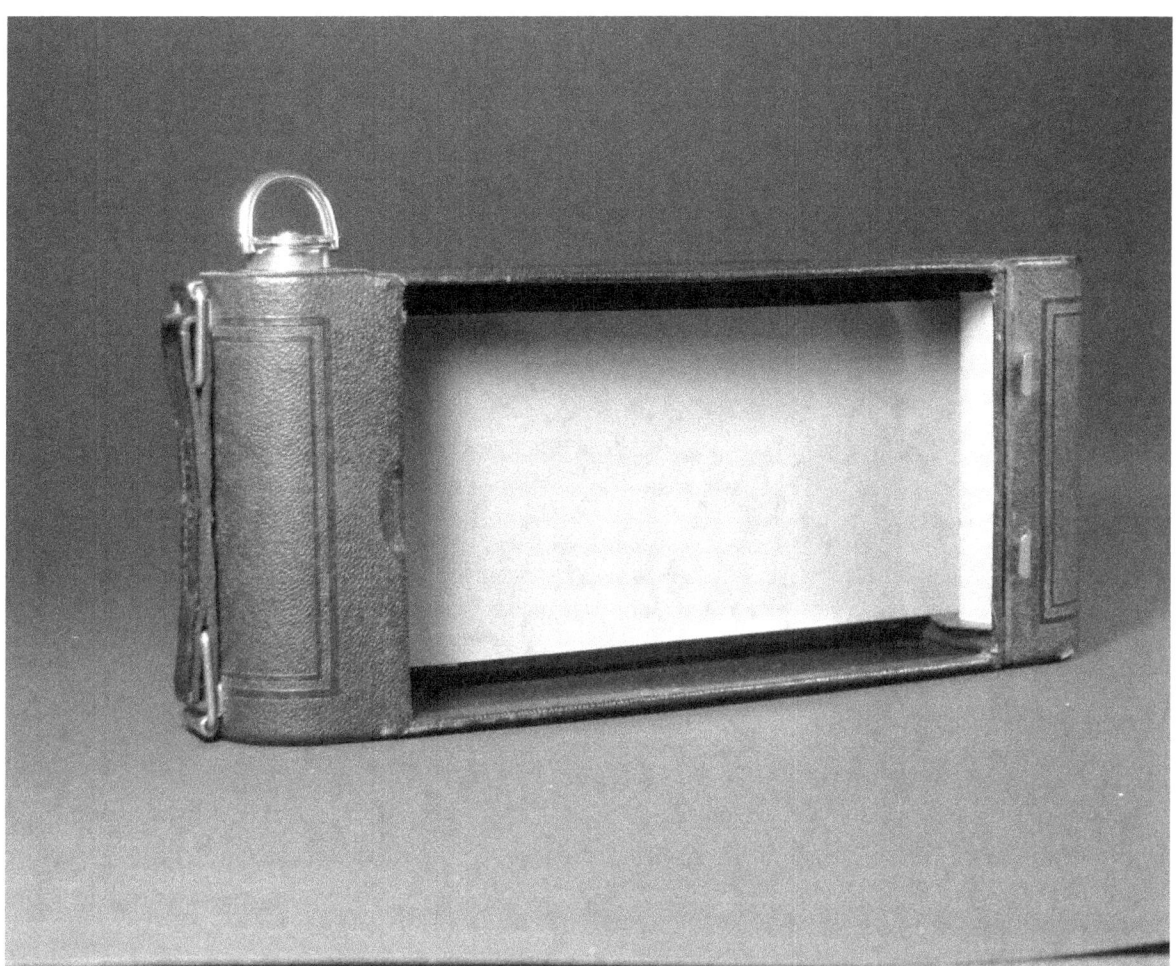

To load film you remove the back. You place the full spool on the right, in this picture, and the empty spool on the left, in this picture. Winding key is in upper left in this picture.

Mamiya 35 S2

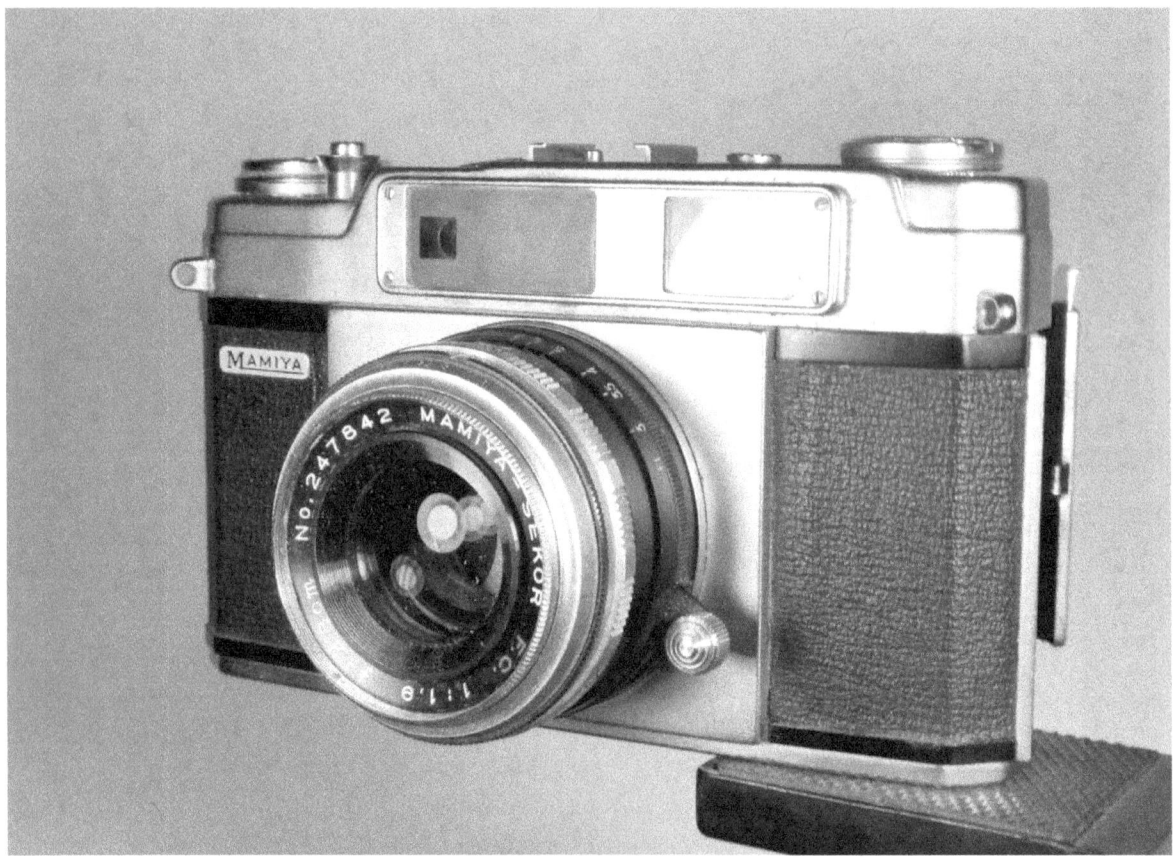

Name: Mamiya 35 S2.
Type: 35MM rangefinder.
Film Size: 35MM.
Year of manufacture: Late 1950s.
Manufacturer:Mamiya.
Country: Japan.
Shutter settings: B, 1 second – 1/500.
Aperture settings: F/1.9 – F/16.
Exposure setting: Manual.
Lens: Mamiya Sekor, 48MM, F/1.9.
Interchangeable lenses? No.
How do you focus? Coupled rangefinder.
Viewfinder: Eye level.
Loading film: Open back, load full cassette, thread into takeup reel.
Automatic film advance? No (manual).
Automatic film rewind? No (manual).
Cable release socket: Yes.
Tripod socket: Yes.
Battery type: None.
Unique features:

Mamiya 35 S2

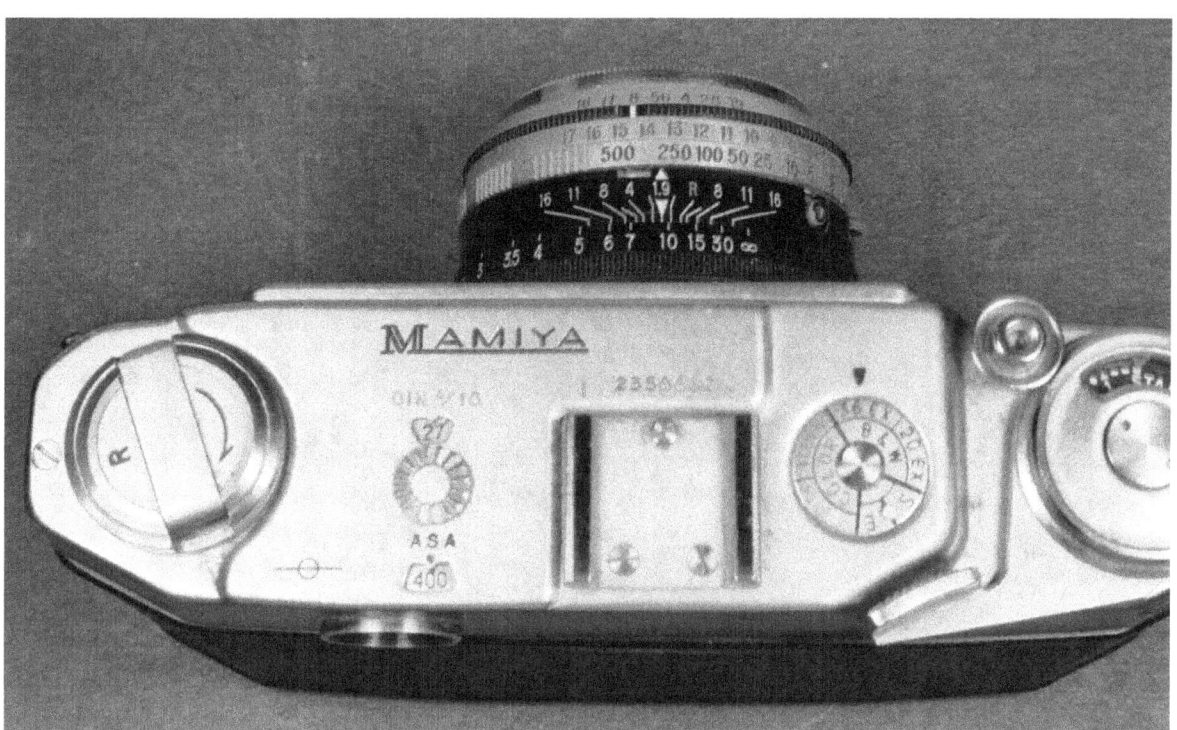

The film plane marker is shown between the rewind knob and the accessory shoe.

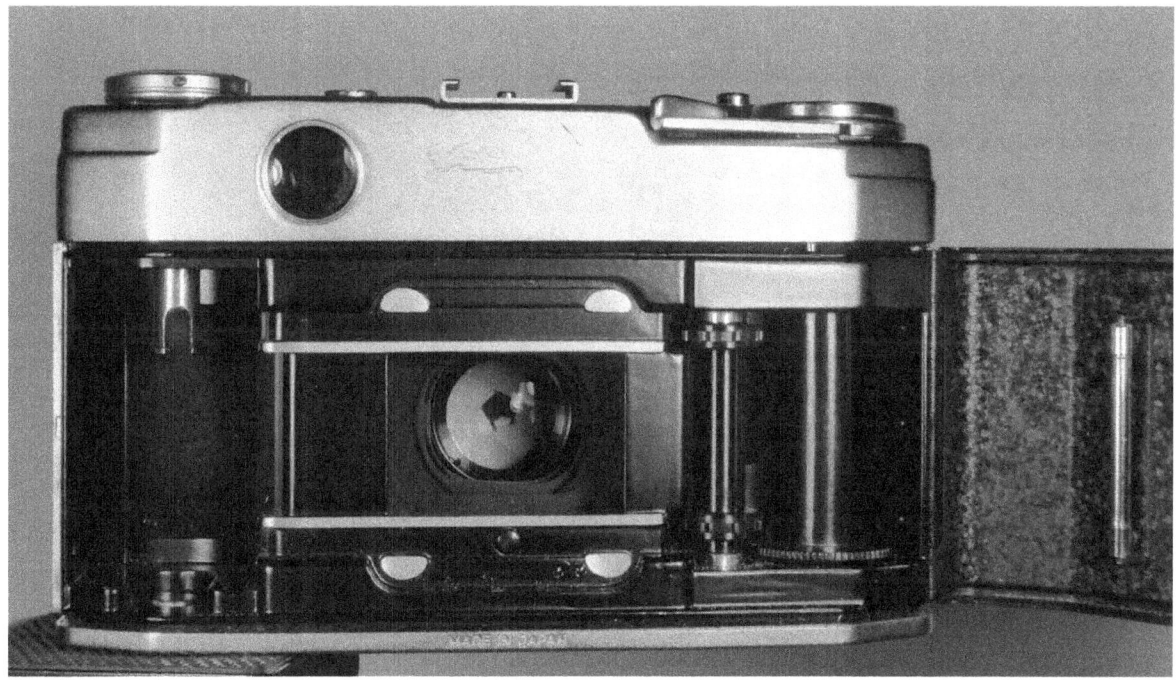

Mamiya Ruby

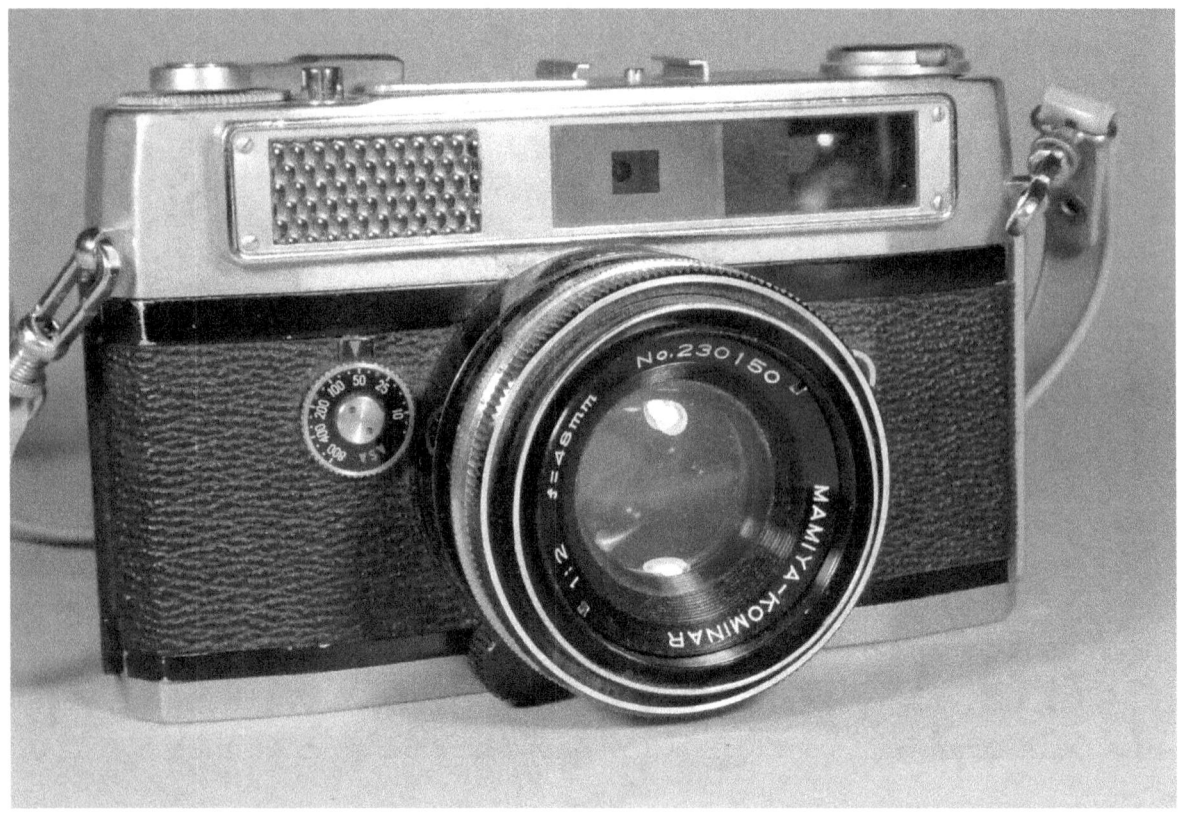

Name: Mamiya Ruby.
Type: 35MM rangefinder.
Film Size: 35MM.
Year of manufacture: 1959.
Manufacturer: Mamiya.
Country: Japan.
Shutter settings: B, 1 second – 1/500.
Aperture settings: F/2 – F/16.
Exposure setting: Photocell. Transfer meter (top of camera) manually to camera.
Lens: Mamiya-Kominar F/2, 48MM.
Interchangeable lenses? No.
How do you focus? Rangefinder through viewfinder.
Viewfinder: Eye level.
Loading film: Open back, load full cassette, thread into takeup reel.
Automatic film advance? No (manual).
Automatic film rewind? No (manual).
Cable release socket: Yes.
Tripod socket: Yes.
Battery type: None.
Unique features: Leaf shutter.

Mamiya Ruby

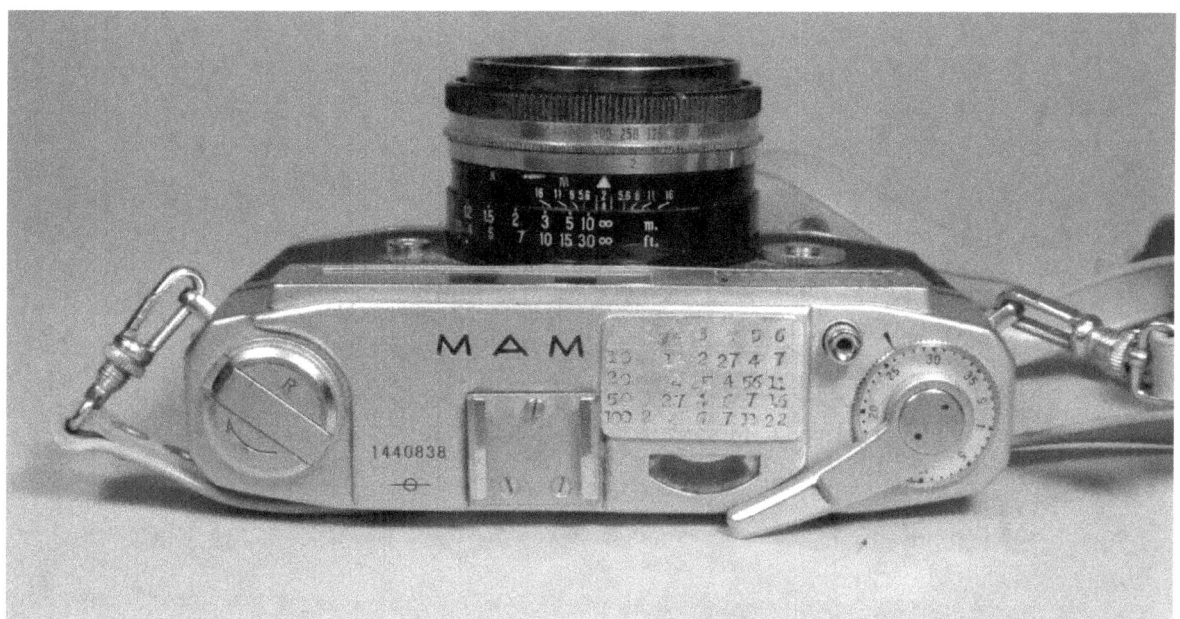

Previous owner attached exposure table to top of this camera. Exposure meter needle is just under it.

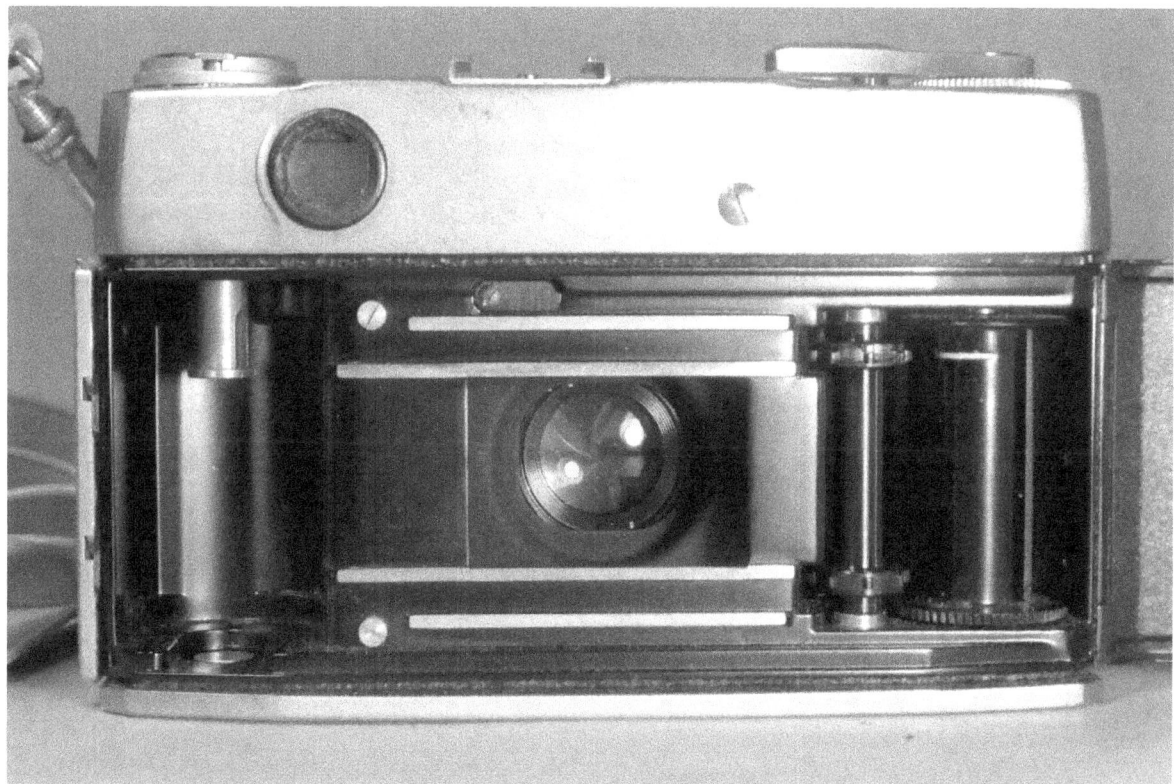

Leaf shutter visible.

Minolta 16 EE II

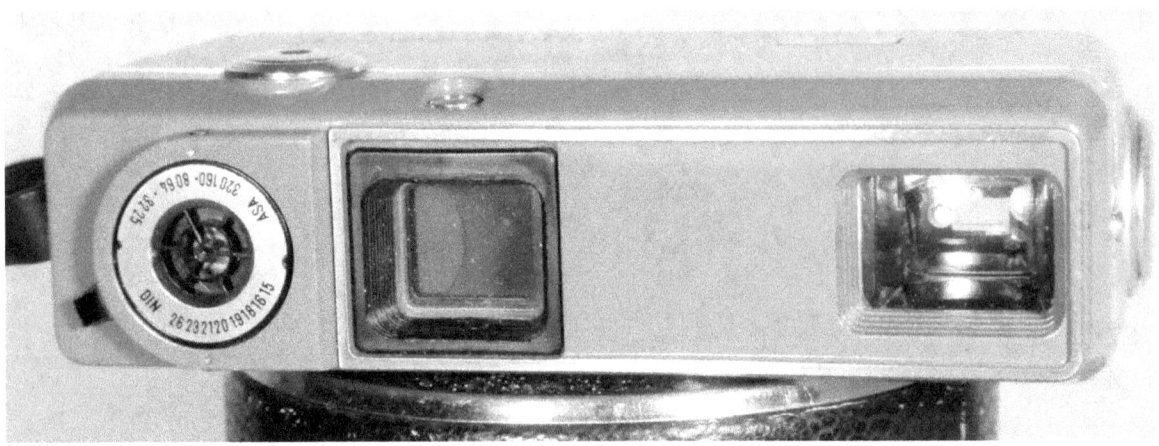

Name: Minolta 16 EE II.
Type: 16MM Subminiature.
Film Size: 16MM cartridge.
Year of manufacture: 1963.
Manufacturer: Minolta.
Country: Japan.
Shutter settings: 1/50 (select "H" on exposure dial), 1/200 (select "L").
 ("F" setting gives F/11 and 1/30, for flash.)
Aperture settings: Automatic. Not under user control.
Exposure setting: Automatic, shutter priority.
Lens: Rokkor F/2.8 25MM.
Interchangeable lenses? No.
How do you focus? Estimate distance by zones, set zone by lever on top of camera.
Viewfinder: Eye level.
Loading film:
 Open back, insert film cartridge.
Automatic film advance? No (manual).
Automatic film rewind? N/A. Film cartridge does not require rewinding.
Cable release socket: No.
Tripod socket: Yes.
Battery type: EPX625.
Unique features:

Minolta 16 EE II

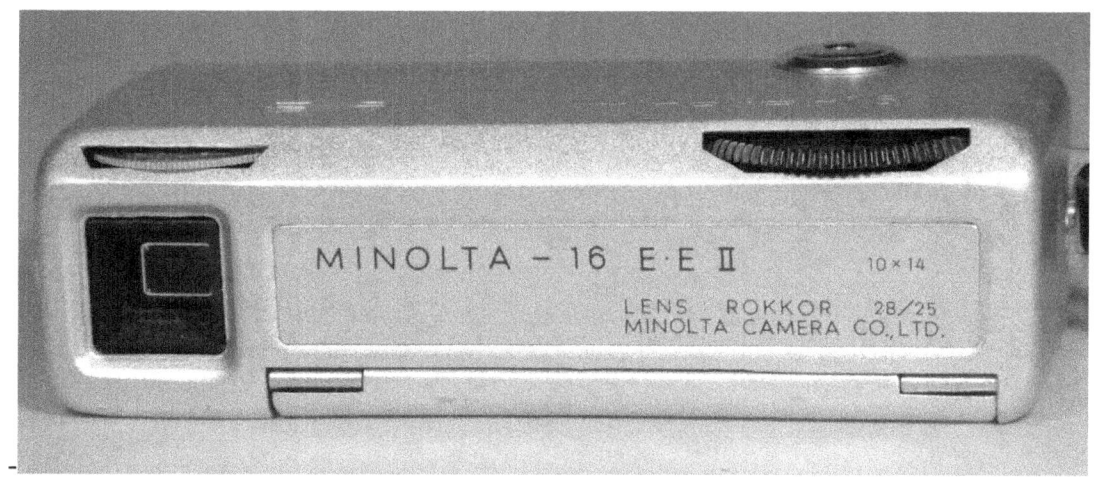

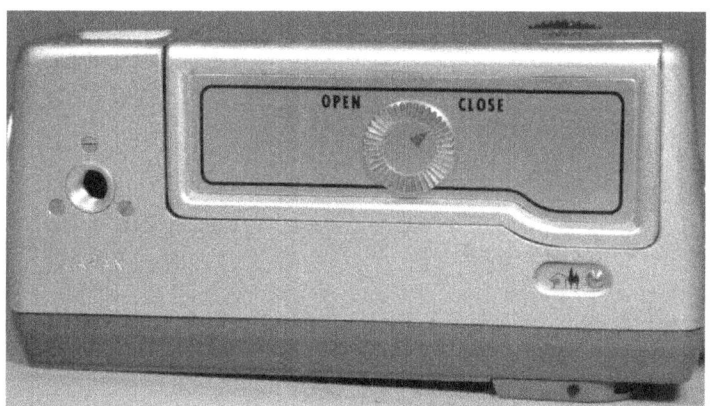

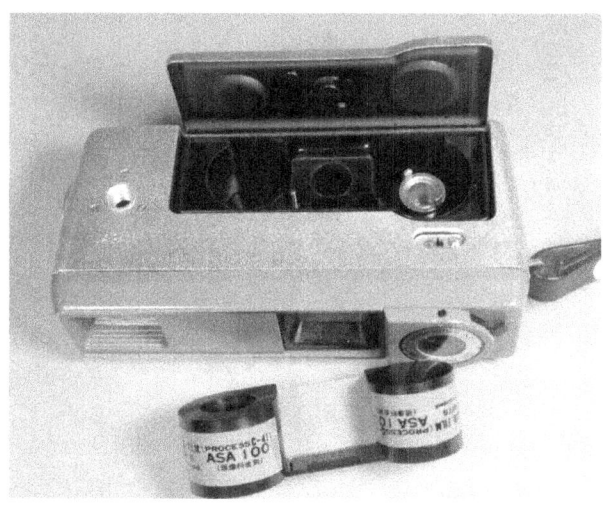

Minolta 16 MG-S

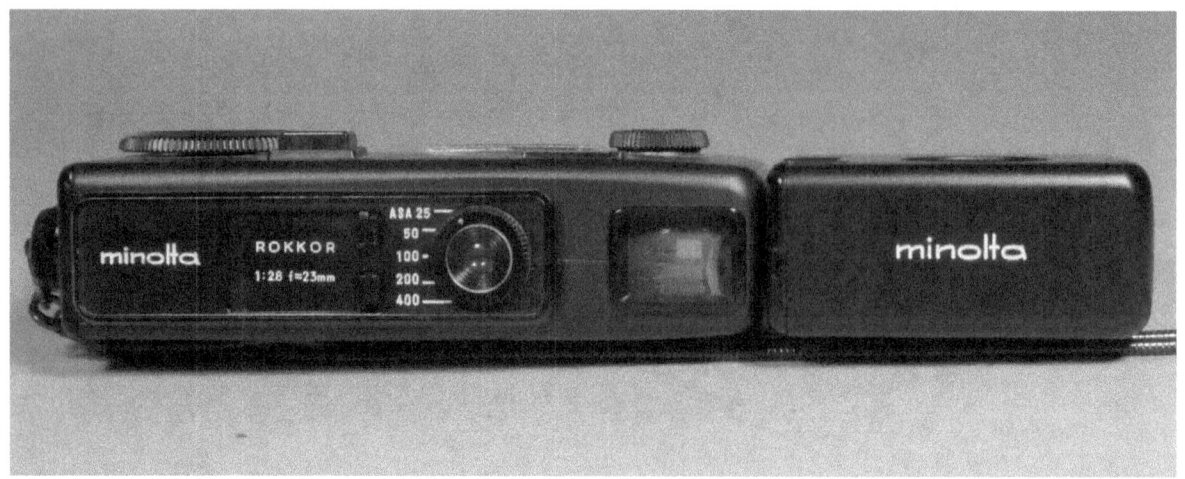

Name: Minolta 16 MG-S.
Type: 16MM subminiature 18 exposure cartridge.
Film Size: 16MM.
Year of manufacture: 1970.
Manufacturer: Minolta.
Country: Japan.
Shutter settings: 1/30 to 1/500.
Aperture settings: F/2.8 – F/16.
Exposure setting: Manual, or automatic shutter priority with CdS metering.
Lens: Rokkor F/2.8 23MM.
Interchangeable lenses? No.
How do you focus? Fixed focus, but sliding door over lens puts closeup element in front of lens. (1.2 M, 4 feet.)
Viewfinder: Eye level.
Loading film:
    Open back, load film cartridge.
Automatic film advance? No (manual). Big wheel on top.
Automatic film rewind? N/A. Film cartridge does not require rewinding.
Cable release socket: No.
Tripod socket: No.
Battery type: Mallory PX-675 or Eveready EPX-675 Mercury 1.35 volts. Required for operation.
Unique features: A dayload/daylight developing tank was made by Minolta.

Minolta 16 MG-S

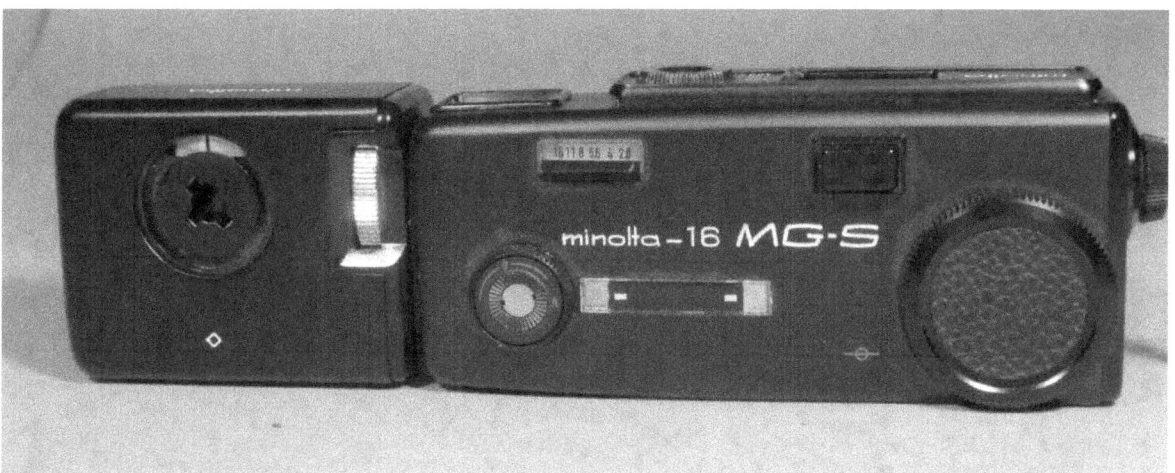

Top, with flash unit attached. Showing exposure needle meter. Exposure control knob is at left; film advance knob at right.

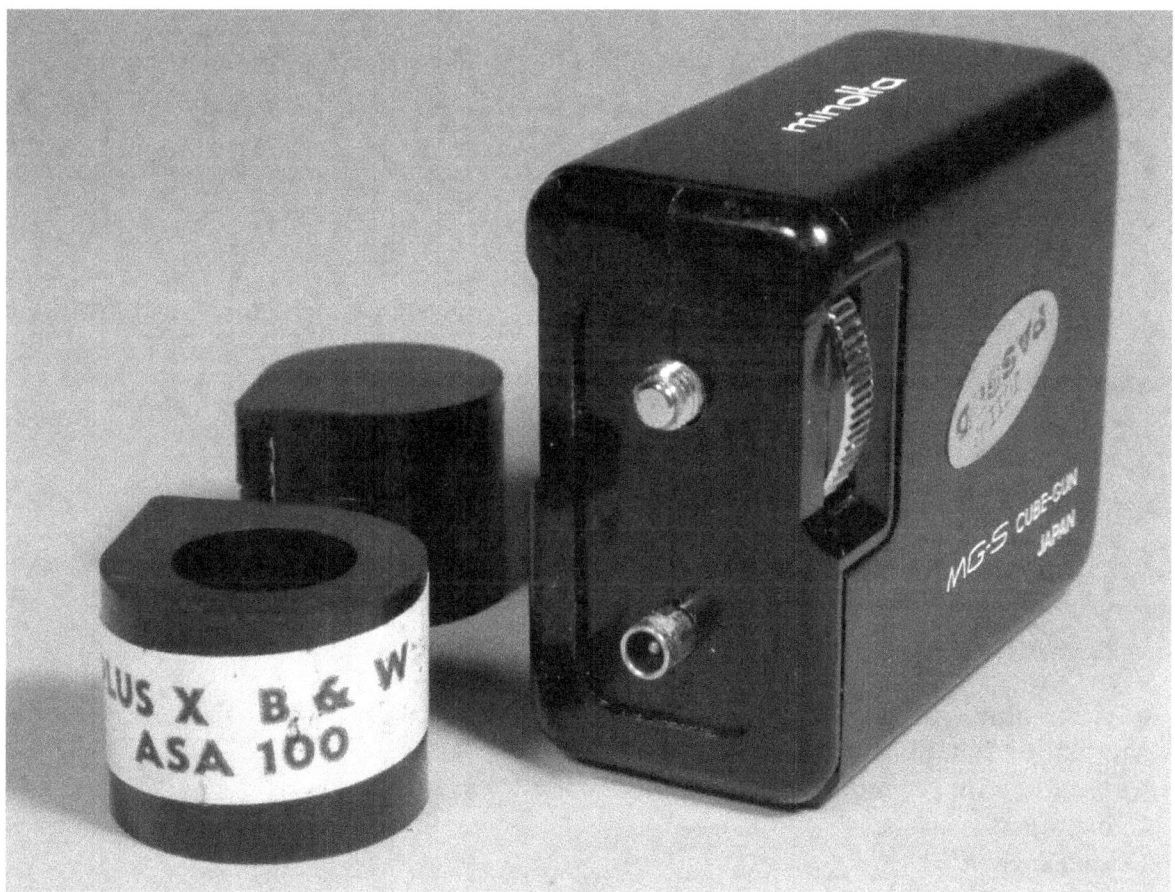

Film is in cassettes. No rewinding is needed.

Minolta AF-Tele

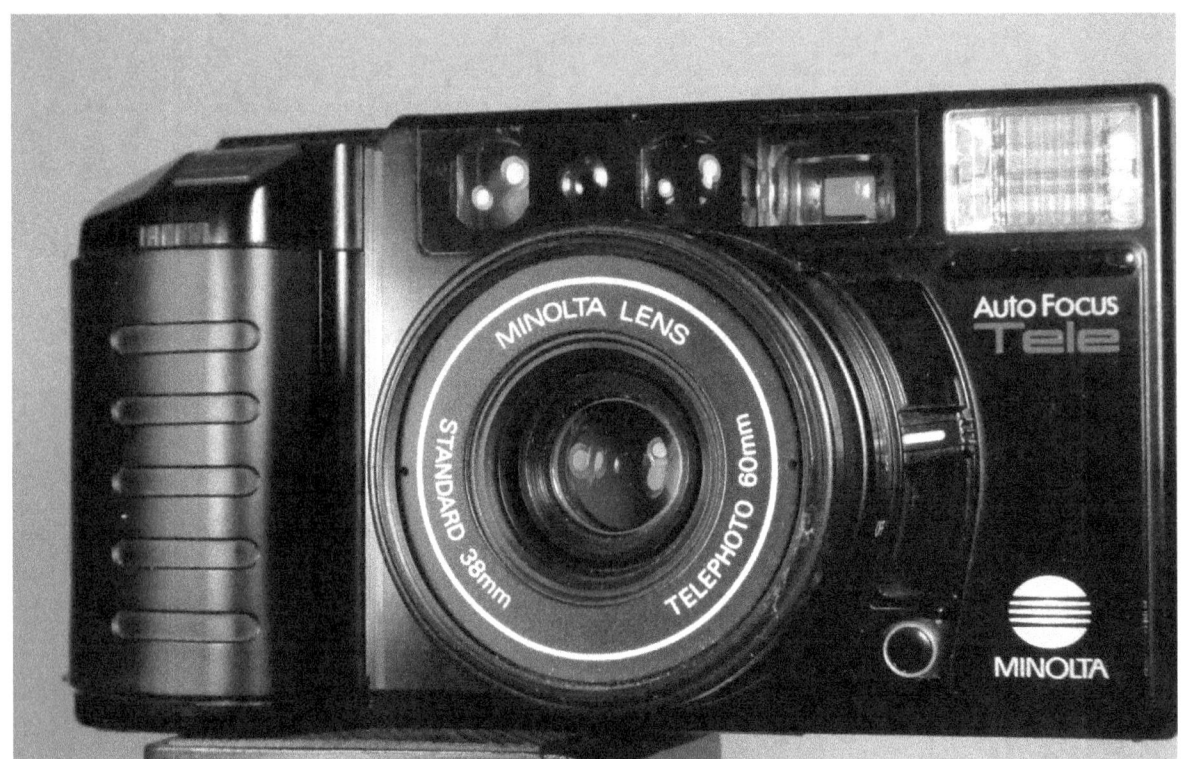

Name: Minolta AF-Tele.
Type: 35MM autofocus.
Film Size: 35MM.
Year of manufacture: 1985.
Manufacturer: Minolta.
Country: Japan.
Shutter settings: Not under user control.
Aperture settings: Not under user control.
Exposure setting: Automatic.
Lens: Minolta 38MM and 60MM, F/2.8.
Interchangeable lenses? No.
How do you focus? Autofocus.
Viewfinder: Eye level.
Loading film: Open back, load full cassette, pull film out, extend to take up reel.
Automatic film advance? Yes.
Automatic film rewind? Yes.
Cable release socket: No.
Tripod socket: Yes.
Battery type: DL 223A, BR-P2P or AA, quantity 2.
Unique features:

Minolta AF-Tele

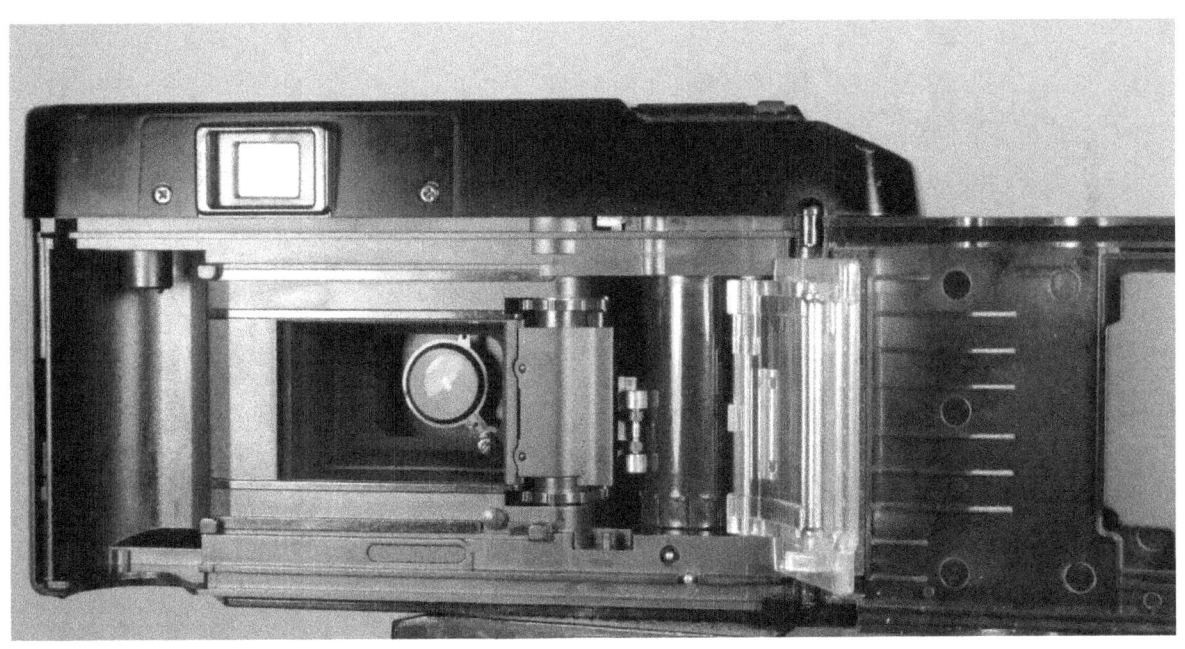

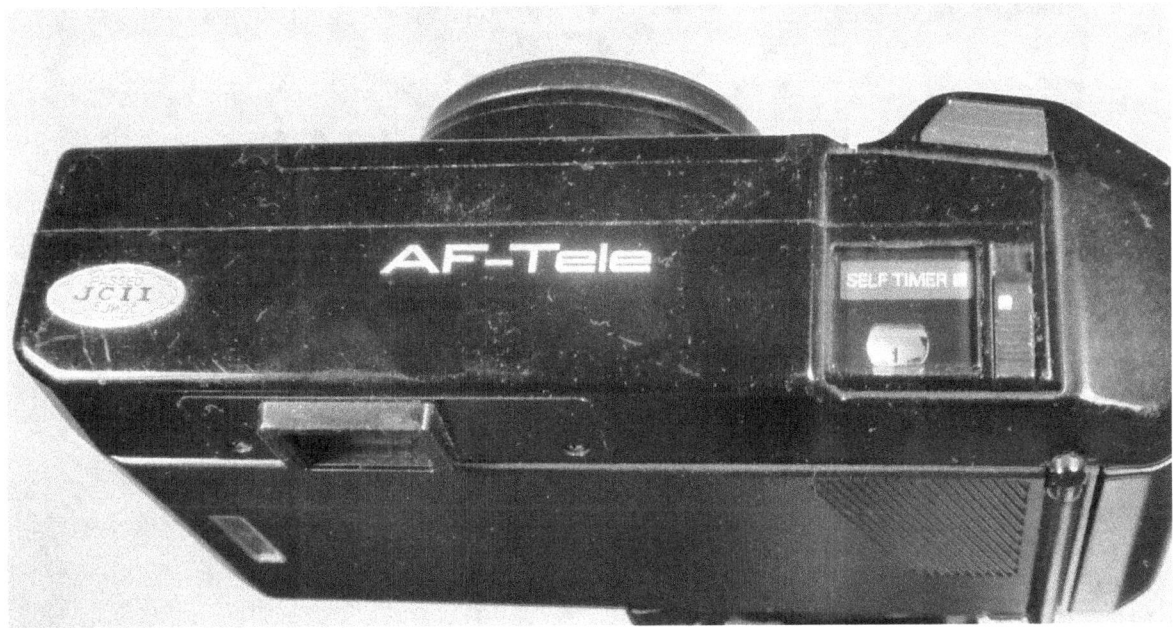

Minolta Autopak 700

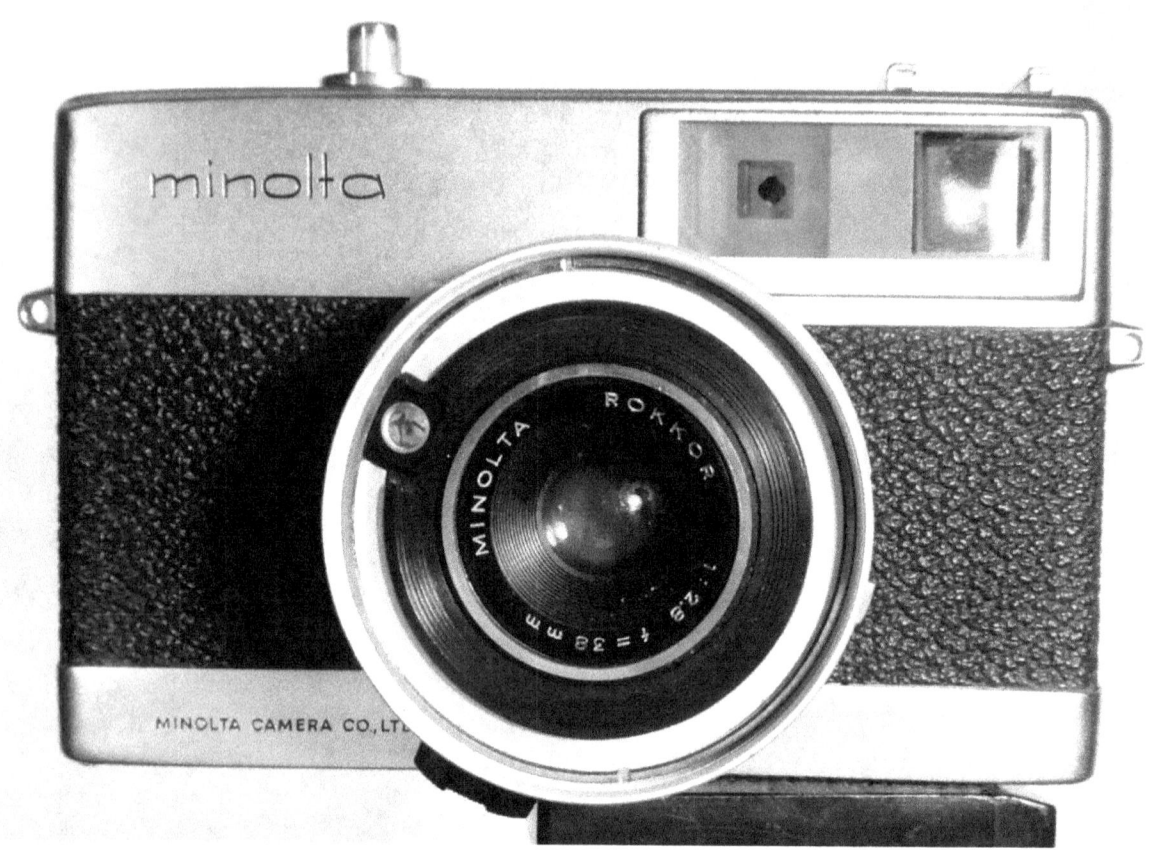

Name: Minolta Autopak 700.
Type: 126 rangefinder.
Film Size: 126 cassette.
Year of manufacture: 1966.
Manufacturer: Minolta.
Country: Japan.
Shutter settings: A, B, 1/30 – 1/250.
Aperture settings: A, F/2.8 – F/22.
Exposure setting: Automatic and manual.
Lens: Rokkor F/2.8 38MM.
Interchangeable lenses? No.
How do you focus? Coupled rangefinder. Turn lever on lens, match split image.
Viewfinder: Eye level.
Loading film: Open back, insert film cartridge.
Automatic film advance? N/A.
Automatic film rewind? N/A. Film cartridge does not require rewinding.
Cable release socket: Yes.
Tripod socket: Yes.
Battery type: PX13, PX625.
Unique features:

Minolta Autopak 700

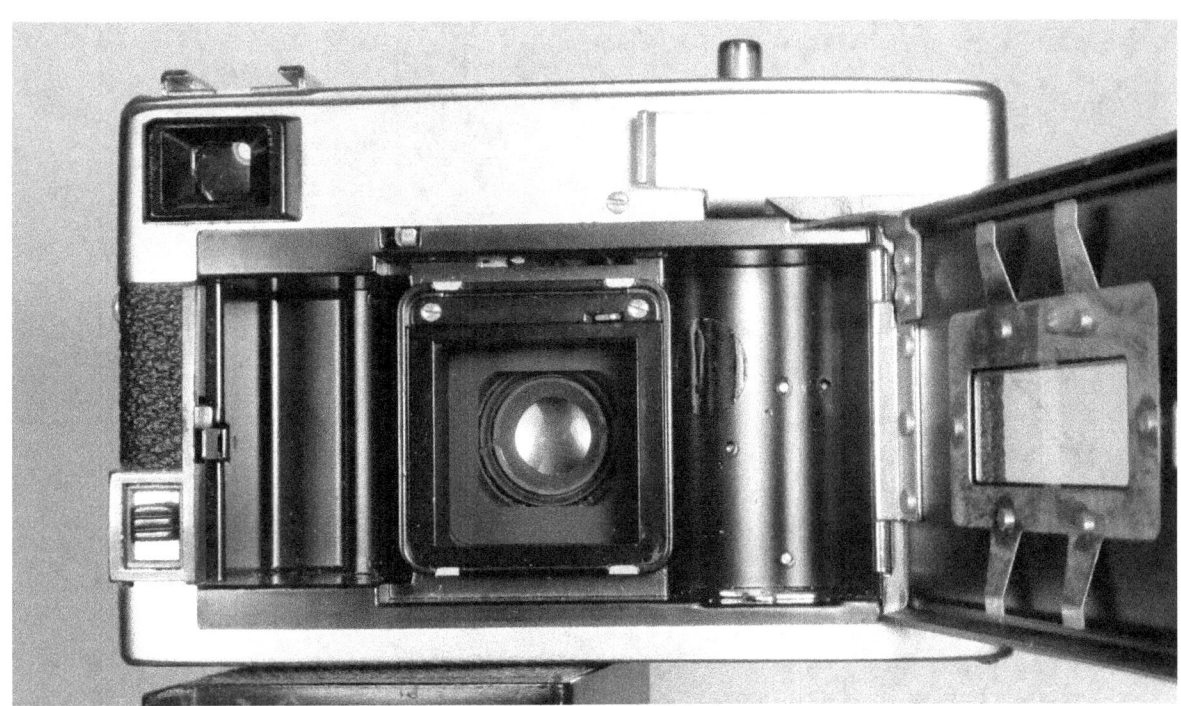

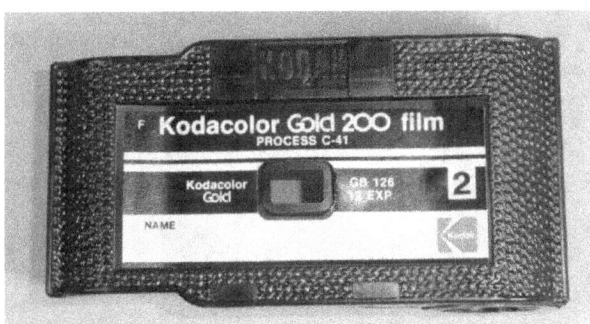

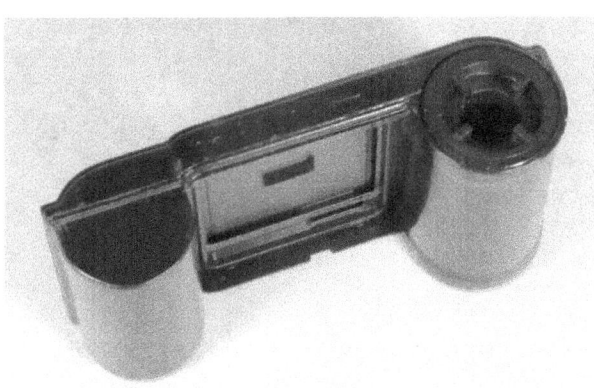

Minolta Maxxum 50

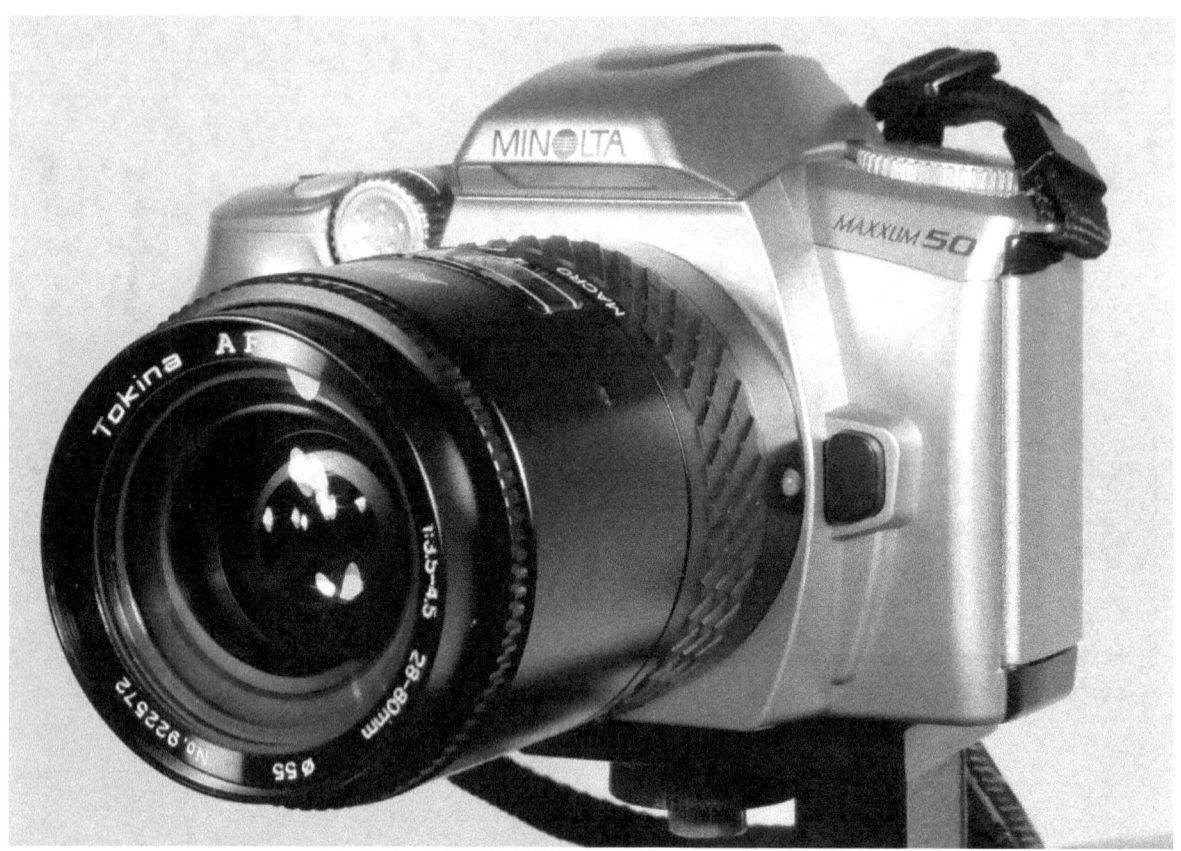

Name: Minolta Maxxum 50.
Type: 35MM SLR autofocus.
Film Size: 35MM.
Year of manufacture: 2004.
Manufacturer: Minolta.
Country: Made in China.
Shutter settings: 30 seconds – 1/2000.
Aperture settings: F/3.5 – F/22.
Exposure setting: Automatic, manual, programmed shooting modes. Aperture or shutter priority.
Lens: Lens on camera is Tokina AF, 28 - 80MM, F/3.5.
Interchangeable lenses? Yes.
How do you focus? Autofocus, manual.
Viewfinder: Eye level.
Loading film: Open back, load full cassette, extend film to mark.
Automatic film advance? Yes.
Automatic film rewind? Automatic, manual.
Cable release socket: No.
Tripod socket: Yes.
Battery type: CR2, quantity 2.
Unique features: Date and time can be set.

Minolta Maxxum 50

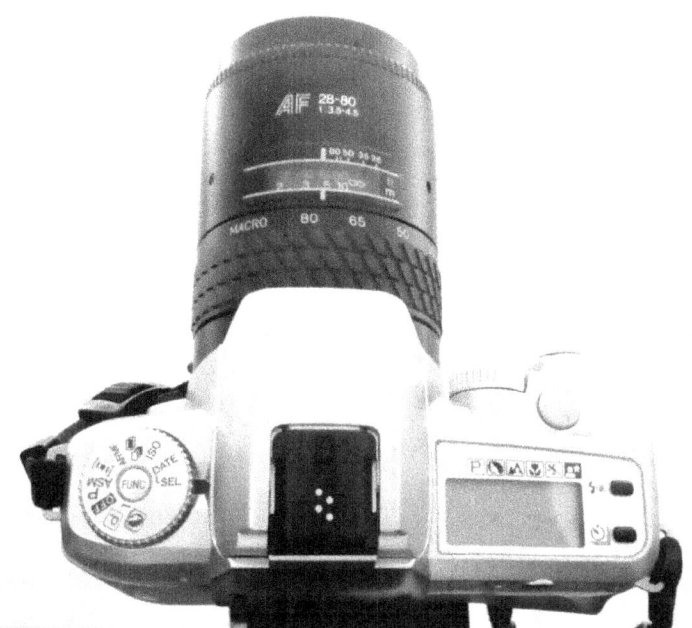

Program dial on left.

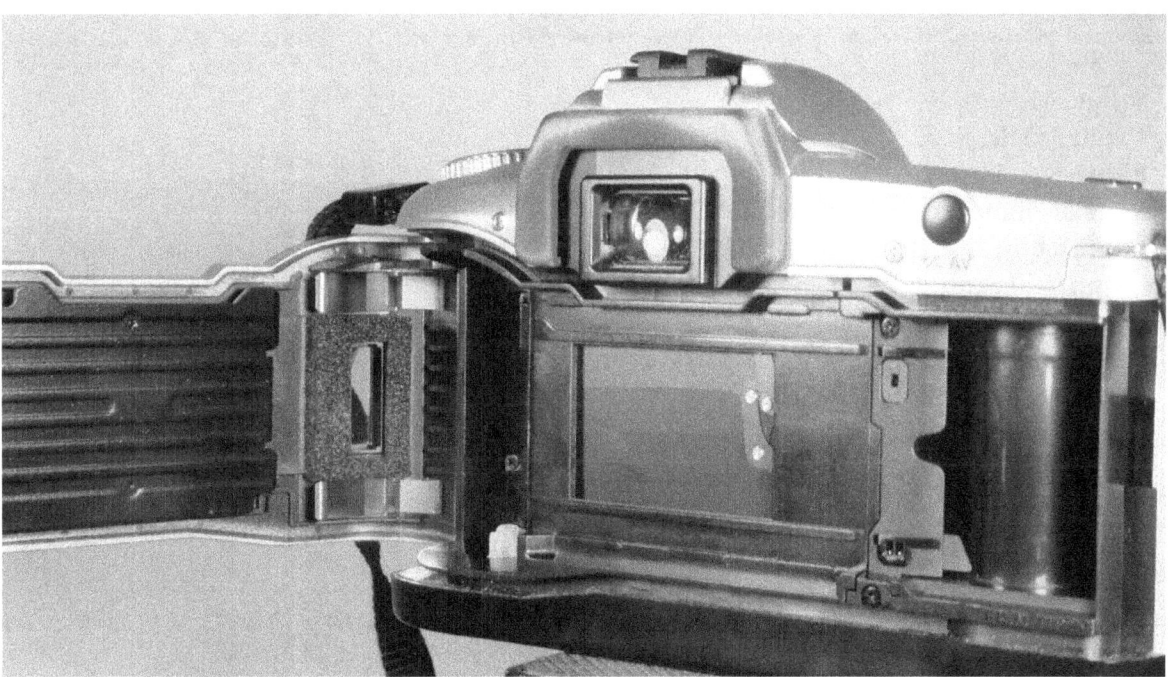

Shutter is electronic, focal plane, vertical movement

Minolta XG-A

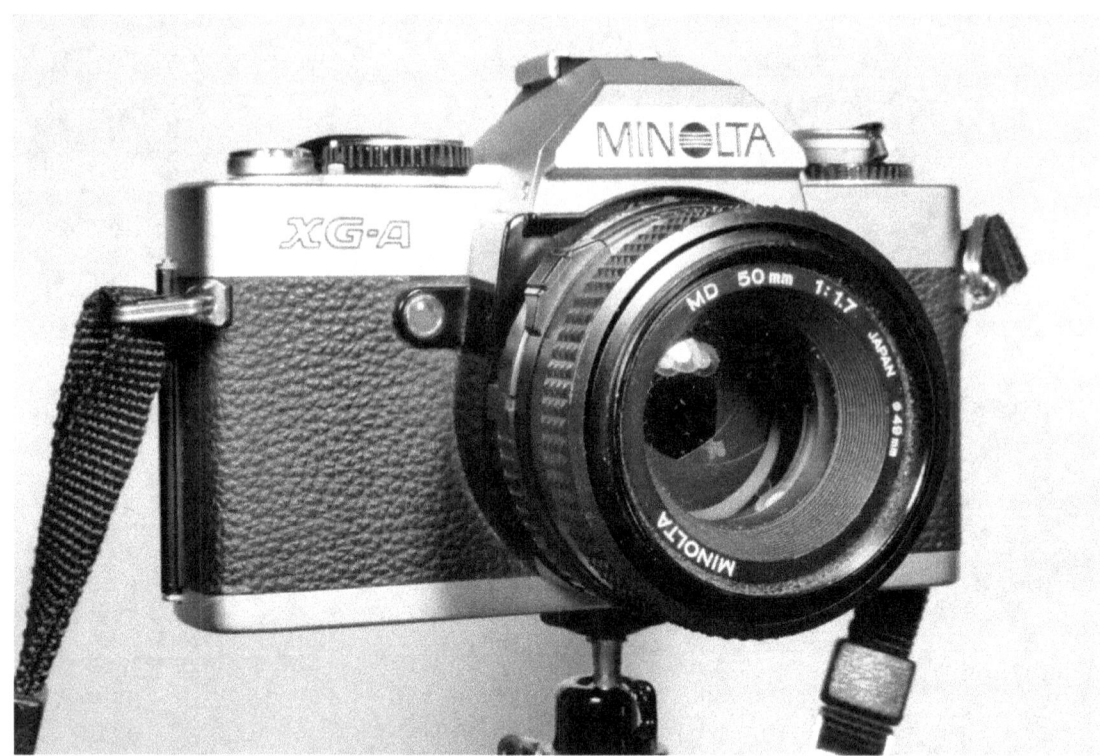

Name: Minolta XG-A.
Type: 35MM SLR.
Film Size: 35MM.
Year of manufacture: Around 1982.
Manufacturer: Minolta.
Country: Japan.
Shutter settings: 1 second – 1/1000, under user control, indirectly. Turn *aperture* ring until desired shutter speed appears in viewfinder.
Aperture settings: F/1.7 – F/22.
Exposure setting: Automatic.
Lens: Lens on camera: Minolta MD, 50MM, F/1.7.
Interchangeable lenses? Yes.
How do you focus? Focus through viewfinder by turning lens ring.
Viewfinder: Eye level.
Loading film: Open back, load full cassette, thread into takeup reel.
Automatic film advance? No (manual).
Automatic film rewind? No (manual).
Cable release socket: Yes.
Tripod socket: Yes.
Battery type: Eveready A-76 or EPX-76/S-76, quantity 2. Required for operation.
Unique features: Shutter release button not very obvious, on top of camera, in middle of dial on right.

Minolta XG-A

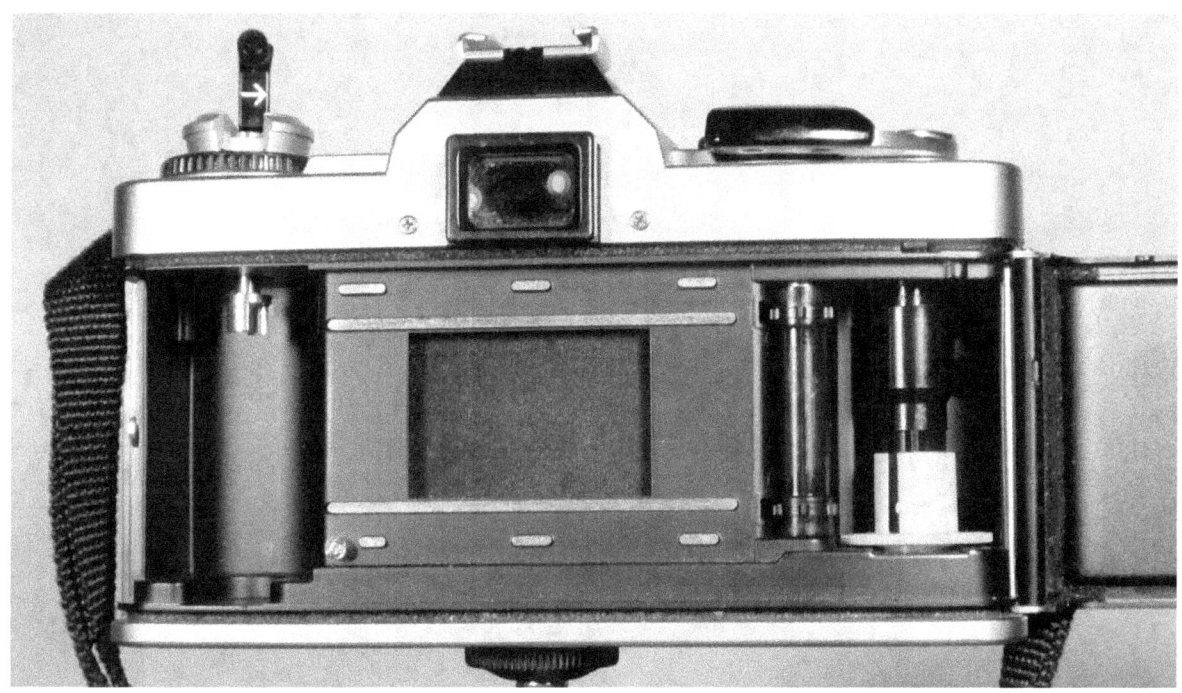

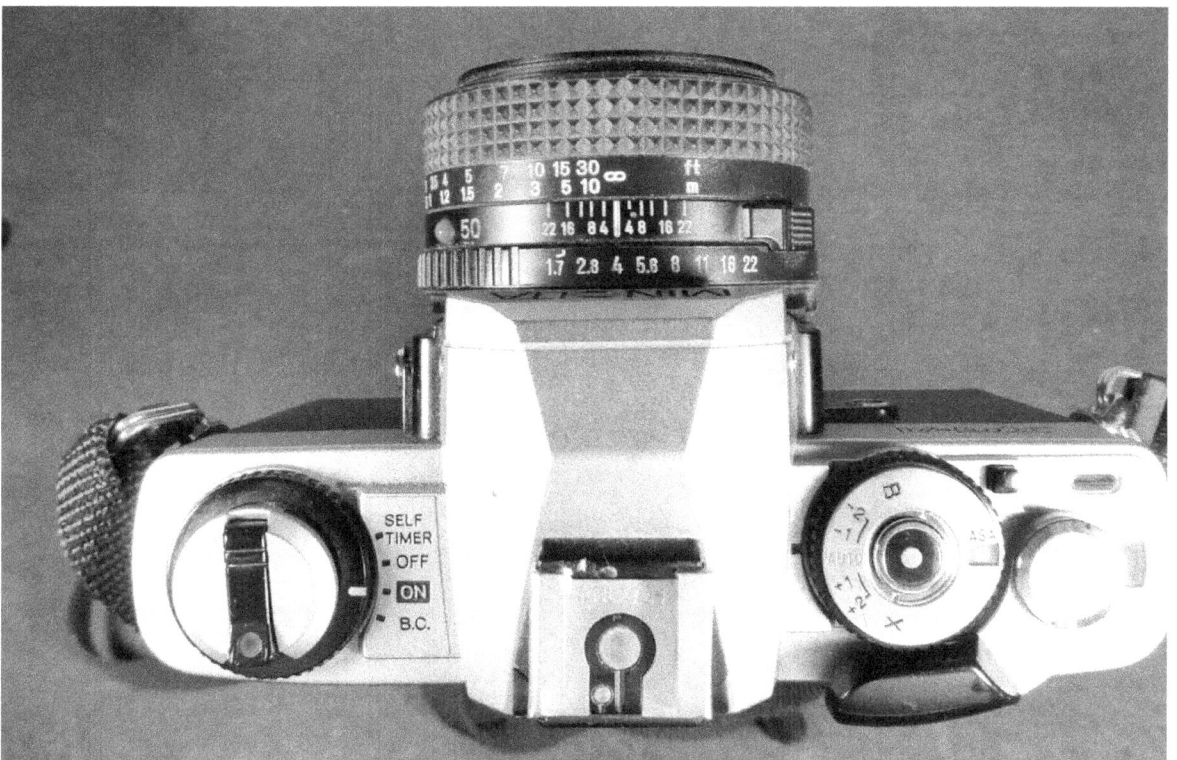

BC stands for "battery check."

Miranda DX3

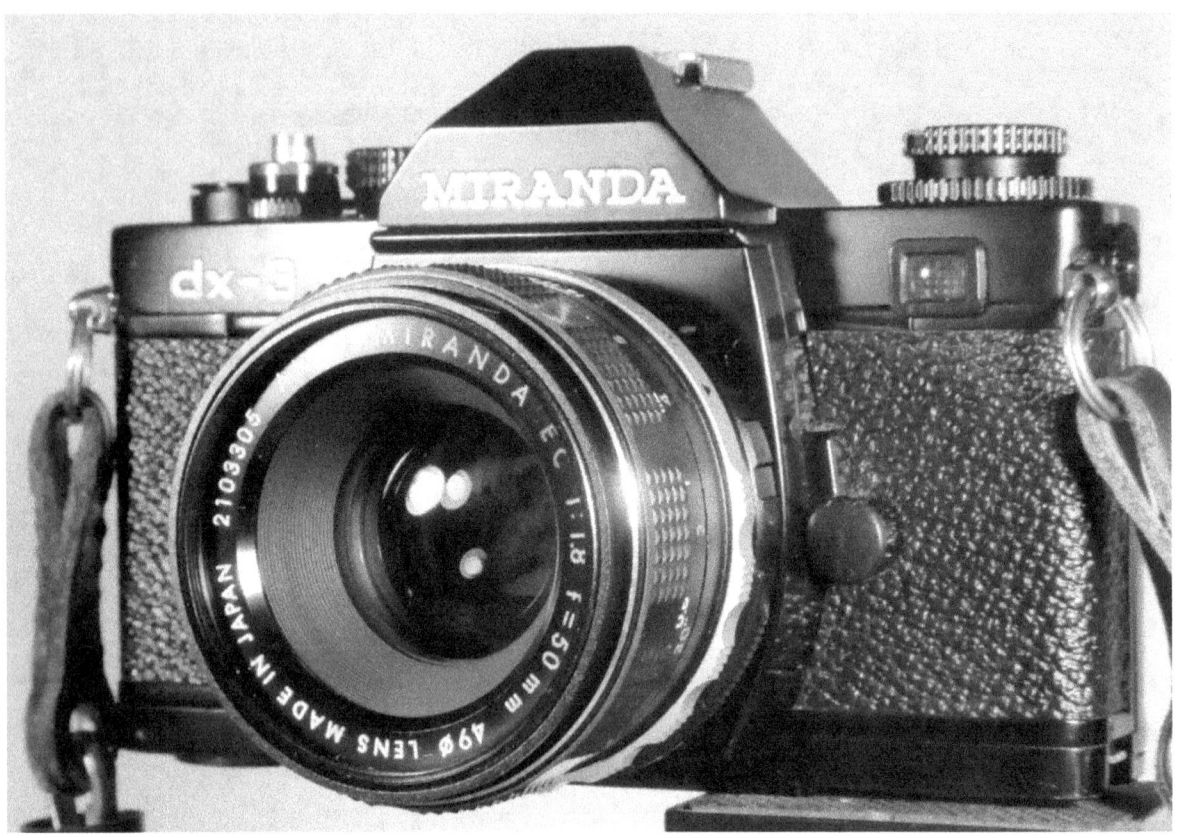

Name: Miranda DX3.
Type: 35MM SLR.
Film Size: 35MM.
Year of manufacture: 1975 - 1976.
Manufacturer: Miranda.
Country: Japan.
Shutter settings: B, 4 seconds – 1/1000.
Aperture settings: F/1.8 – F/16.
Exposure setting: Automatic.
Lens: Lens on camera: Auto Miranda F/1.8, 50MM.
Interchangeable lenses? Yes.
How do you focus? Through viewfinder.
Viewfinder: Eye level.
Loading film: Open back, load full cassette, thread into takeup reel.
Automatic film advance? No (manual).
Automatic film rewind? No (manual).
Cable release socket: Yes.
Tripod socket: Yes.
Battery type: Eveready S76, Mallory MS 76, 1.5 volt silver oxide, quantity 4.
Unique features: Can be used as a manual camera without batteries, but shutter will operate only on one speed.

Miranda DX3

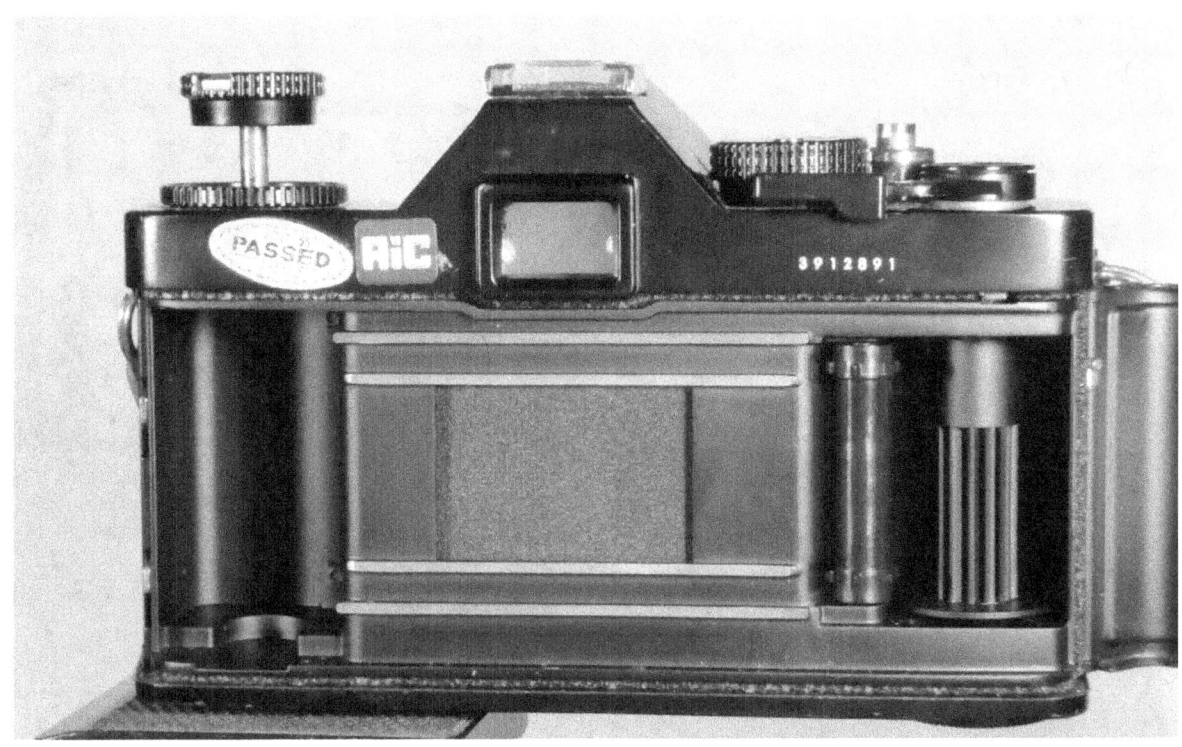

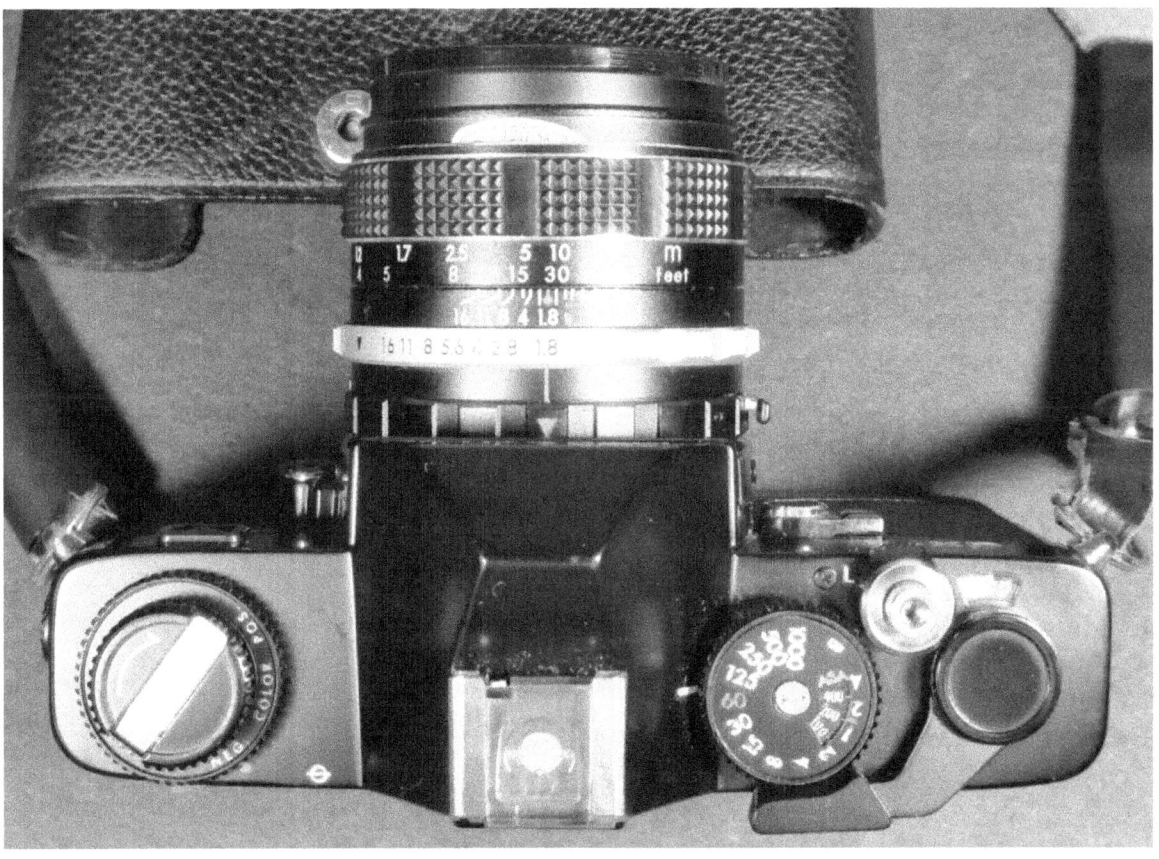

Nikon L35 AD2

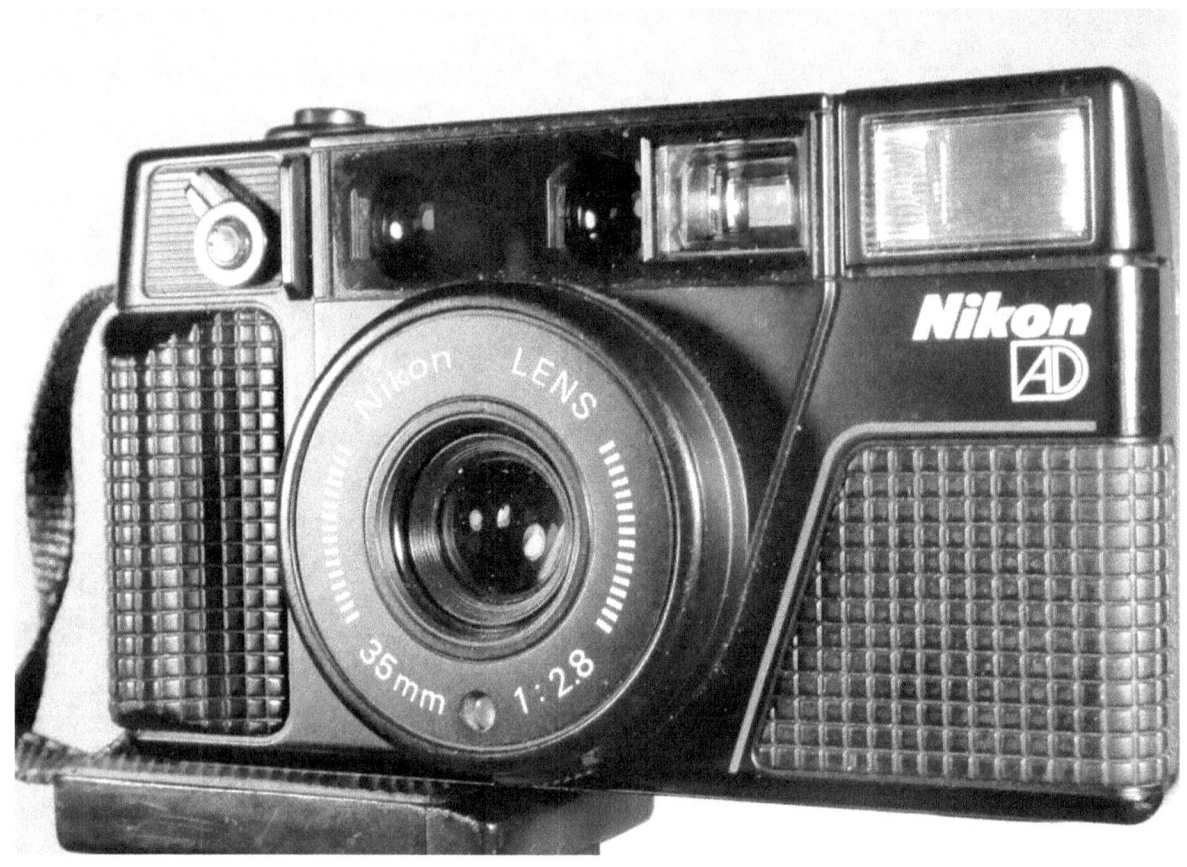

Name: Nikon L35 AD2.
Type: 35MM autofocus.
Film Size: 35MM.
Year of manufacture: 1983.
Manufacturer: Nikon.
Country: Japan.
Shutter settings: Not under user control.
Aperture settings: Not under user control.
Exposure setting: Automatic.
Lens: Nikon 35MM, F/2.8.
Interchangeable lenses? No.
How do you focus? Autofocus.
Viewfinder: Eye level.
Loading film: Open back, load full cassette, extend film to mark.
Automatic film advance? Yes.
Automatic film rewind? Yes. Activated by button.
Cable release socket: No.
Tripod socket: Yes.
Battery type: AA, quantity 2.
Unique features: Has autodate function.

Nikon L35 AD2

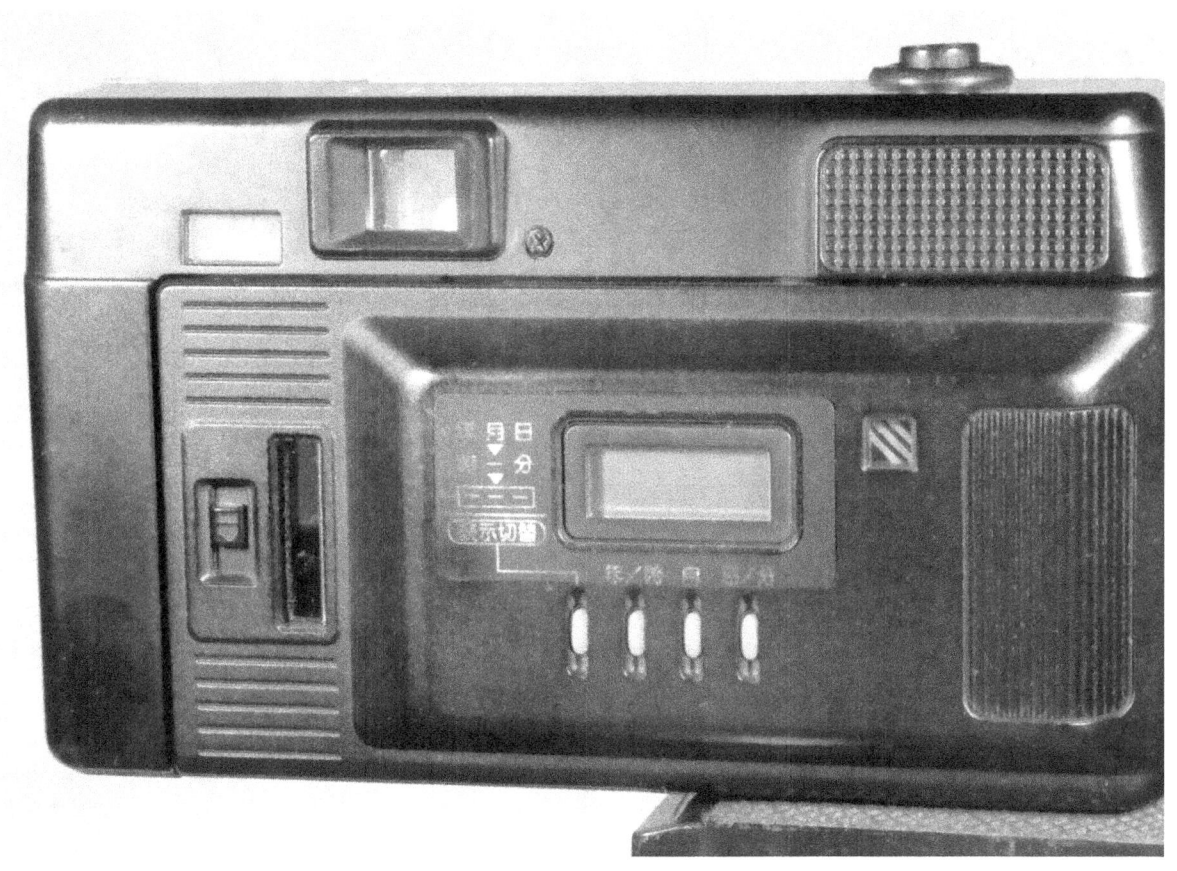

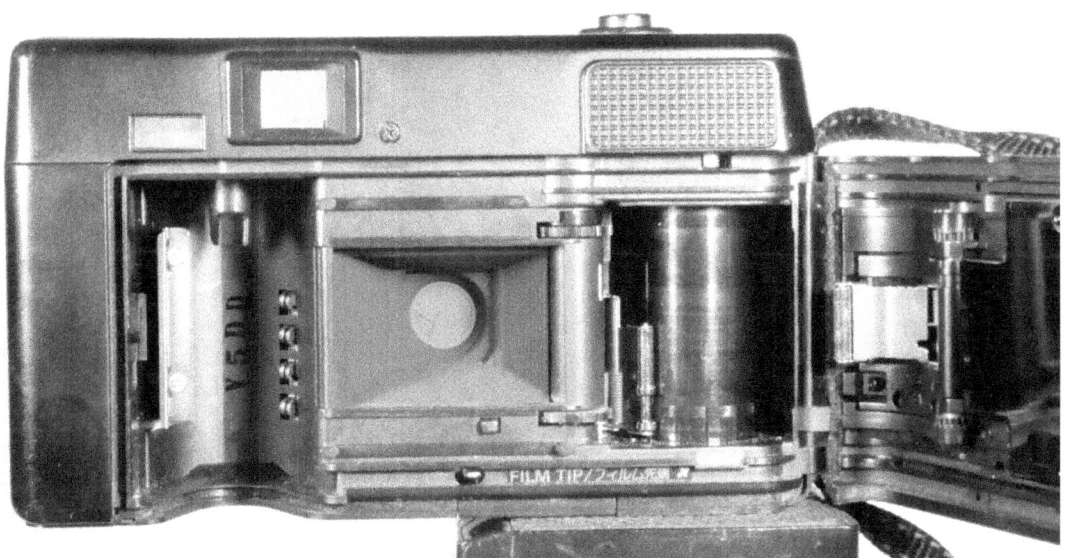

Arrow shows how far to extend film leader when loading.

Nikon Light Touch Zoom 120ED

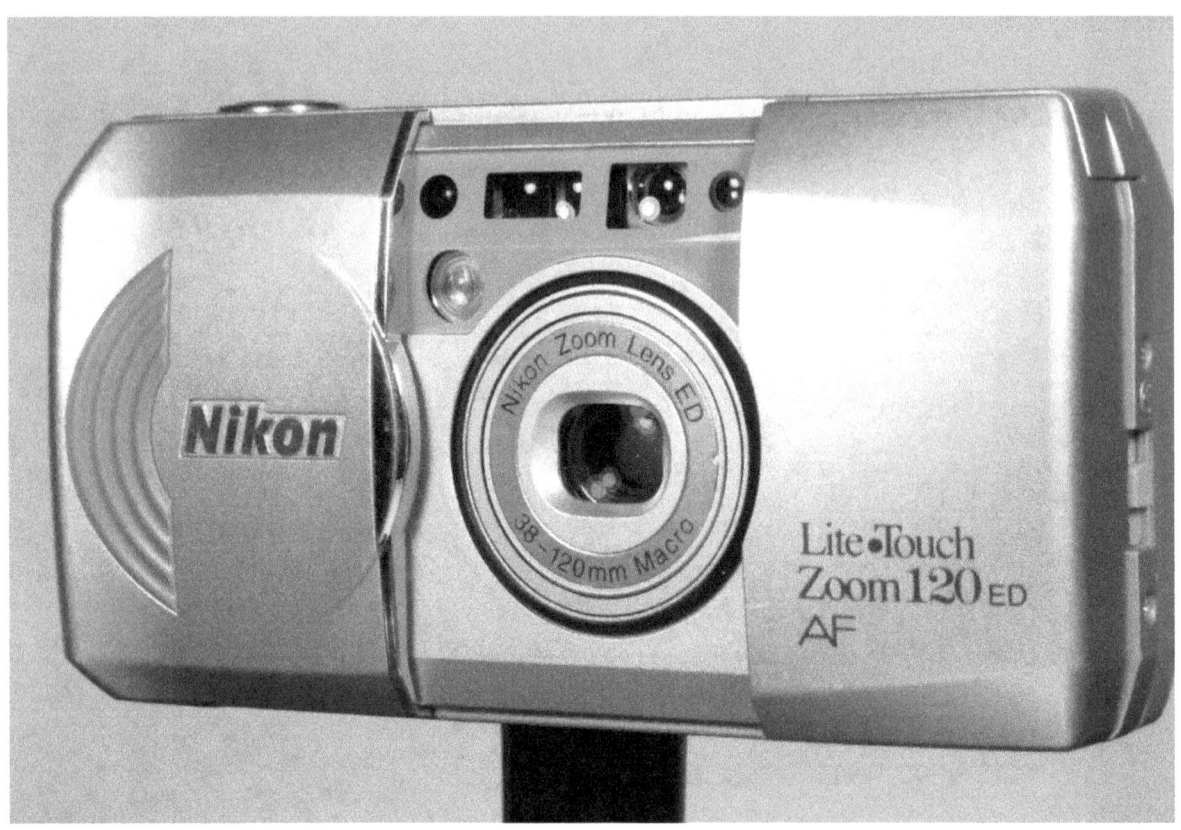

Name: Nikon Light Touch Zoom 120ED.
Type: 35MM compact Point and Shoot.
Film Size: 35MM.
Year of manufacture: 2000.
Manufacturer: Nikon.
Country: China.
Shutter settings: Not under user control.
Aperture settings: Not under user control.
Exposure setting: Automatic.
Lens: Nikon Zoom Lens ED, 38 - 120MM Around F/3.5.
Interchangeable lenses? No.
How do you focus? Autofocus. Macro capable.
Viewfinder: Eye level.
Loading film: Open back, load full cassette, pull film out to index mark.
Automatic film advance? Yes.
Automatic film rewind? Yes.
Cable release socket: No.
Tripod socket: Yes.
Battery type: DL123A, CR123A.
Unique features:
    Date imprinting, panorama mode.

Nikon Light Touch Zoom 120ED

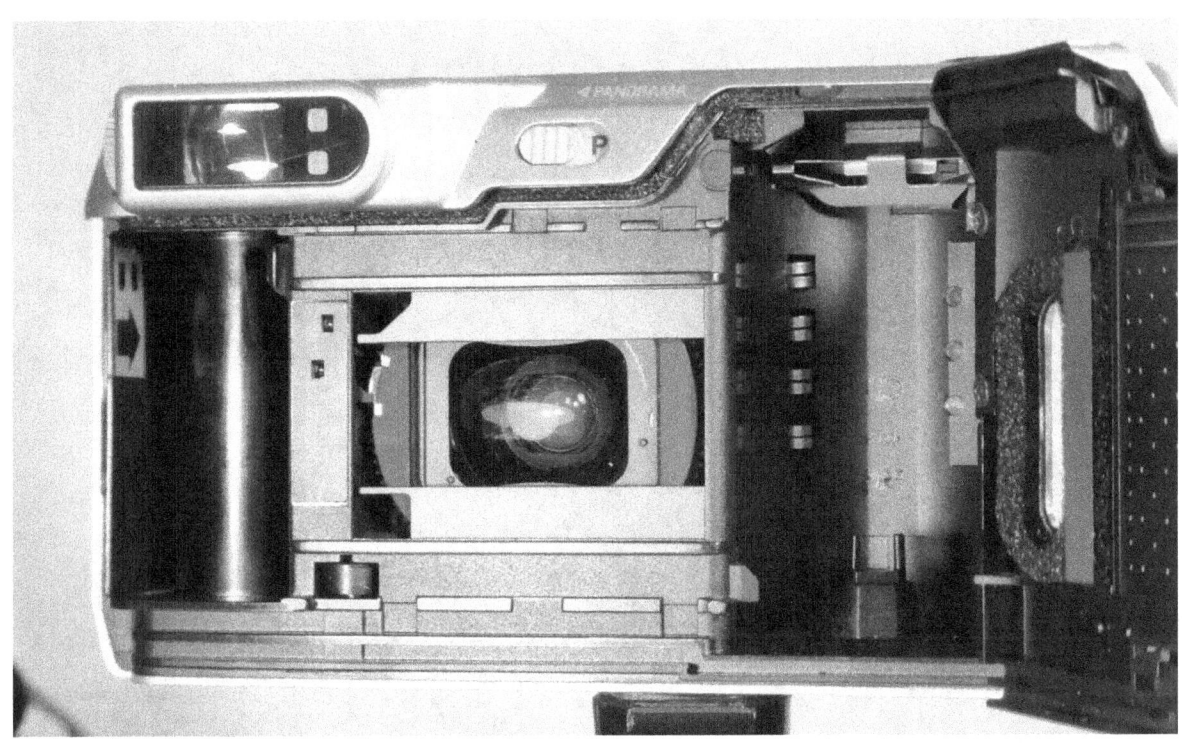

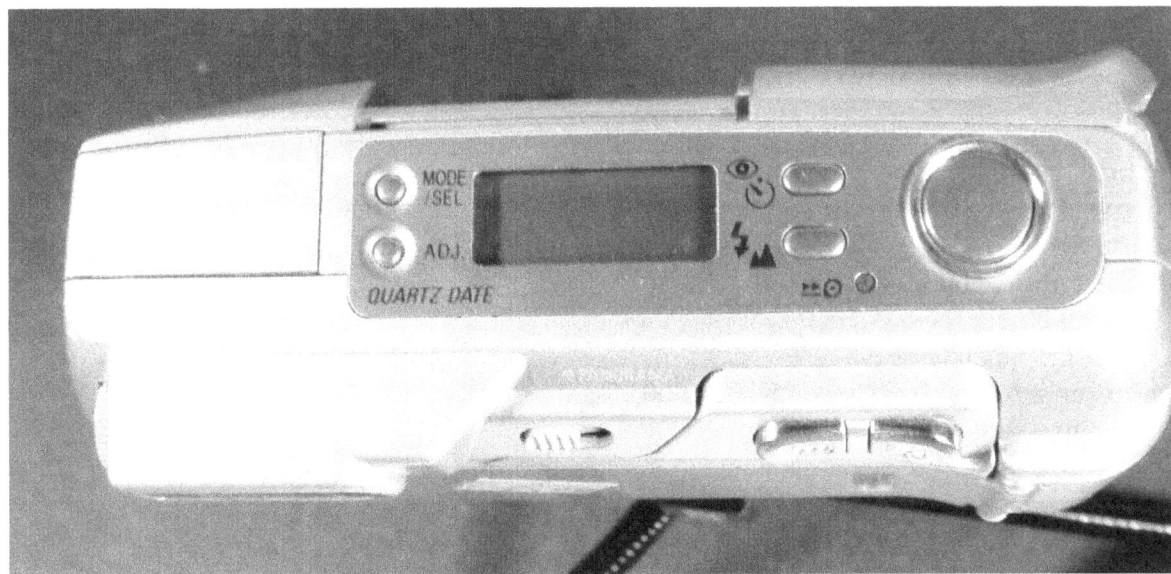

Nikon N6006

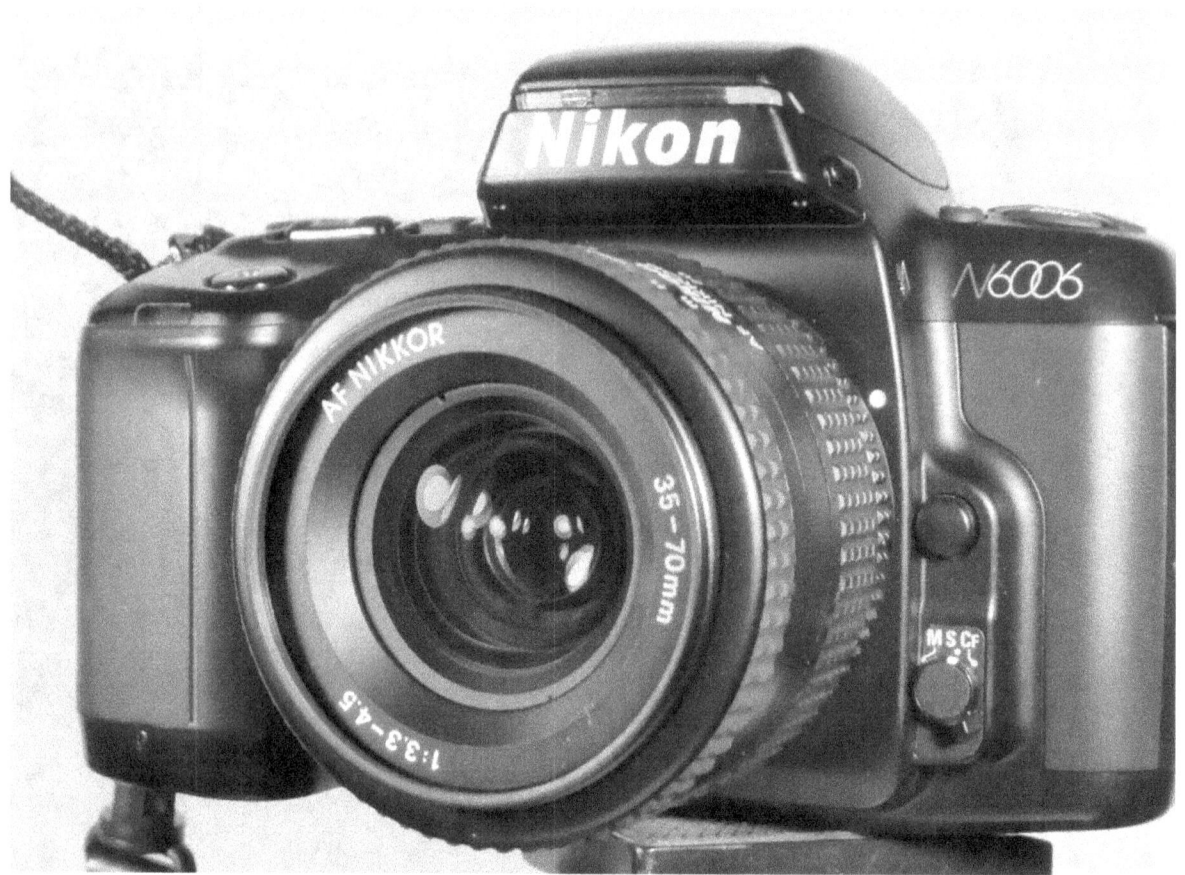

Name: Nikon N6006.
Type: 35MM SLR.
Film Size: 35MM.
Year of manufacture: 1990.
Manufacturer: Nikon.
Country: Japan.
Shutter settings: B, 30 seconds – 1/2000.
Aperture settings: F/3.5 – F/22.
Exposure setting: Automatic, manual. Shutter, aperture priority, program mode.
Lens: Lens on camera: AF Nikkor 35 – 70MM, F/3.3.
Interchangeable lenses? Yes.
How do you focus? Autofocus, manual through lens in viewfinder.
Viewfinder: Eye level.
Loading film: Open back, load full cassette, extend to mark.
Automatic film advance? Yes.
Automatic film rewind? Yes.
Cable release socket: Yes.
Tripod socket: Yes.
Battery type: DL223A, CR-P2.
Unique features:

Nikon N6006

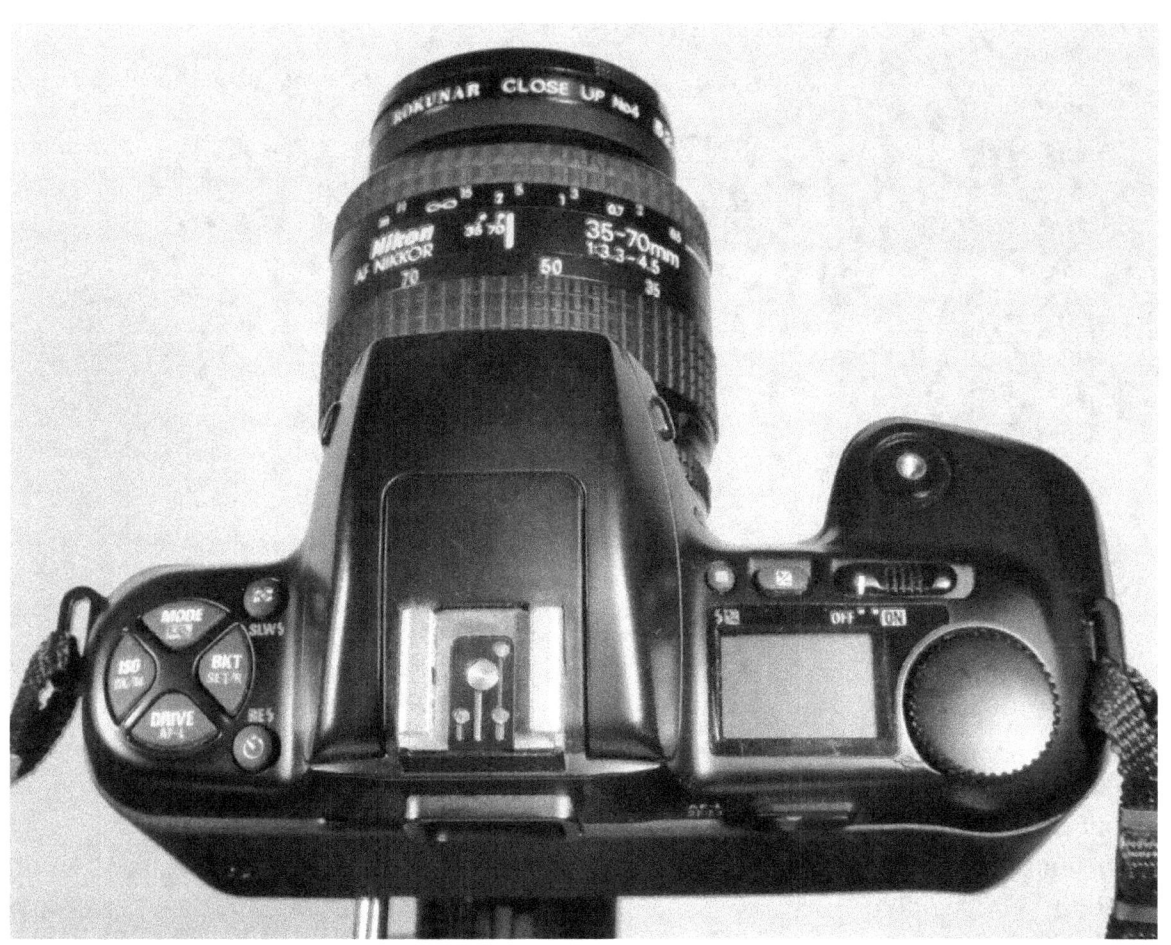

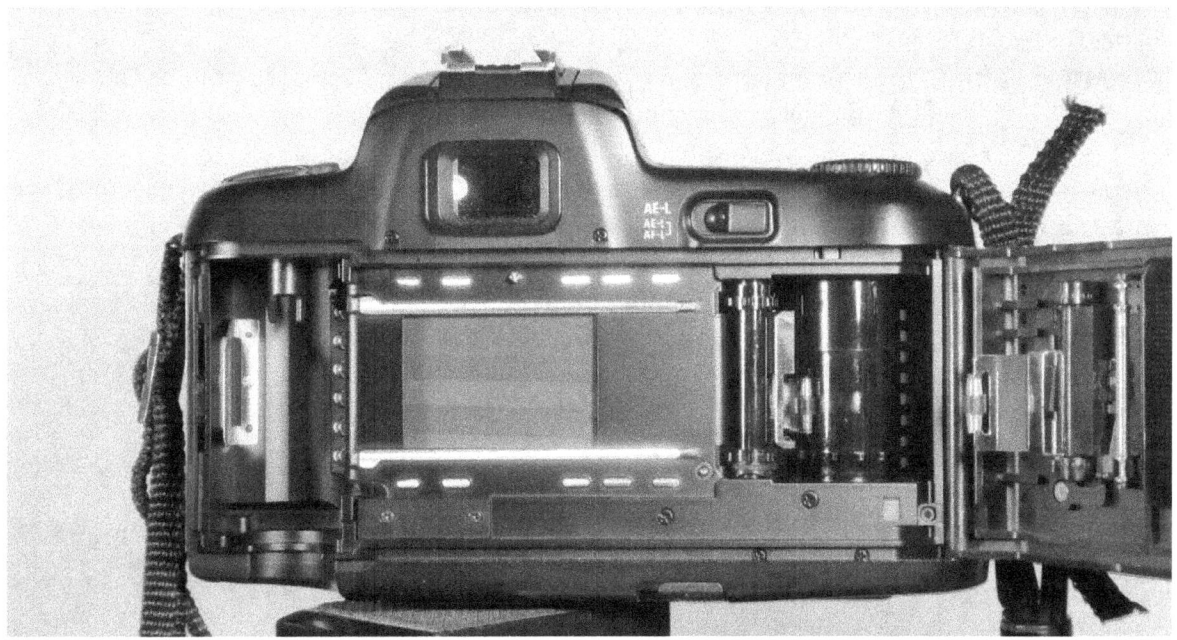

Olympus 35 SP

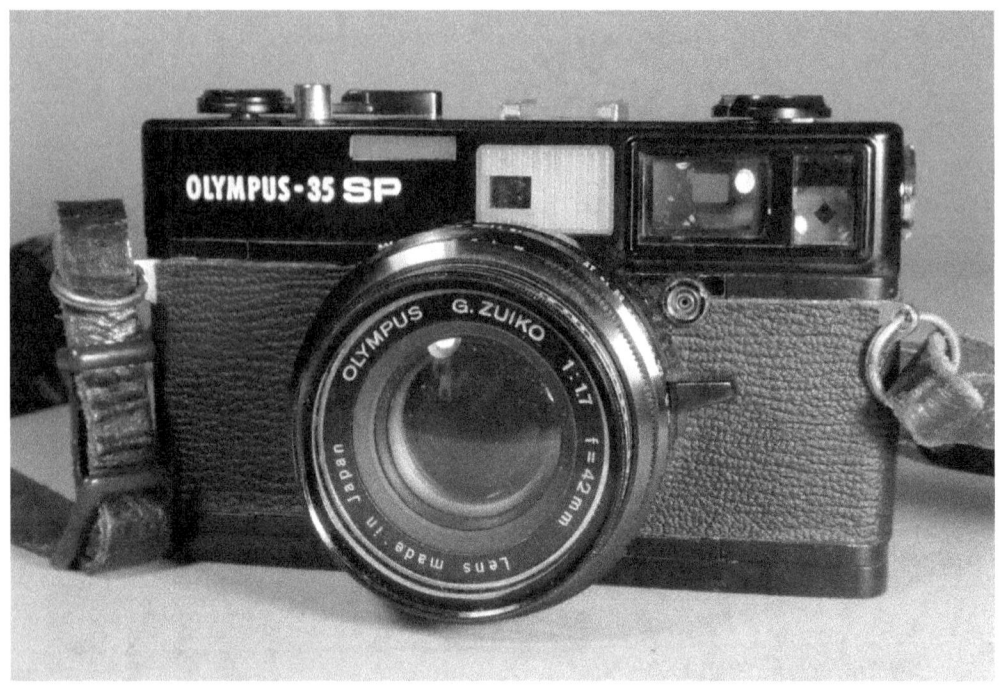

Name: Olympus 35 SP.
Type: 35MM rangefinder.
Film Size: 35MM.
Year of manufacture: 1969.
Manufacturer: Olympus.
Country: Japan.
Shutter settings: B, 1 second - 1/500.
Aperture settings: F/1.7 – F/16.
Exposure setting: Built-in meter. Center-weighted average metering. Spot meter button.
 Set "A" for automatic exposure.
 ASA (ISO) setting knob.
Lens: Zuiko F/1.7, 42MM.
Interchangeable lenses? No.
How do you focus? Rangefinder, lens ring.
Viewfinder: Eye level combined with rangefinder.
Loading film: Open back, load full cassette, thread into takeup reel.
Automatic film advance? No (manual).
Automatic film rewind? N/A.
Cable release socket: No.
Tripod socket: Yes.
Battery type: EPX 625, PX13.
Unique features:

Olympus 35 SP

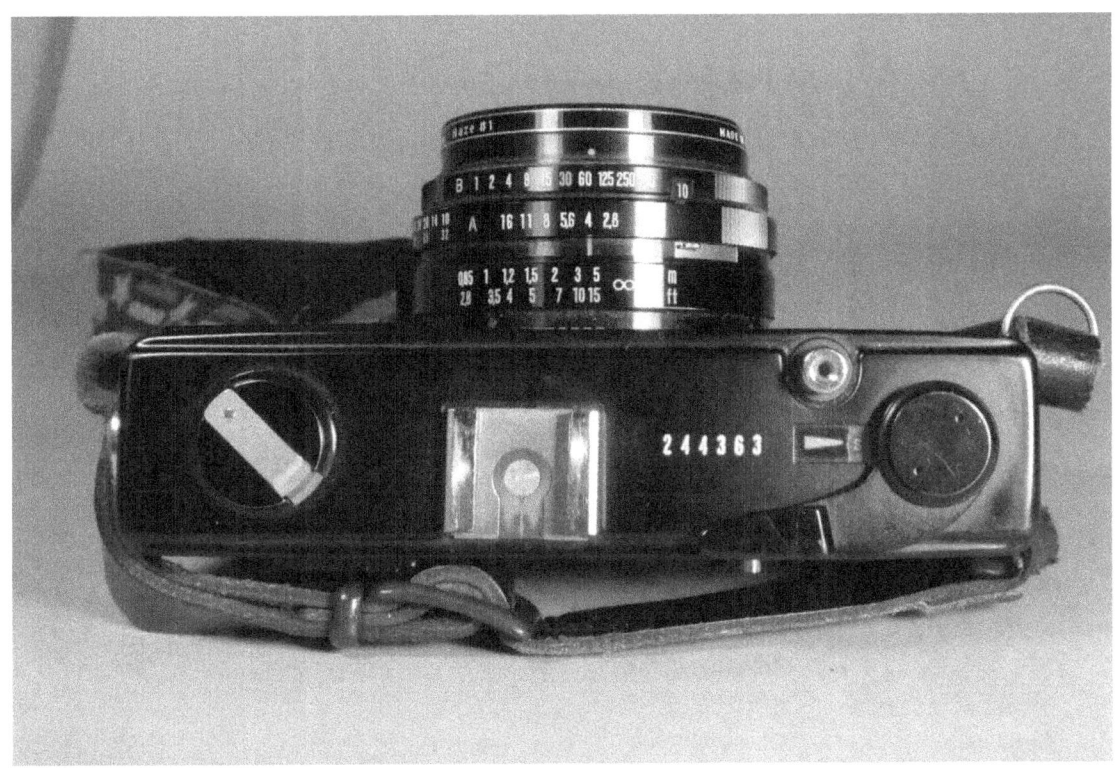

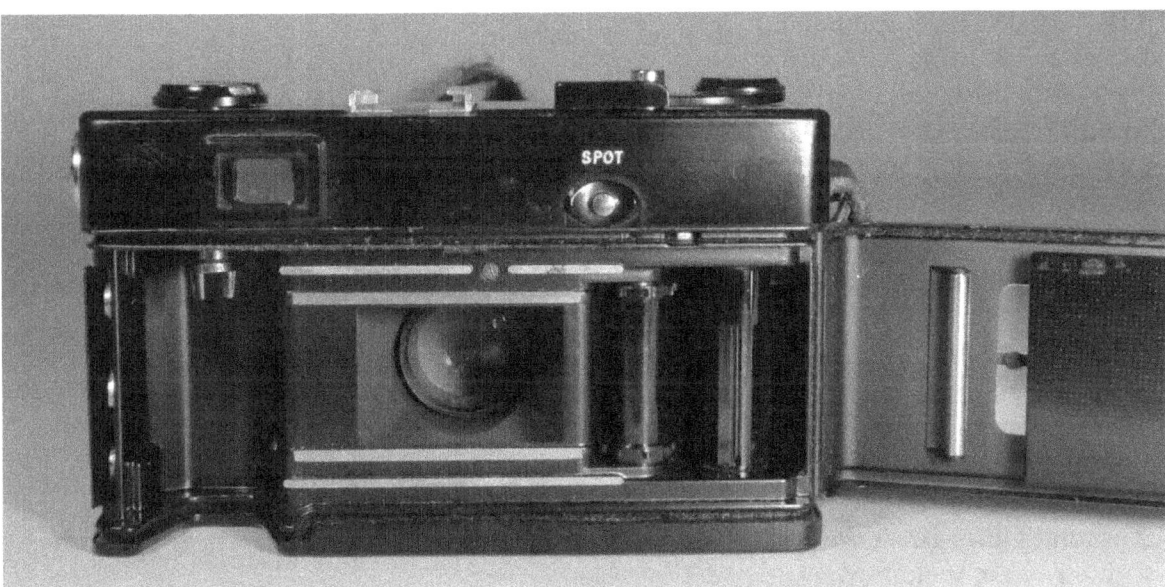

SPOT button gives spot metering while it is pressed.

Olympus Infinity Stylus

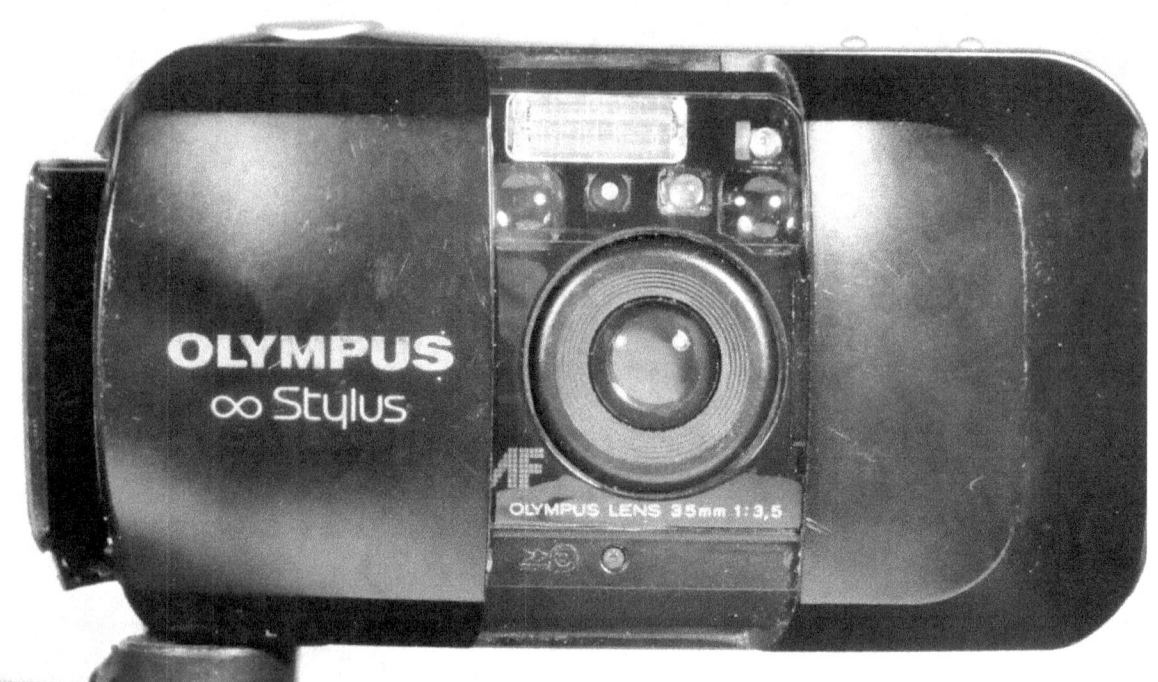

Name: Olympus Infinity Stylus.
Type: 35MM Point and Shoot.
Film Size: 35MM.
Year of manufacture: 1991.
Manufacturer: Olympus.
Country: Hong Kong.
Shutter settings: Not under user control.
Aperture settings: Not under user control.
Exposure setting: Automatic.
Lens: Olympus 35MM, F/3.5.
Interchangeable lenses? No.
How do you focus? Autofocus.
Viewfinder: Eye level.
Loading film: Open back, load full cassette, pull film out to index mark.
Automatic film advance? Yes.
Automatic film rewind? Yes.
Cable release socket: No.
Tripod socket: Yes.
Battery type: CR123A, DL123A.
Unique features:

Olympus Infinity Stylus

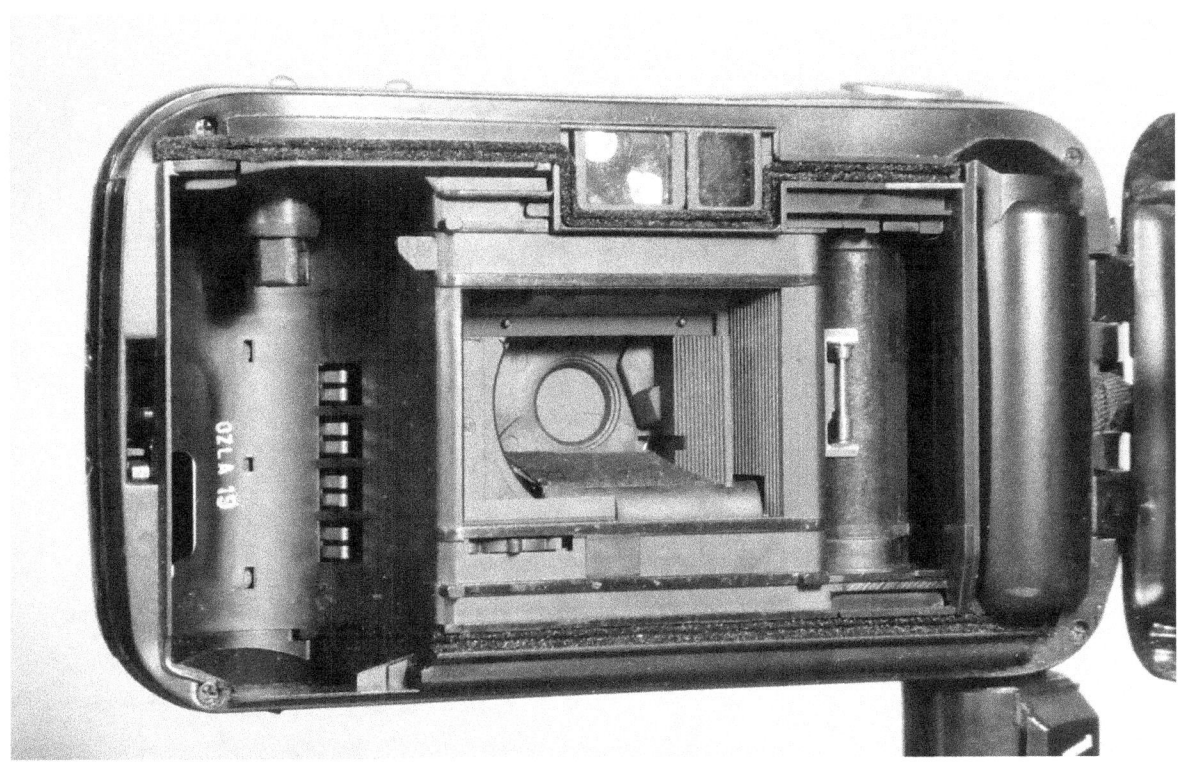

Olympus Infinity Twin

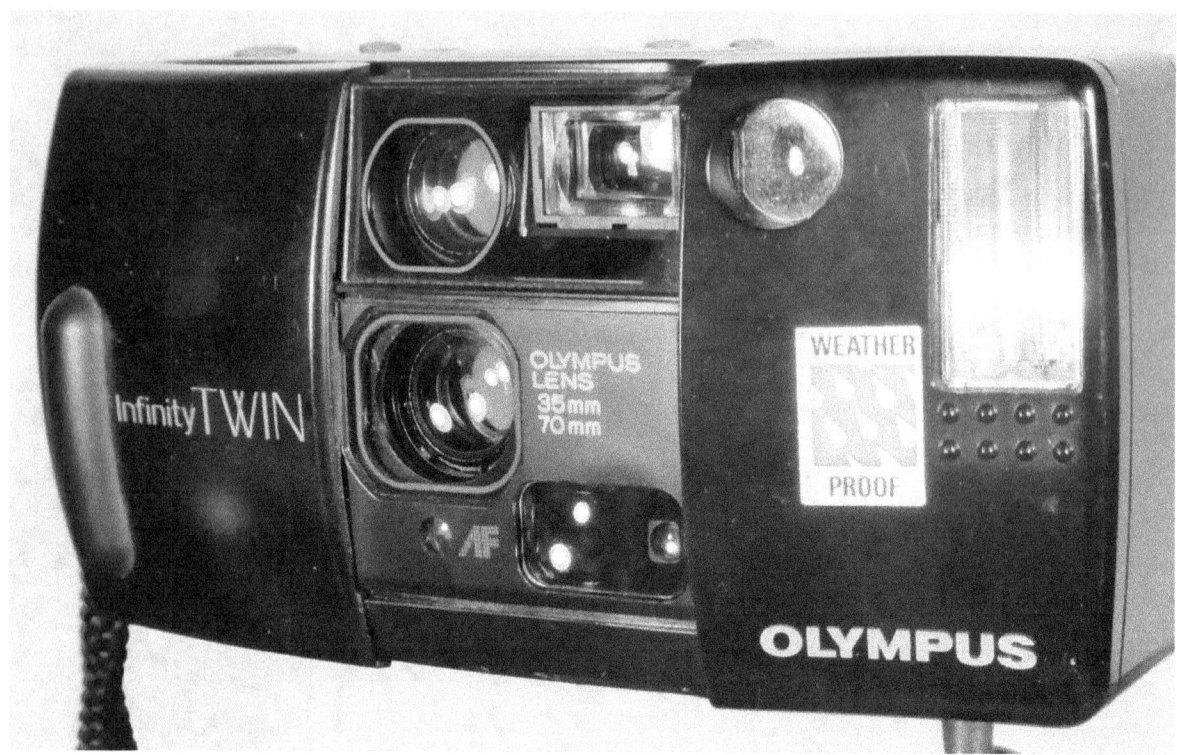

Name: Olympus Infinity Twin.
Type: 35MM Point and Shoot.
Film Size: 35MM.
Year of manufacture: 1989.
Manufacturer: Olympus.
Country: Japan.
Shutter settings: Not under user control.
Aperture settings: Not under user control.
Exposure setting: Automatic.
Lens: Olympus 35MM F/3.5 and 70MM F/6.3.
Interchangeable lenses? No.
How do you focus? Autofocus.
Viewfinder: Eye level.
Loading film: Open back, load full cassette, extend film to index mark.
Automatic film advance? Yes.
Automatic film rewind? Yes.
Cable release socket: No.
Tripod socket: Yes.
Battery type: CR123A, DL123A.
Unique features: Twin lenses. One for 35MM, the other for 70MM.

Olympus Infinity Twin

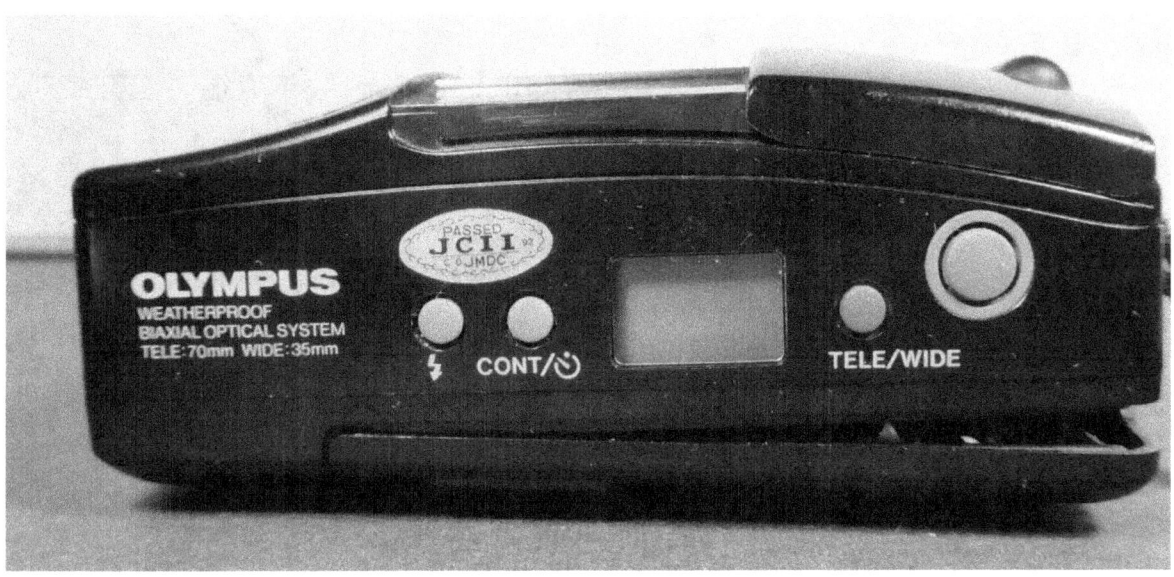

Olympus Infinity Zoom 2000

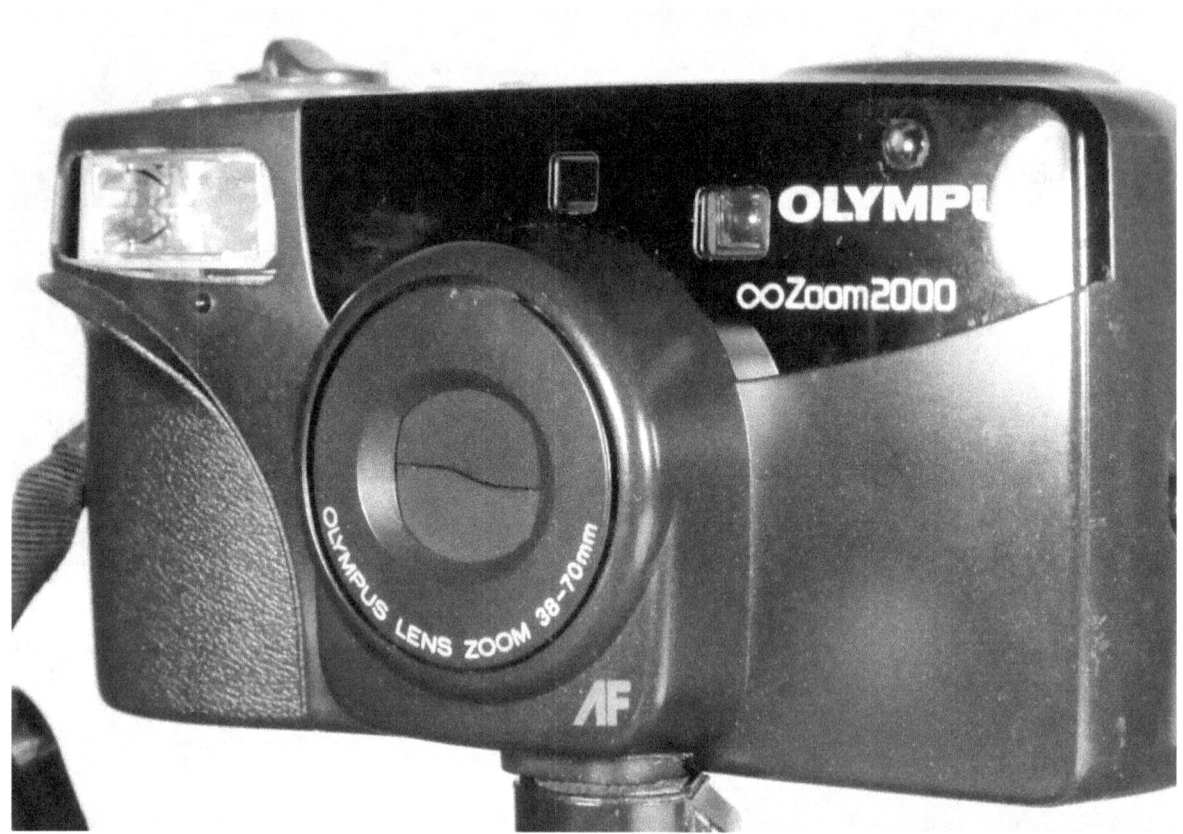

Name: Olympus Infinity Zoom 2000.
Type: 35MM Point and Shoot.
Film Size: 35MM.
Year of manufacture: Around 1995.
Manufacturer: Olympus.
Country: Japan.
Shutter settings: Not under user control.
Aperture settings: Not under user control.
Exposure setting: Automatic.
Lens: Olympus 38 - 70MM.
Interchangeable lenses? No.
How do you focus?. Autofocus.
Viewfinder: Eye level.
Loading film: Open back, load full cassette, pull film out to index mark.
Automatic film advance? Yes.
Automatic film rewind? Yes.
Cable release socket: No.
Tripod socket: Yes.
Battery type: CR123A, DL123A, AA quantity 2.
Unique features:

Olympus Infinity Zoom 2000

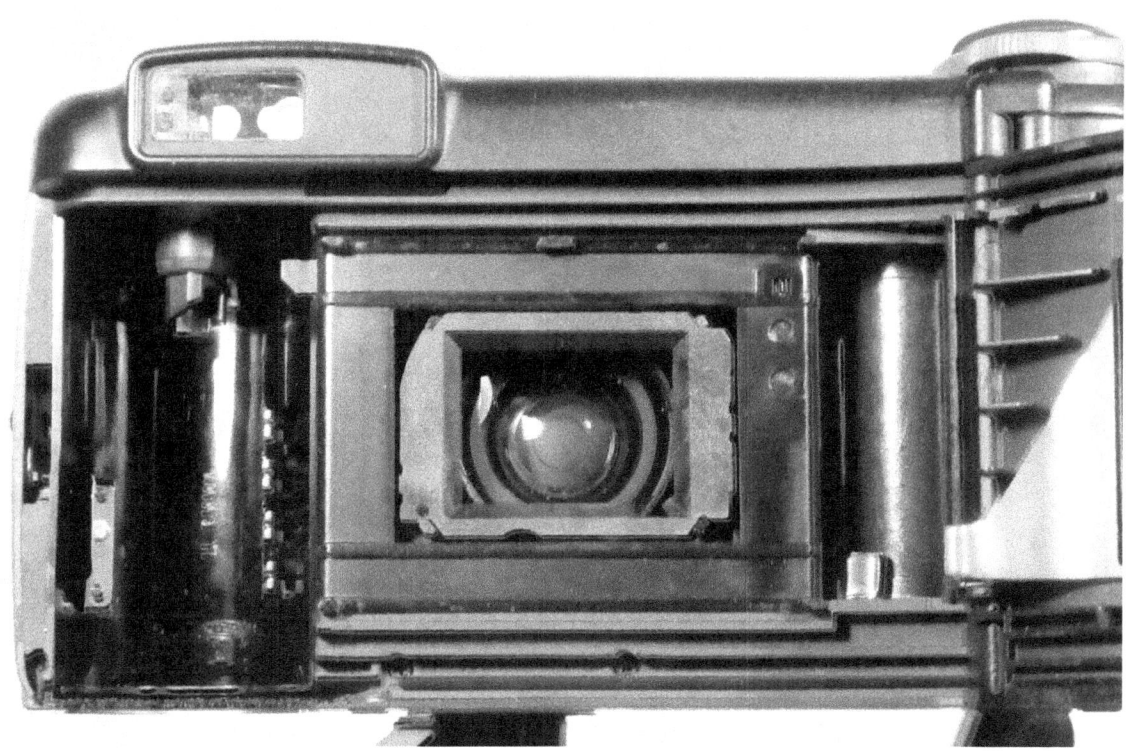

Olympus OM 10

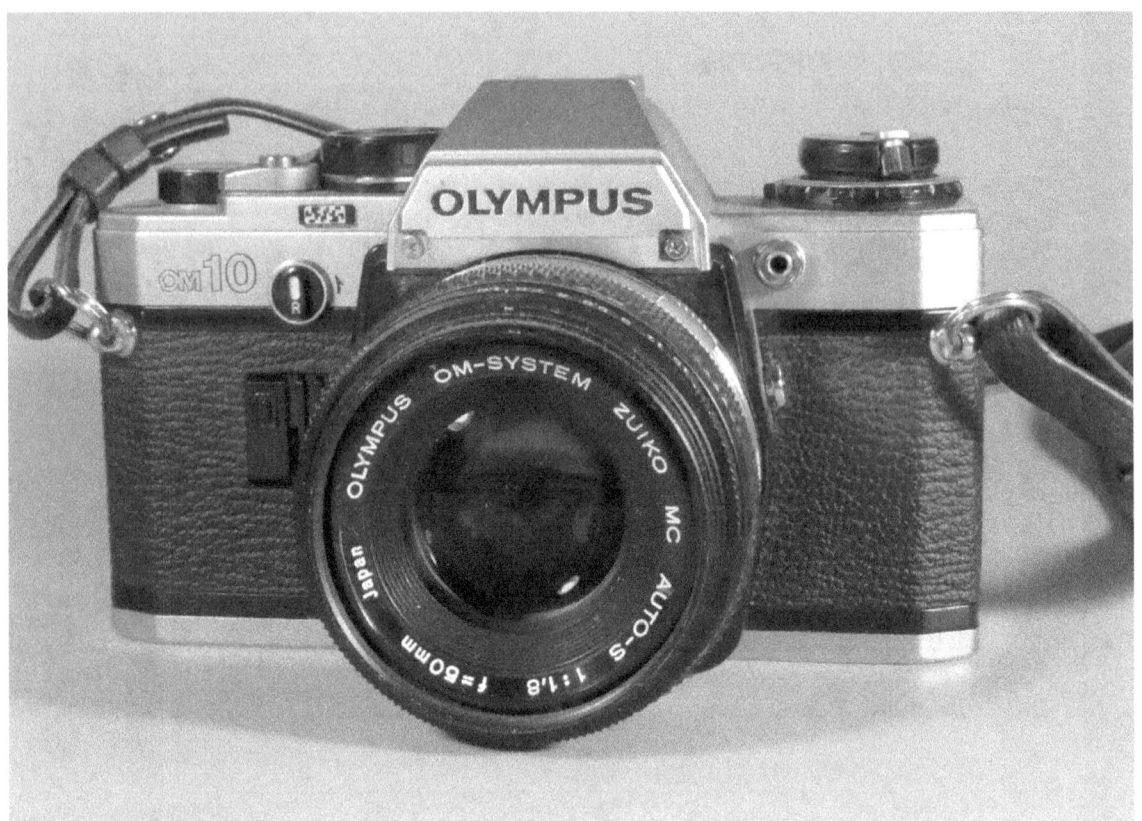

Name: Olympus OM-10.
Type: 35MM SLR.
Film Size: 35MM.
Year of manufacture: 1979.
Manufacturer: Olympus.
Country: Japan.
Shutter settings: B, 1/25 -1/1600.
Aperture settings: F/1.8 – F/16.
Exposure setting: Metered. Aperture priority, shutter priority. Manual available, with attachment.
Lens: Lens on camera: Olympus Zuiko, F/1.8, 50MM.
Interchangeable lenses? Yes.
How do you focus? With viewfinder. Focusing ring on lens.
Viewfinder: Eye level pentaprism.
Loading film: Open back, load full cassette, thread into takeup reel.
Automatic film advance? No (manual).
Automatic film rewind? No (manual).
Cable release socket:Yes.
Tripod socket: Yes.
Battery type: Two 1.5 V batteries, LR44 (A76, EPX76). Required for shutter to operate.
Unique features:

Olympus OM 10

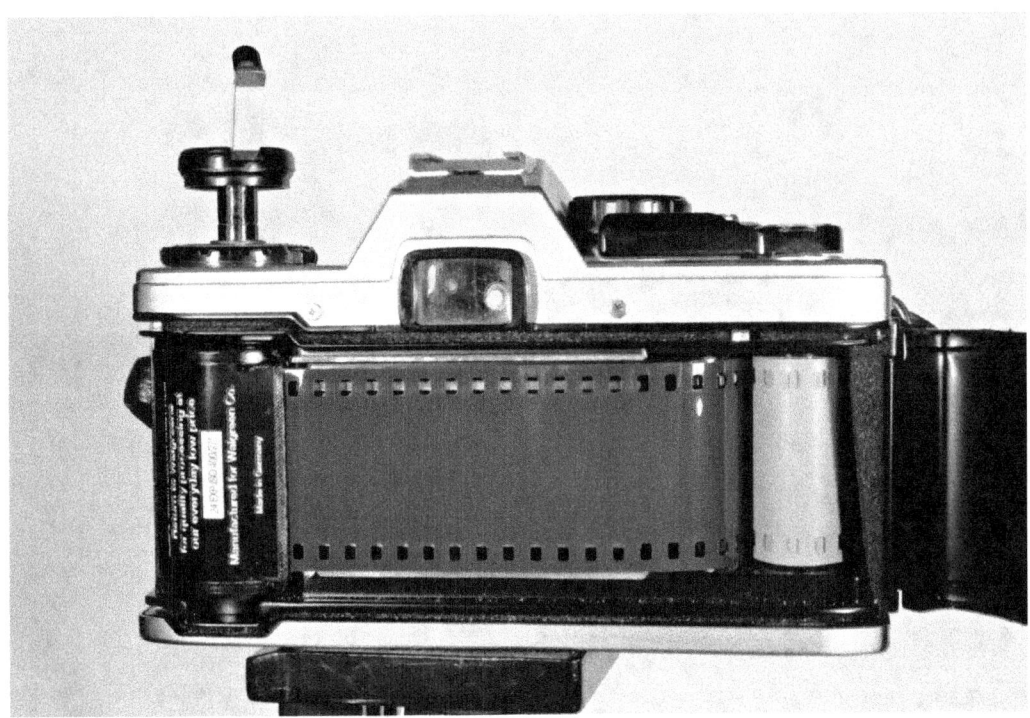

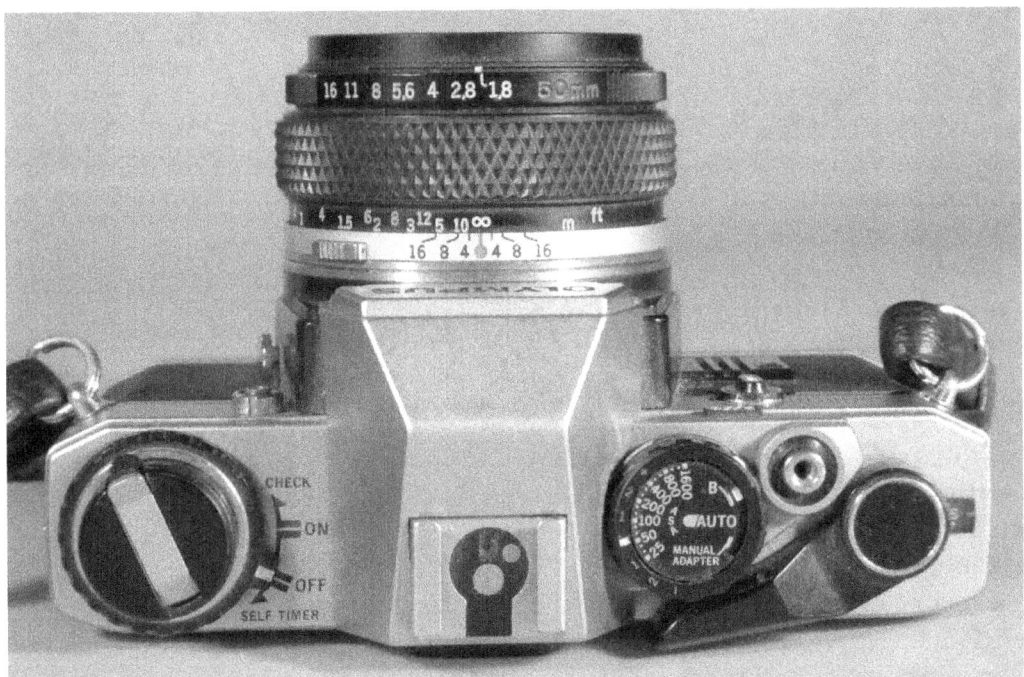

"Check," on left dial is for battery check. Light in front, left of camera turns on if battery is OK. An optional manual adapter is available to attach to the camera.

Olympus Trip 35

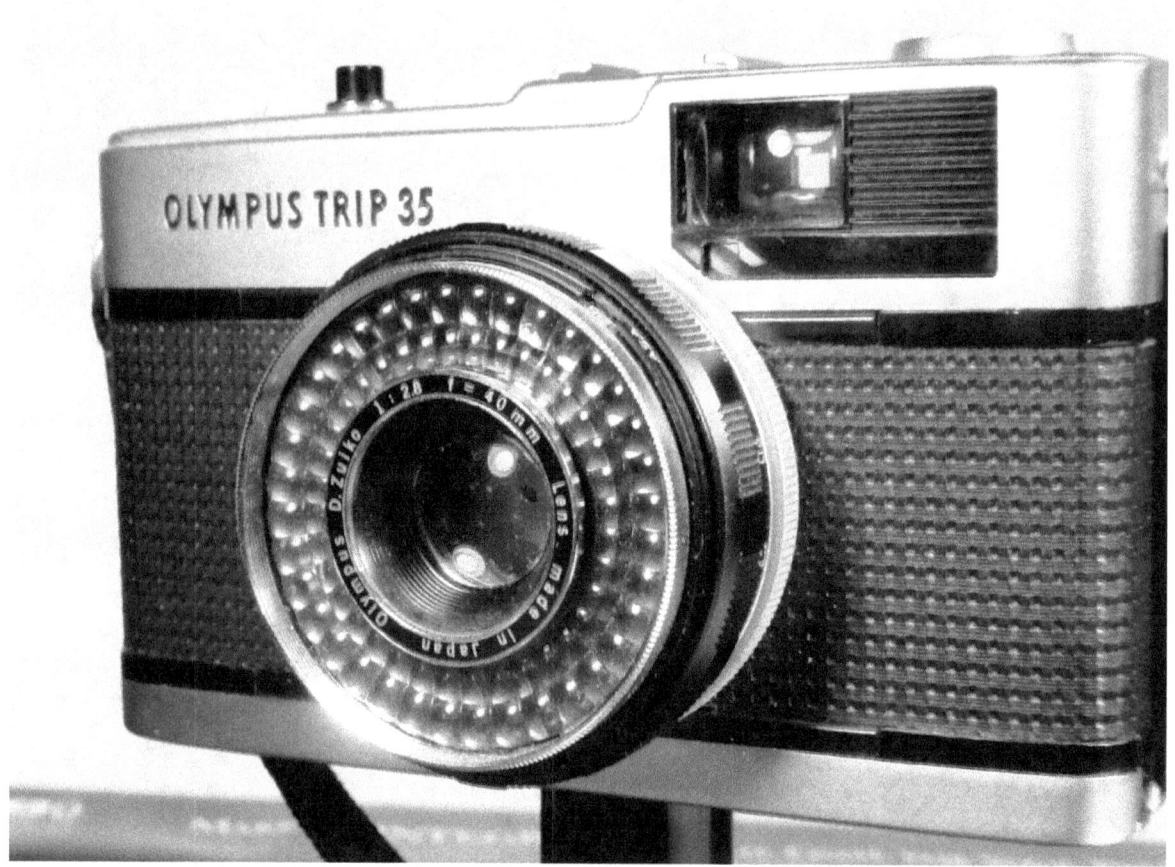

Name: Olympus Trip 35.
Type: 35MM Point and Shoot.
Film Size: 35MM.
Year of manufacture: 1967.
Manufacturer: Olympus.
Country: Japan.
Shutter settings: 1/40, 1/200. Set automatically.
Aperture settings: F/2.8– F/22. Set automatically.
Exposure setting: Automatic metered, manual.
Lens: Zuiko 40MM, F/2.8.
Interchangeable lenses? No.
How do you focus? Zone focus. Estimate distance, set zone on lens.
Viewfinder: Eye level.
Loading film: Open back, load full cassette, thread into takeup reel.
Automatic film advance? No (manual).
Automatic film rewind? No (manual).
Cable release socket: Yes.
Tripod socket: Yes.
Battery type: None. Light meter does not need a battery.
Unique features: Filter thread on lens. 43.5MM.

Olympus Trip 35

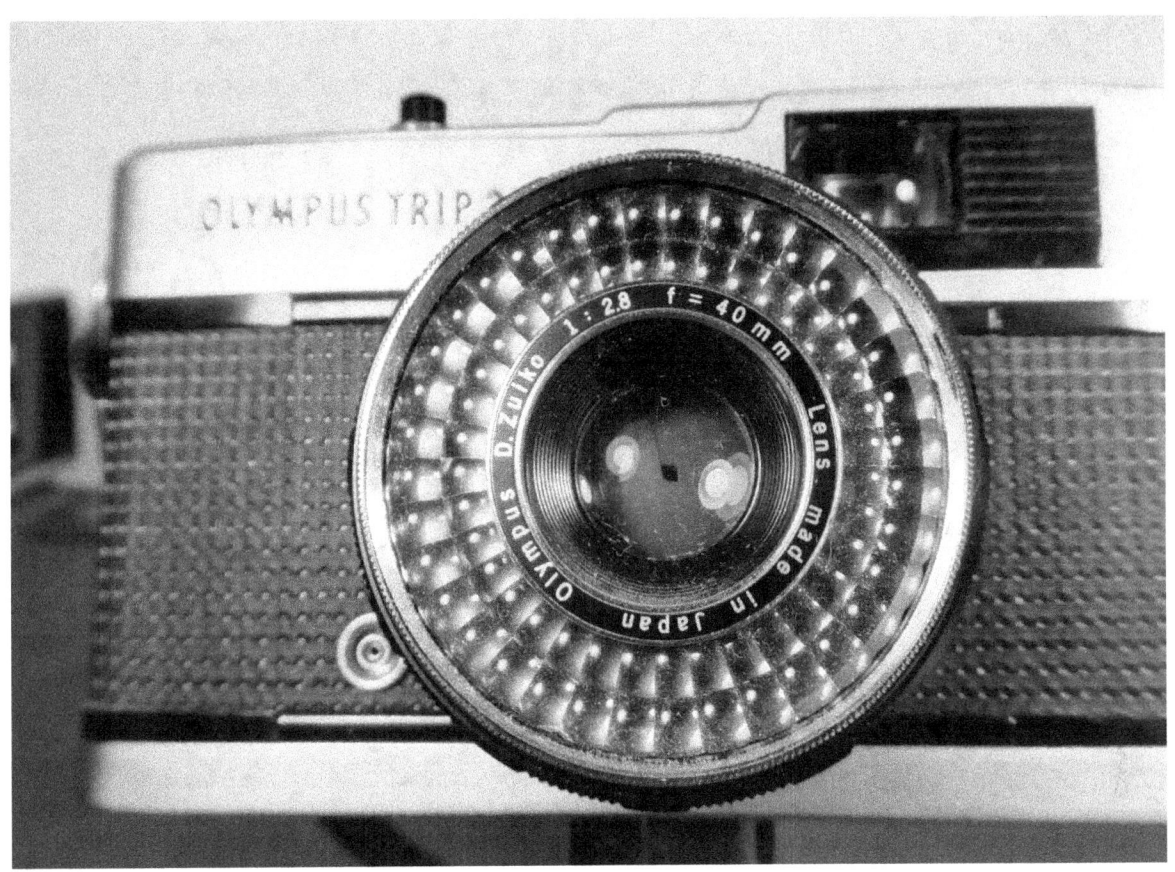

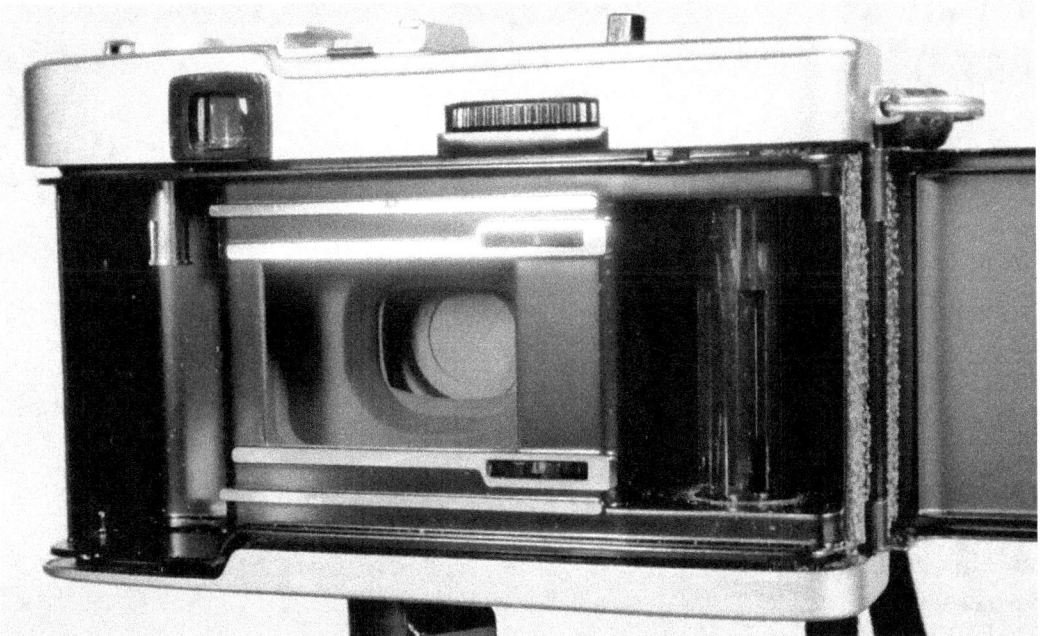

Film advance wheel is in upper center of this picture.

Pentax K1000

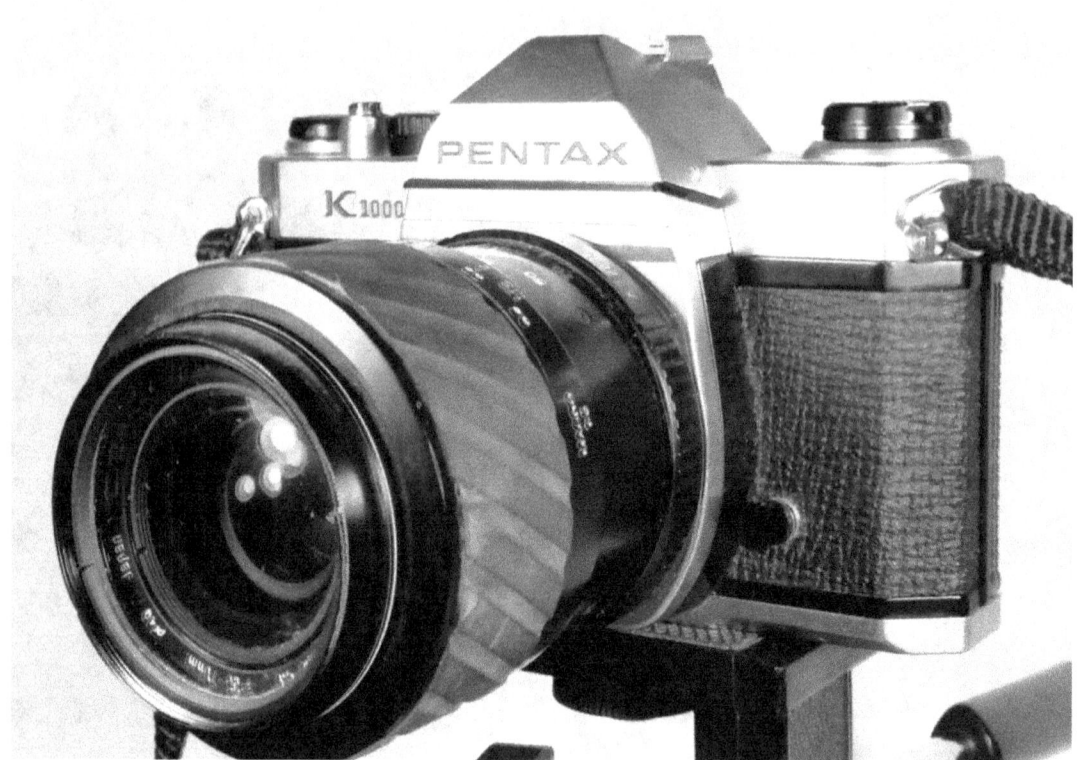

Name: Pentax K1000.
Type: 35MM SLR.
Film Size: 35MM.
Year of manufacture: 1970s.
Manufacturer: Pentax.
Country: USA.
Shutter settings: B, 1 second – 1/1000.
Aperture settings: F/3.5– F/22.
Exposure setting: Semiautomatic. Change shutter speed or F/stop until needle in viewfinder indicates correct exposure.
Lens: Pentax K bayonet mount. Lens on camera: Craig Optics auto zoom macro F/3.5 70MM.
Interchangeable lenses? Yes, K mount.
How do you focus? Focus through lens on ground glass or split-image.
Viewfinder: Eye level.
Loading film: Open back, load full cassette, thread into takeup reel.
Automatic film advance? No (manual).
Automatic film rewind? No (manual).
Cable release socket: Yes.
Tripod socket: Yes.
Battery type: LR44, SR44. Silver oxide, 1.5 volt, quantity 1.
Unique features:
    No on/off switch for exposure meter.

Pentax K1000

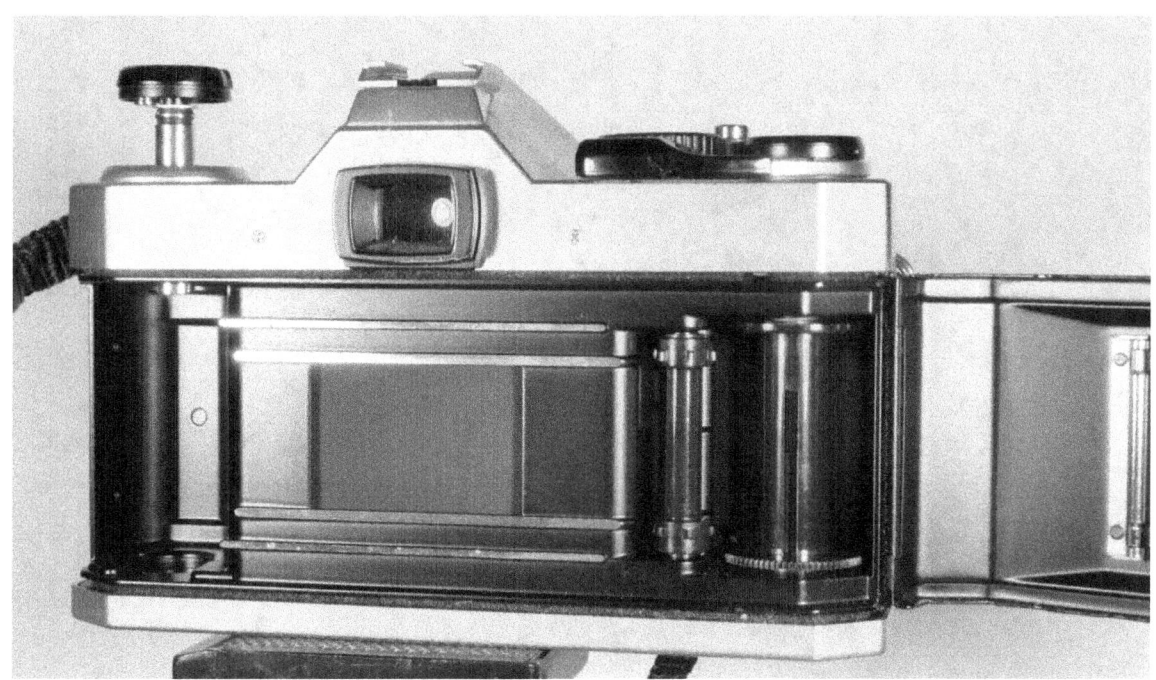

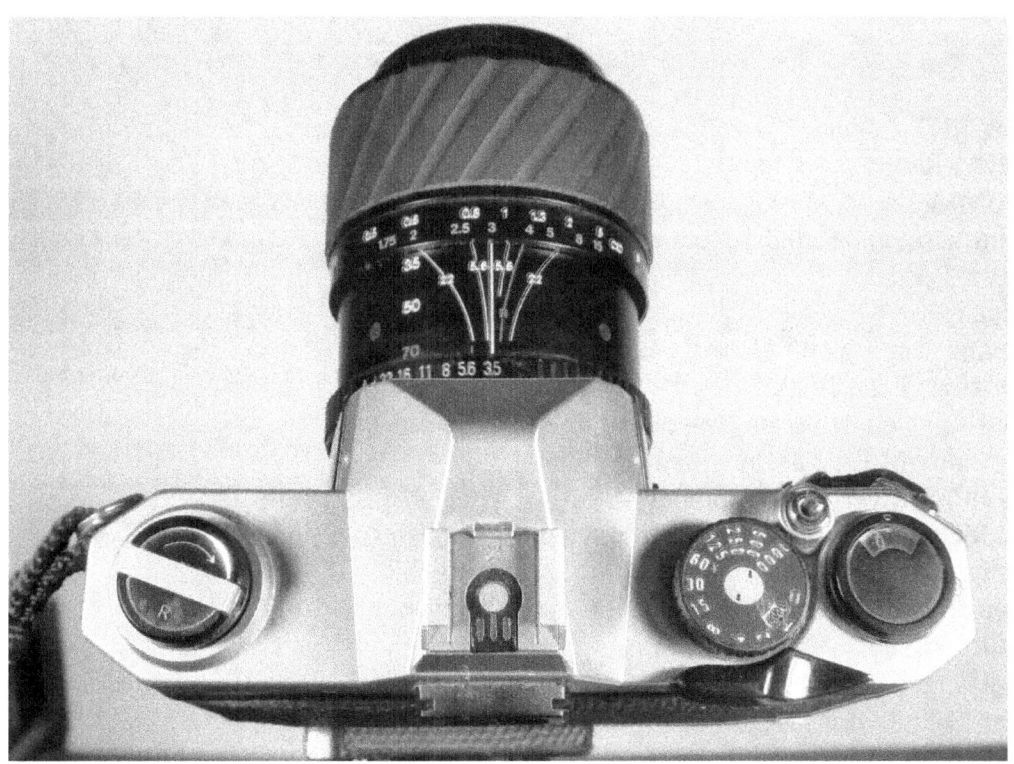

Pentax ME - Super

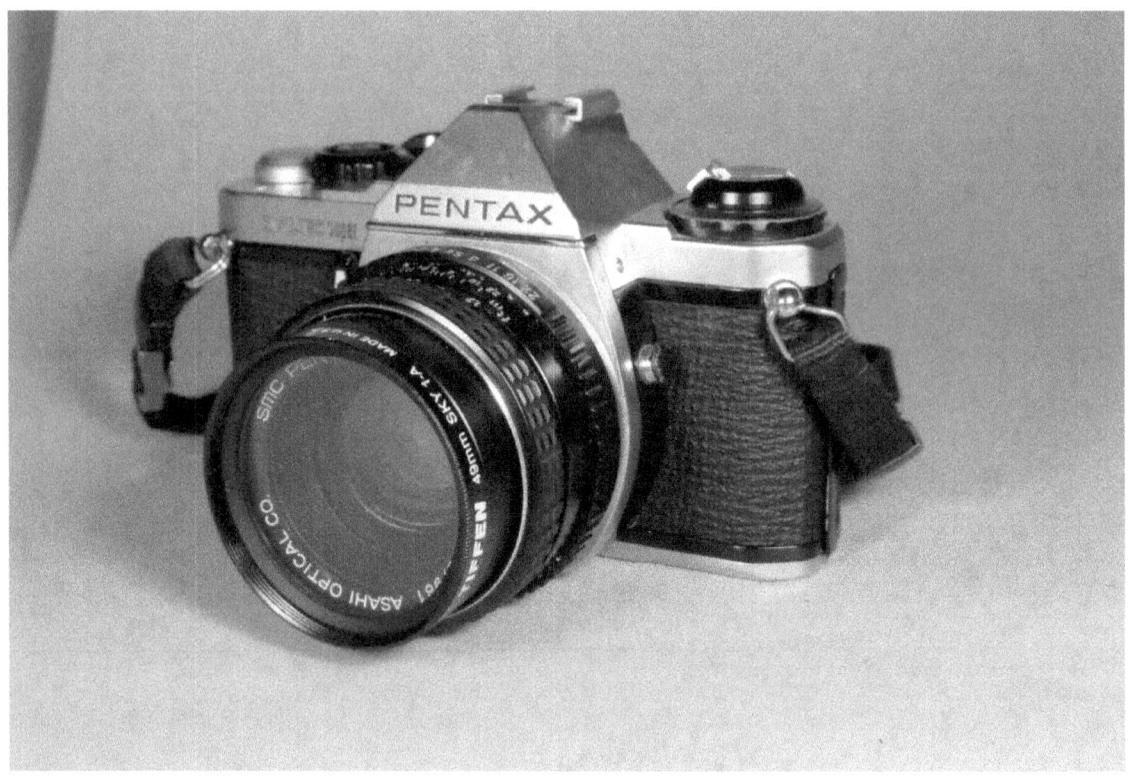

Name: Pentax ME - Super.
Type: 35MM SLR.
Film Size: 35MM.
Year of manufacture: Around 1980.
Manufacturer: Pentax.
Country: Japan.
Shutter settings: 4 seconds – 1/2000. Flash sync at 1/125.
Aperture settings: F/2 – F/22.
Exposure setting: Coupled exposure meter. Aperture priority.
Lens: SMC Pentax-M F/2 50MM. (Standard lens.)
Interchangeable lenses? Yes. K-mount.
How do you focus? Through groundglass in viewfinder, also split image.
Viewfinder: Eye level.
Loading film: Open camera back, thread film into takeup spool.
Automatic film advance? No (manual).
Automatic film rewind? No (manual).
Cable release socket: Yes.
Tripod socket: Yes.
Battery type: LR-44, quantity 2.
Unique features:

Pentax ME - Super

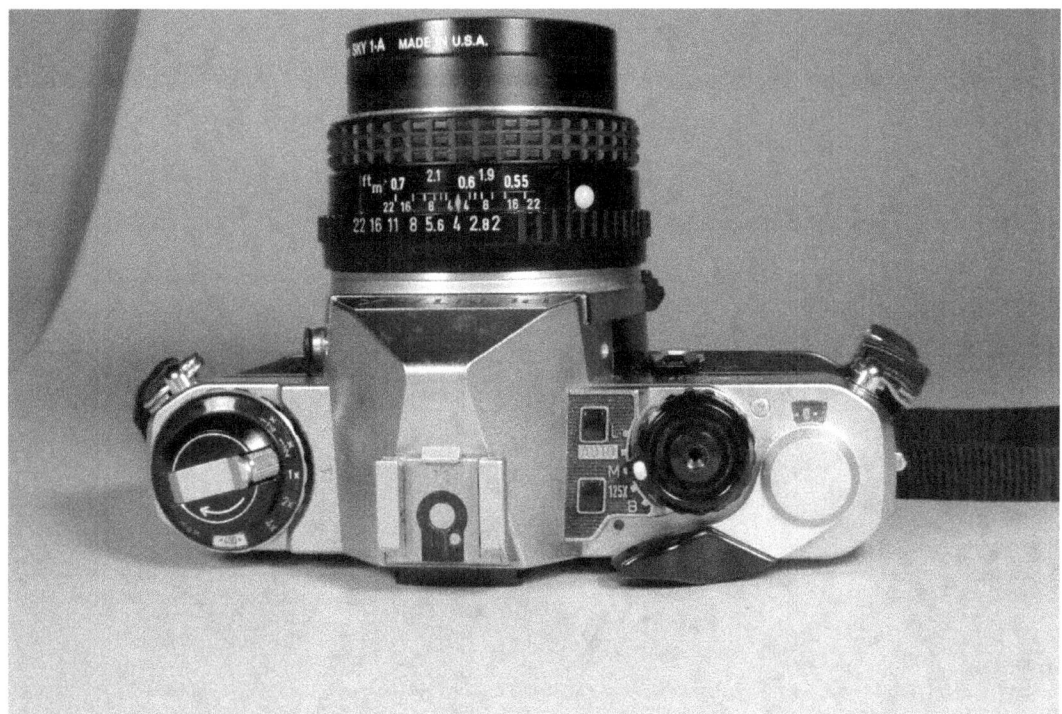

Auto: you select aperture, camera sets shutter speed. 125X is electronic flash sync. "L" locks the shutter release. "M" allows you to select a specific shutter speed shown in the viewfinder. Buttons to select shutter speed are at left of mode select wheel.

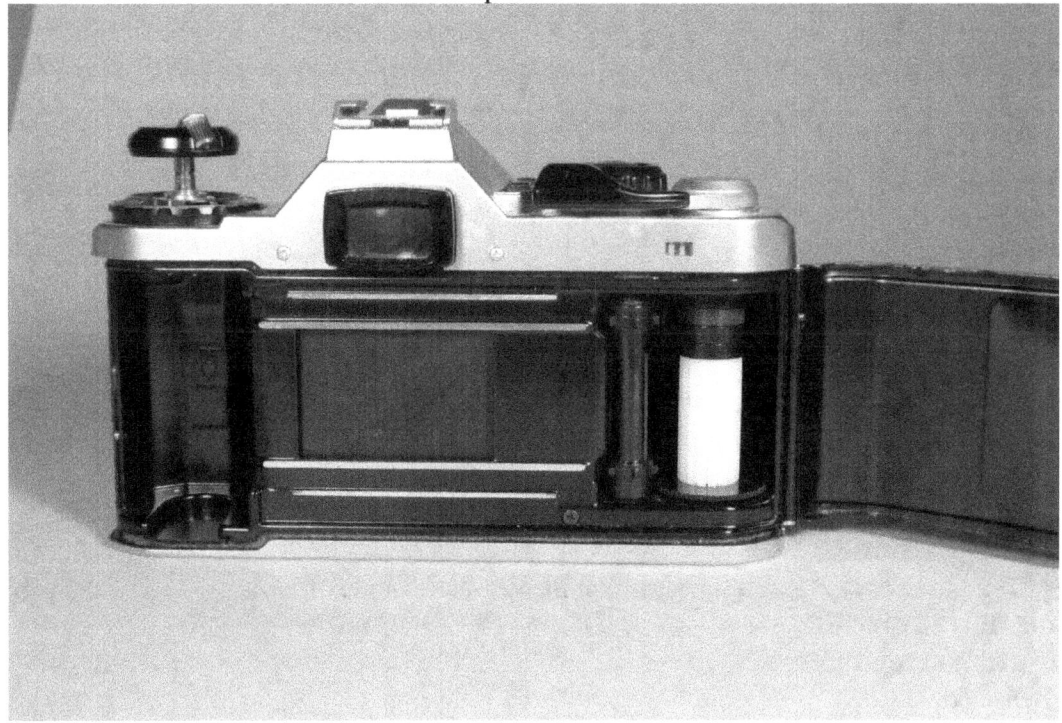

Pentax ZX-30

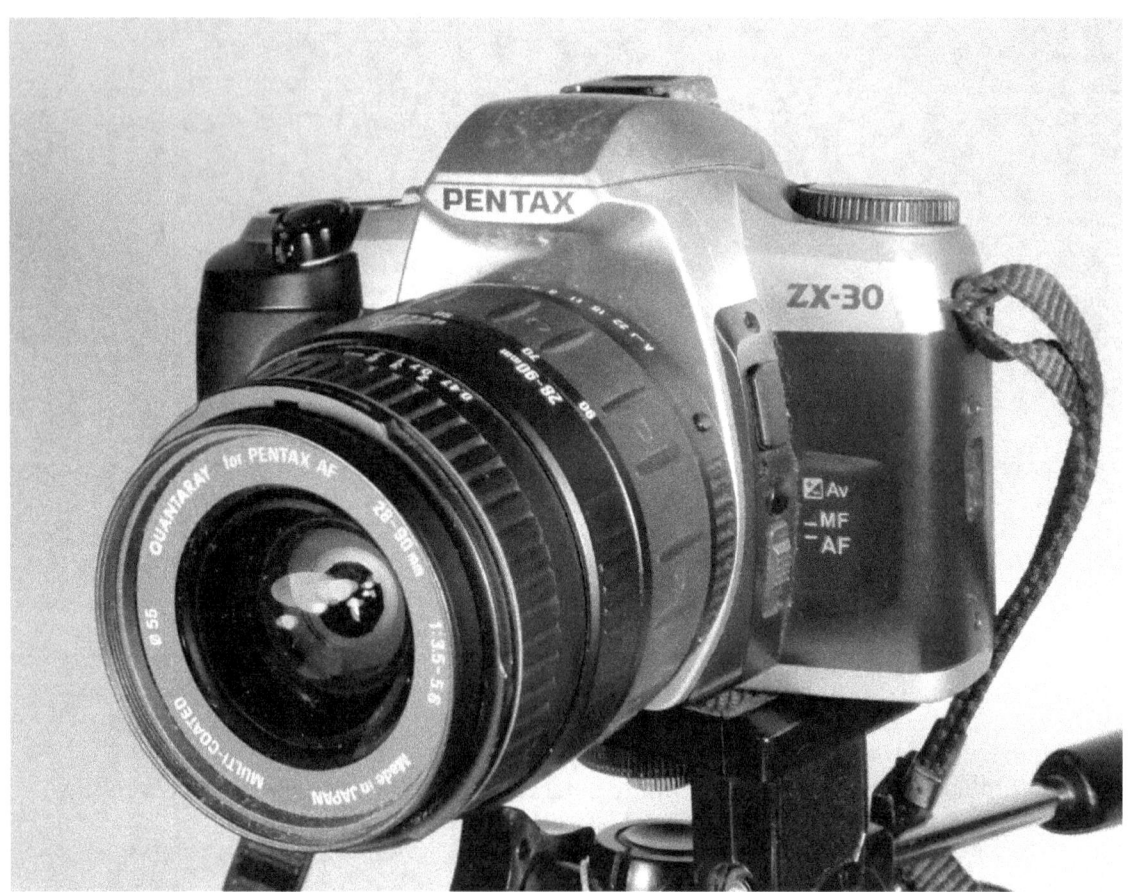

Name: Pentax ZX-30.
Type: 35MM SLR.
Film Size: 35MM.
Year of manufacture: 2000.
Manufacturer: Pentax.
Country: Japan.
Shutter settings: B, 1/30 – 1/2000.
Aperture settings: A, F/3.5– F/22.
Exposure setting: Automatic, metered. (Green operation mode.)
Lens: Lens on camera: Quantaray for Pentax, F/3.5 28 – 90MM.
Interchangeable lenses? Yes.
How do you focus? Autofocus, manually through the lens on ground glass.
Viewfinder: Eye level.
Loading film: Open back, load full cassette, pull film out to index mark.
Automatic film advance? Yes.
Automatic film rewind? Yes.
Cable release socket: No.
Tripod socket: Yes.
Battery type: CR2, 3 volt. Quantity 2.
Unique features: Date back.

Pentax ZX-30

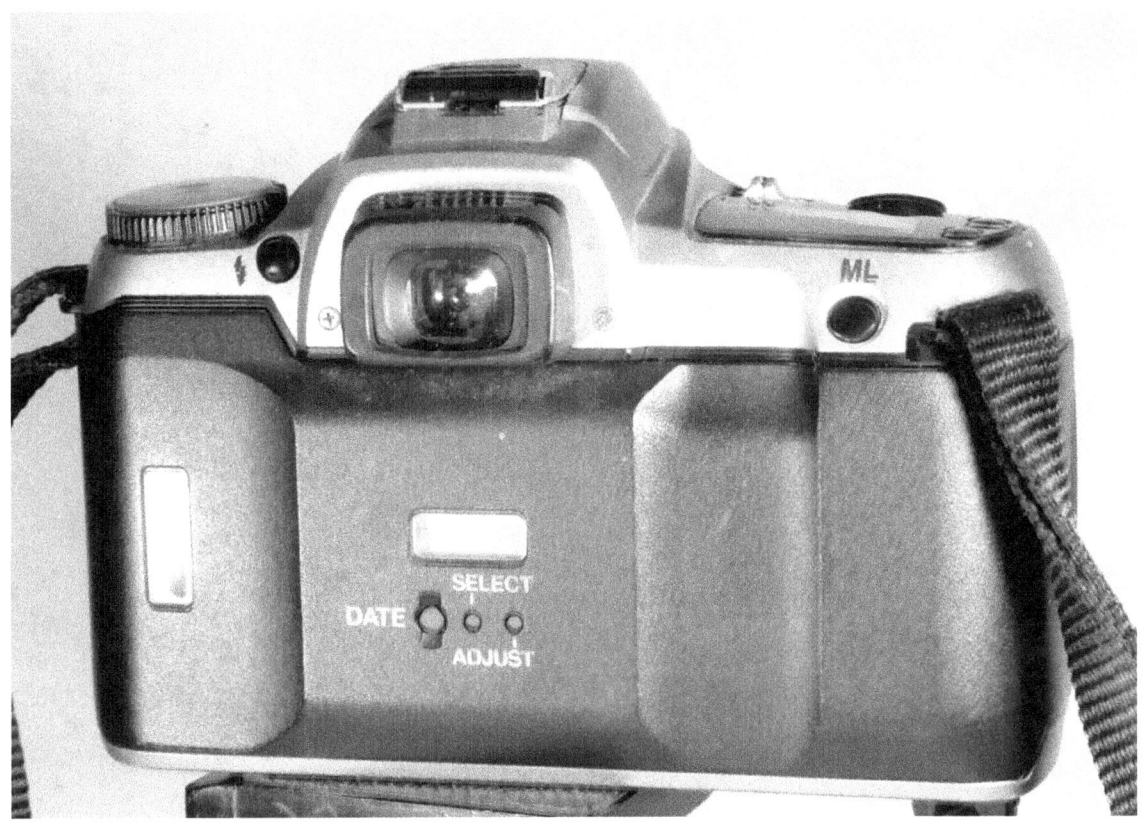

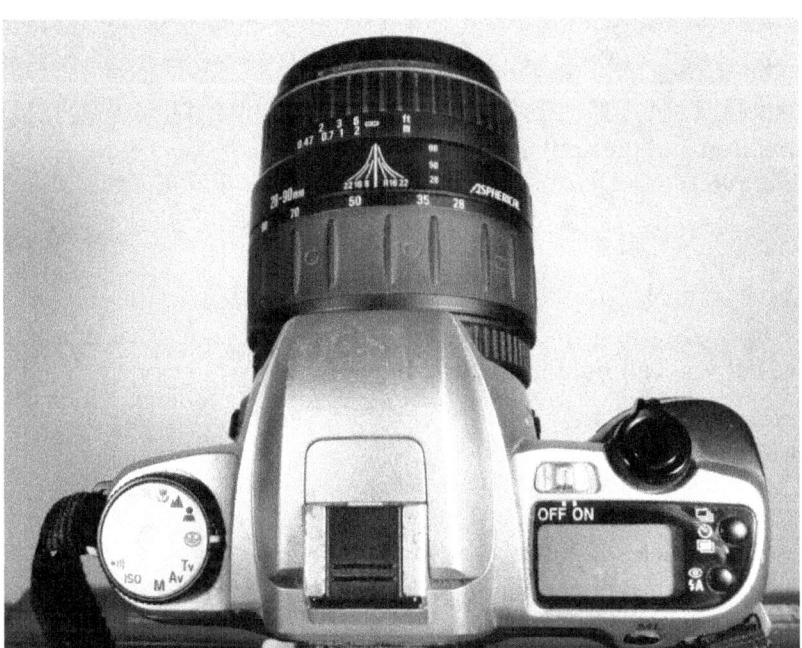

Mode dial on left, LCD panel on right. With the mode dial you select "green" – automatic, portrait, landscape, sports action, close up, night scene, and flash-disabled mode.

Polaroid 230

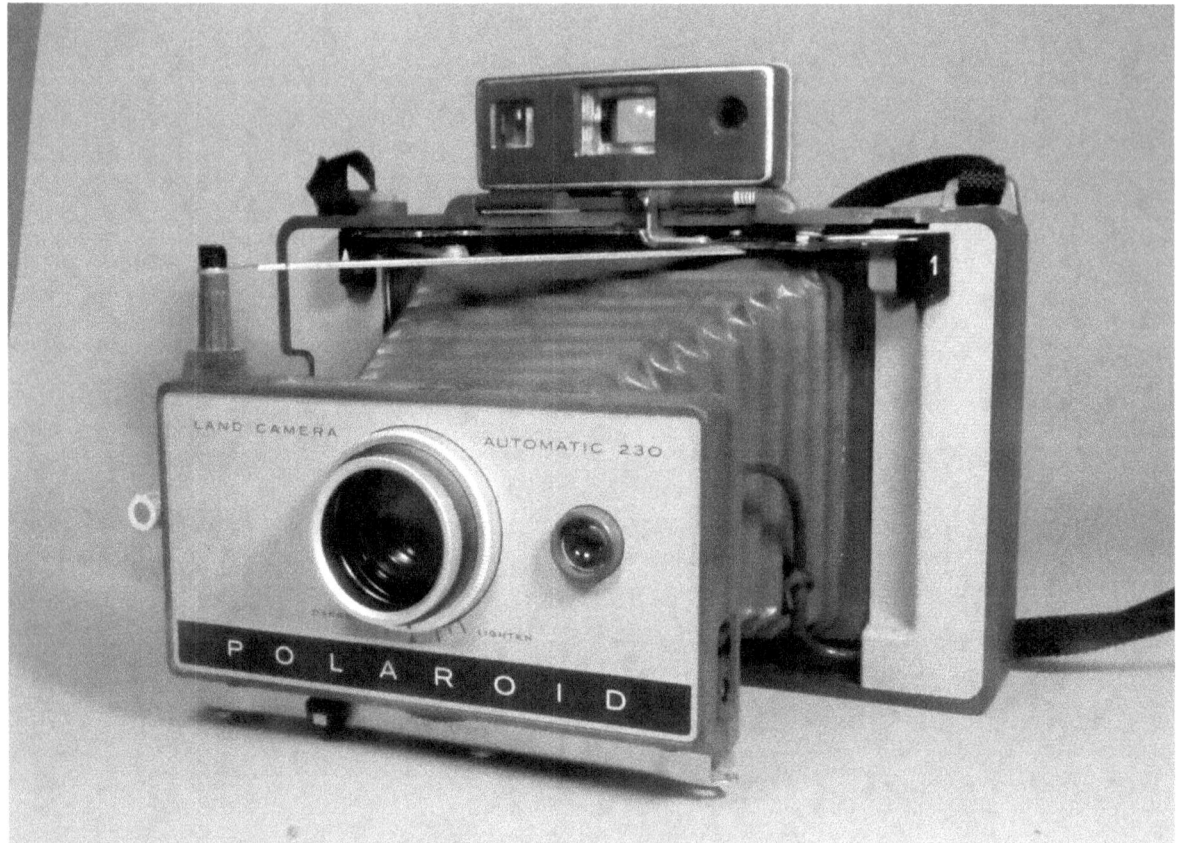

Name: Polaroid 230.
Type: Instant, color or black and white.
Film Size: Film pack, 8 exposures. Type 107 – ISO 3000 Black and White, Type 108, ISO 75 color. Available at Ebay, expired and unusable.
Year of manufacture: Around 1967.
Manufacturer: Polaroid.
Country: USA.
Shutter settings: Not under user control.
Aperture settings: Not under user control.
Exposure setting: Automatic, but you can lighten or darken exposure.
Lens: F8.8 114MM.
Interchangeable lenses? No.
How do you focus? Auxiliary rangefinder attachment.
Viewfinder: Eyelevel.
Loading film: Open back, load film pack. Method specific to this camera.
Automatic film advance? Pull tab to start development, advances film.
Automatic film rewind? N/A.
Cable release socket: No.
Tripod socket: No.
Battery type: Eveready 531 4.5 V, Exell A19PX
Unique features: Instant photo.

Polaroid 230

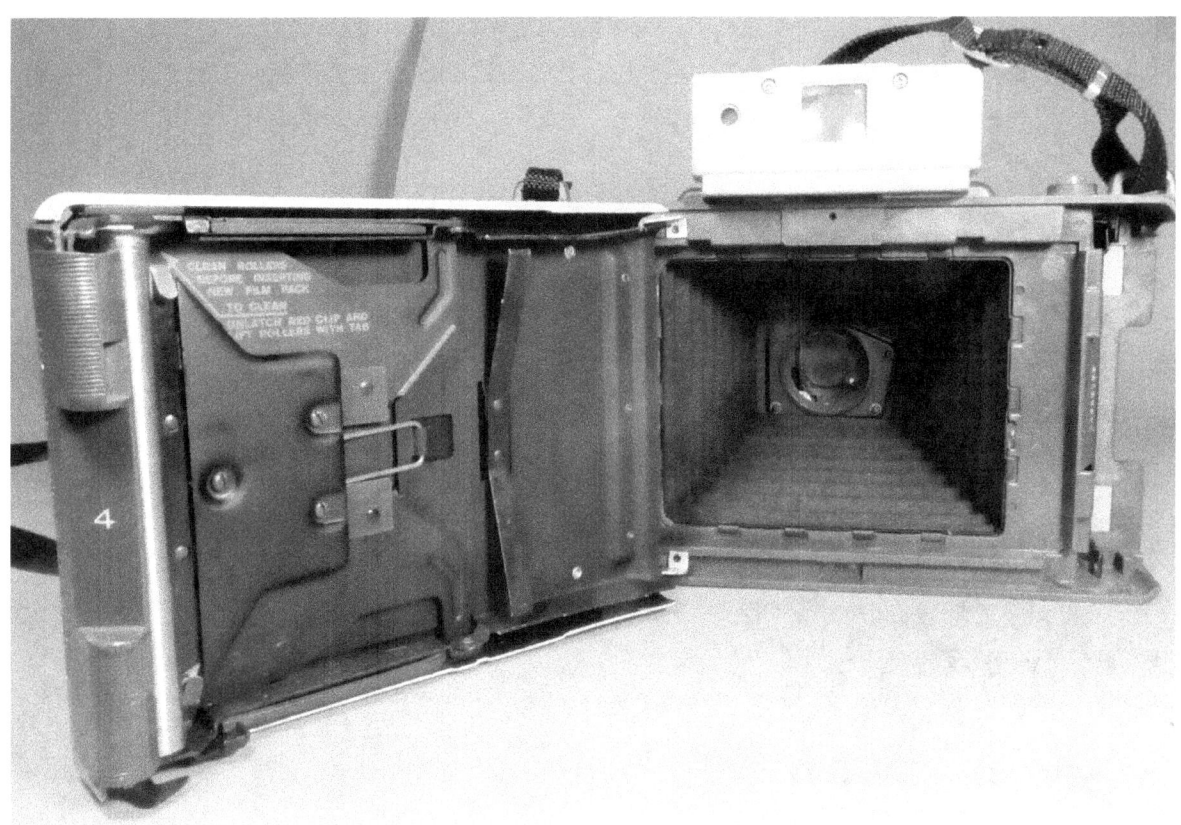

Polaroid Highlander, Model 80A

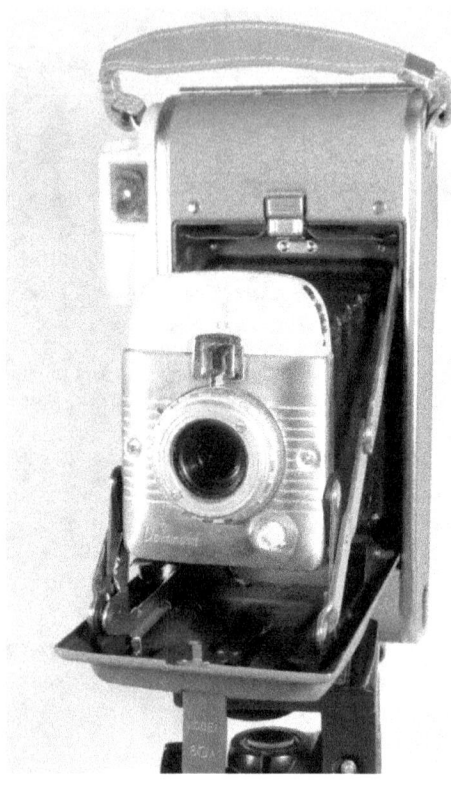

Name: Polaroid Highlander, Model 80A.
Type: Folding bellows, instant print.
Film Size: Specific to this camera. No longer available.
Year of manufacture: 1957.
Manufacturer: Polaroid Corporation.
Country: USA.
Shutter settings: B, I. (Actual shutter speed varies from 1/25 – 1/100.)
Aperture settings: Exposure Values (EV) from 11 – 18.
    An *equivalent* exposure for EV11 is 1/30 at F/8,
      with each additional EV corresponding to +1 F stop.
Exposure setting: Manual.
Lens: 100MM, F/8.8.
Interchangeable lenses? No.
How do you focus? Estimate distance, rotate front lens element.
Viewfinder: Eyelevel.
Loading film: Open back, load film. Specific to this camera and this film.
Automatic film advance? Pull tab to develop, advances film.
Automatic film rewind? N/A.
Cable release socket: Yes.
Tripod socket: Yes.
Battery type: None.
Unique features: Instant black and white photo.

Polaroid Highlander, Model 80A

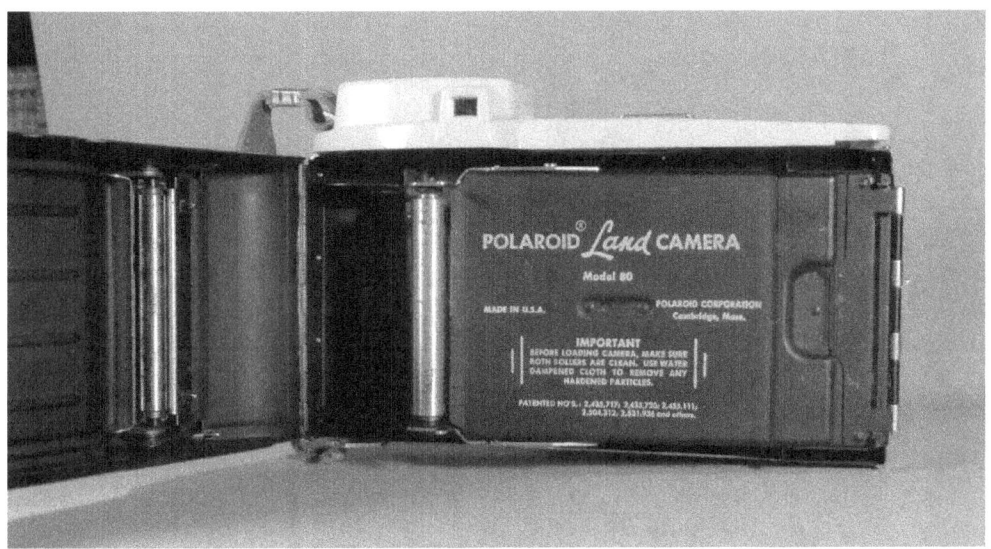

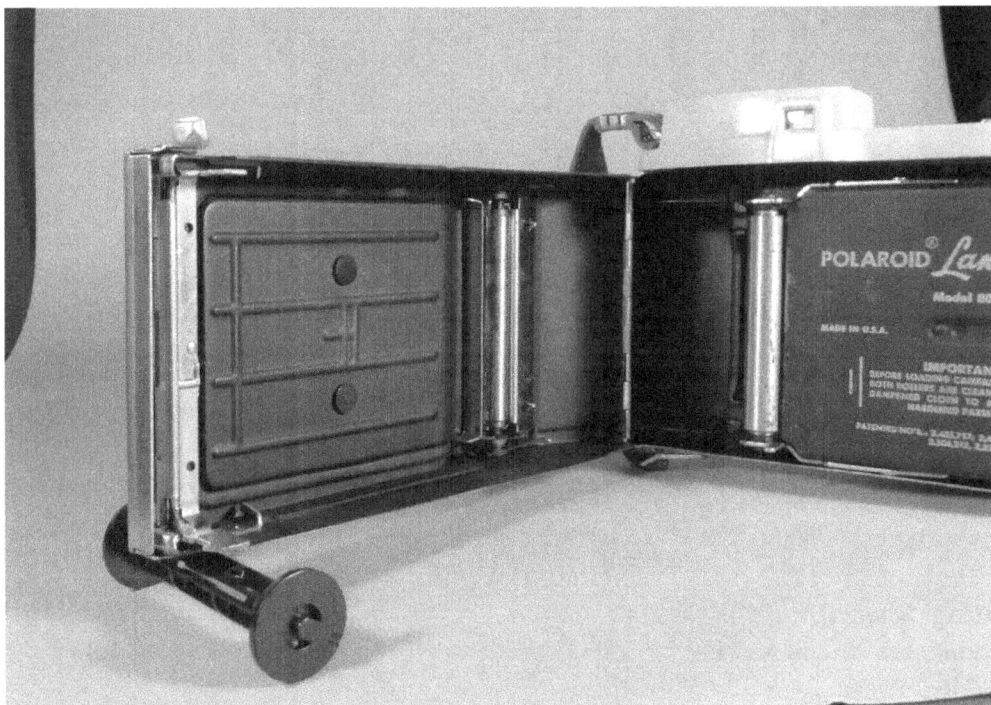

The take up reel is not needed. It is included in each film pack.

Practica FX

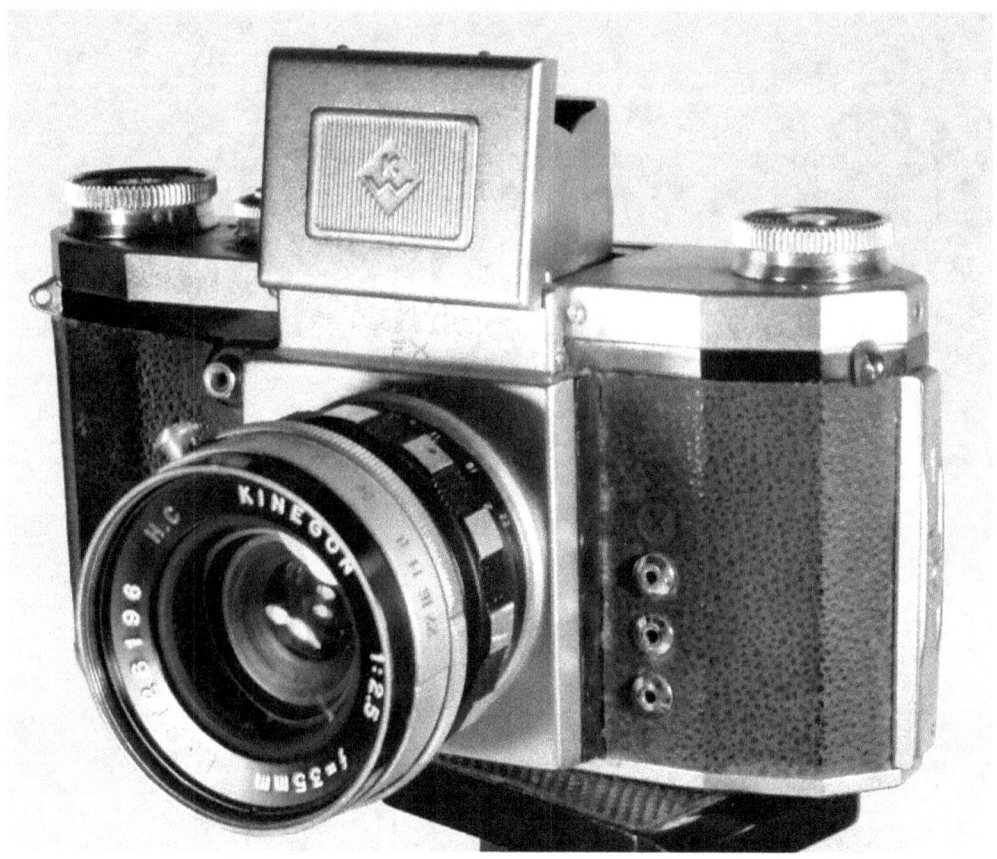

Name: Practica FX.
Type: 35MM SLR.
Film Size: 35MM.
Year of manufacture: 1952.
Manufacturer: VEB KameraWerke.
Country: Germany.
Shutter settings: B, 1/2 – 1/500.
Aperture settings: F/3.5– F/22.
Exposure setting: Manual.
Lens: Lens on camera is Kinegon F.2.5 35MM.
Interchangeable lenses? Yes.
How do you focus? Focus using ground glass. Magnifier available to assist. Eye level sports finder.
Viewfinder: Waist level, through the lens ground glass.
Loading film: Open back, load full cassette, thread into takeup reel.
Automatic film advance? No (manual).
Automatic film rewind? No (manual).
Cable release socket: Yes.
Tripod socket: Yes.
Battery type: None.
Unique features:

Practica FX

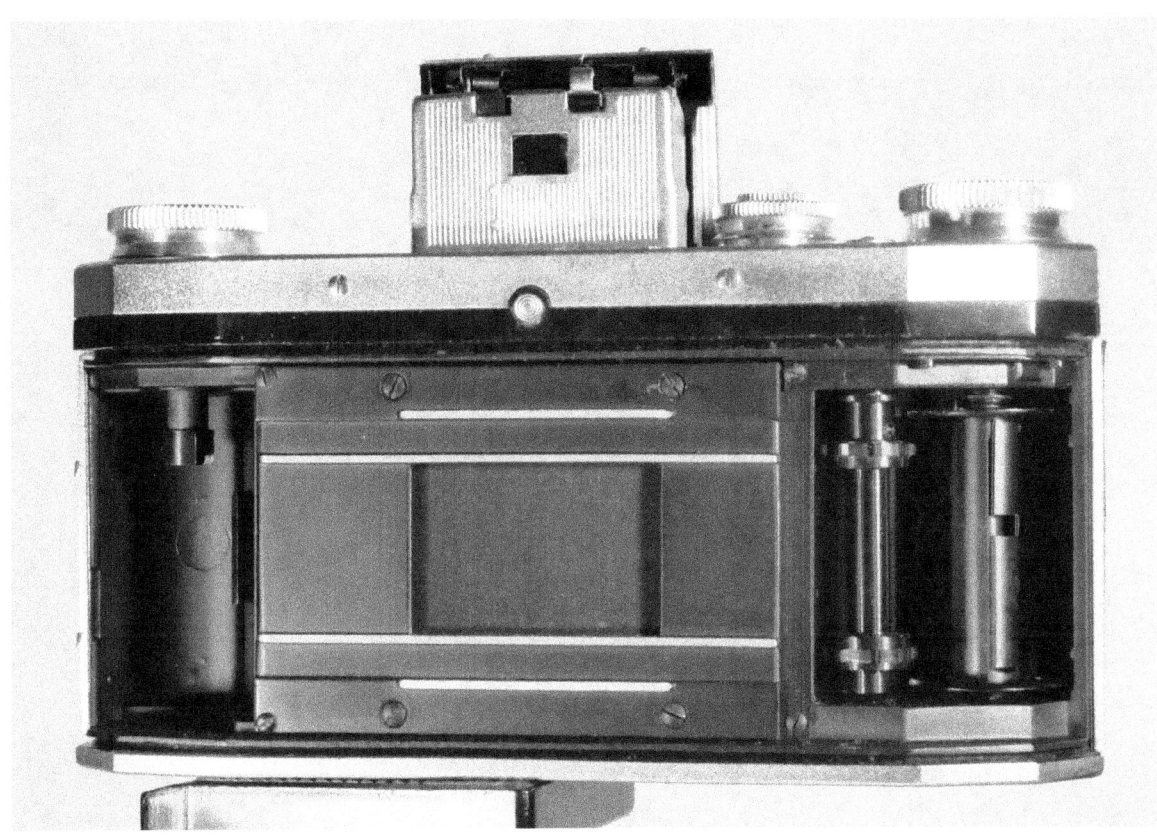

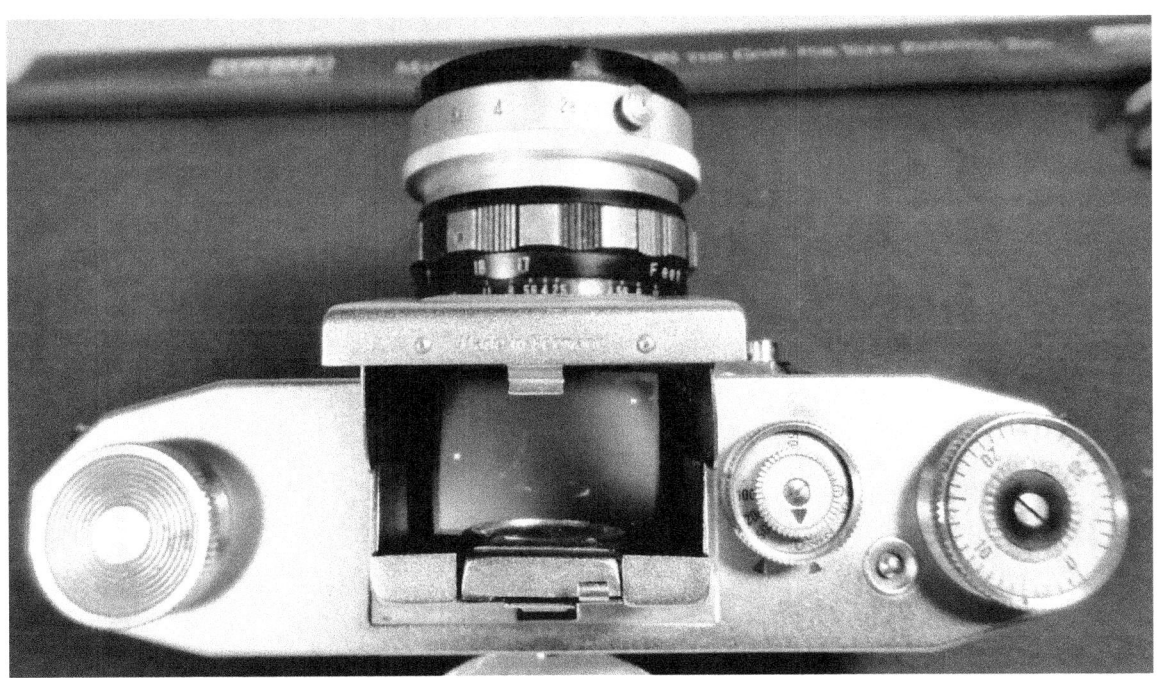

Revere Eight Model Seventy-Seven

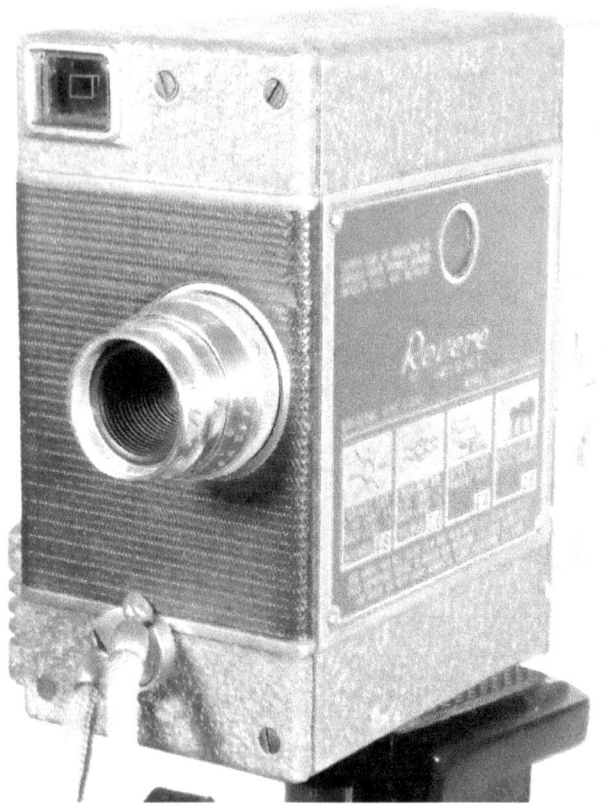

Name: Revere Eight Model Seventy-Seven.
Type: 8MM movie camera.
Film Size: 8MM magazine.
Year of manufacture: Probably 1940s.
Manufacturer: Revere.
Country: USA.
Shutter settings: Not under user control.
Aperture settings: Not under user control.
Exposure setting: Automatic.
Lens: Kodak zoom, 13MM, F/2.7.
Interchangeable lenses? No.
How do you focus? Estimate distance, turn ring on lens.
Viewfinder: Eye level.
Loading film: Open back, load full magazine.
Automatic film advance? N/A.
Automatic film rewind? N/A.
Cable release socket: No
Tripod socket: Yes.
Battery type: None.
Unique features:

Revere Eight Model Seventy-Seven

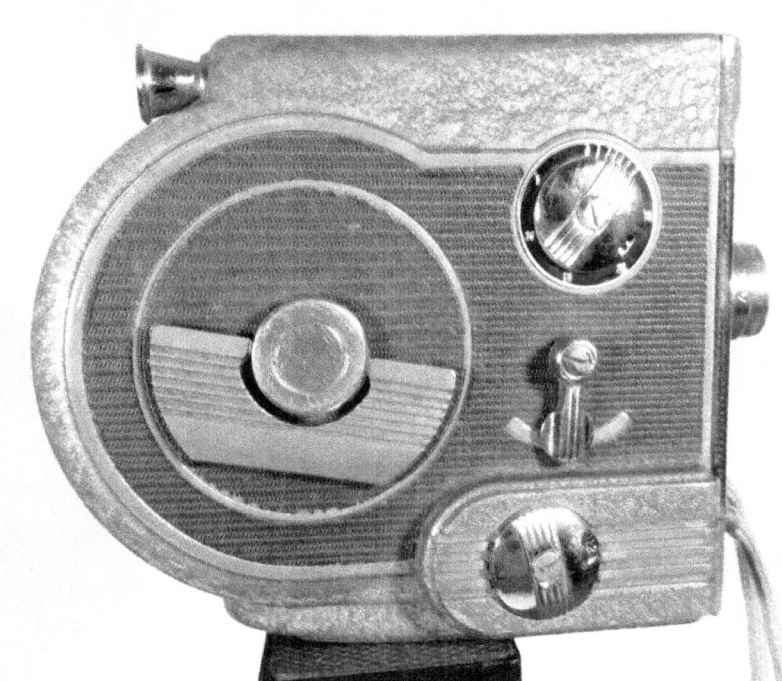

Dials are, clockwise, motor winding key, how many feet of film remain on magazine, shutter release (pull back for movie, push forward for single frame), motor speed selector: 12 or 48. (48 is high speed, for slow motion filming.)

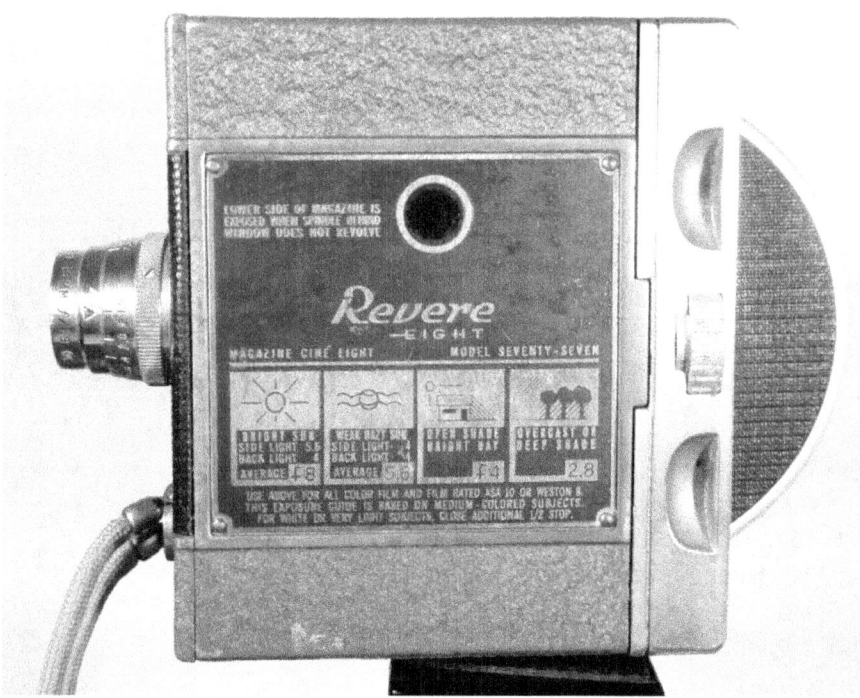

Ricoh 500

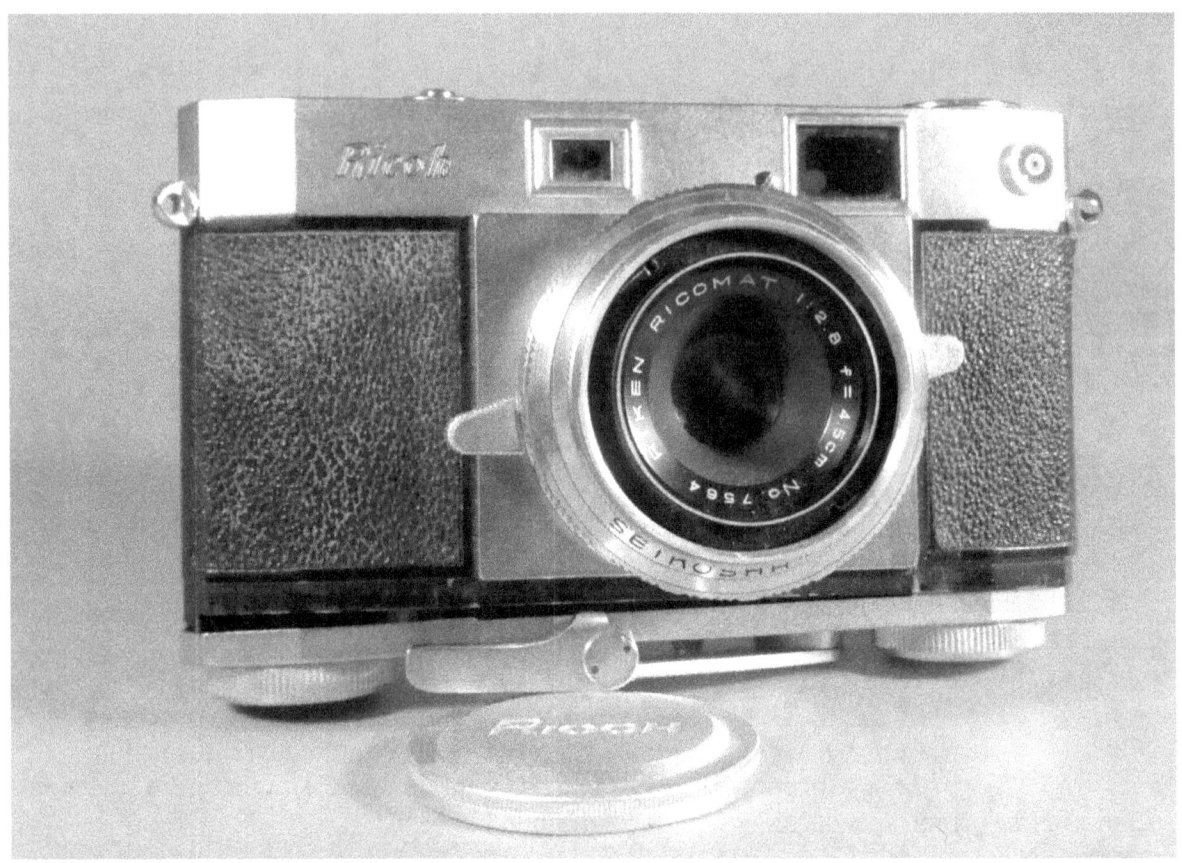

Name: Ricoh 500.
Type: 35MM rangefinder.
Film Size: 35MM.
Year of manufacture: 1957.
Manufacturer: Ricoh.
Country: Japan..
Shutter settings: B, 1 second to 1/500.
Aperture settings: F/2.8 – F/22.
Exposure setting: Manual.
Lens: Ricomat, 45MM.
Interchangeable lenses? No.
How do you focus? Coupled rangefinder.
Viewfinder: Eye level.
Loading film: Open back, load film.
Automatic film advance? No (manual with lever at bottom).
Automatic film rewind? N/A.
Cable release socket: No.
Tripod socket: Yes.
Battery type: LR44W.
Unique features:

Ricoh 500

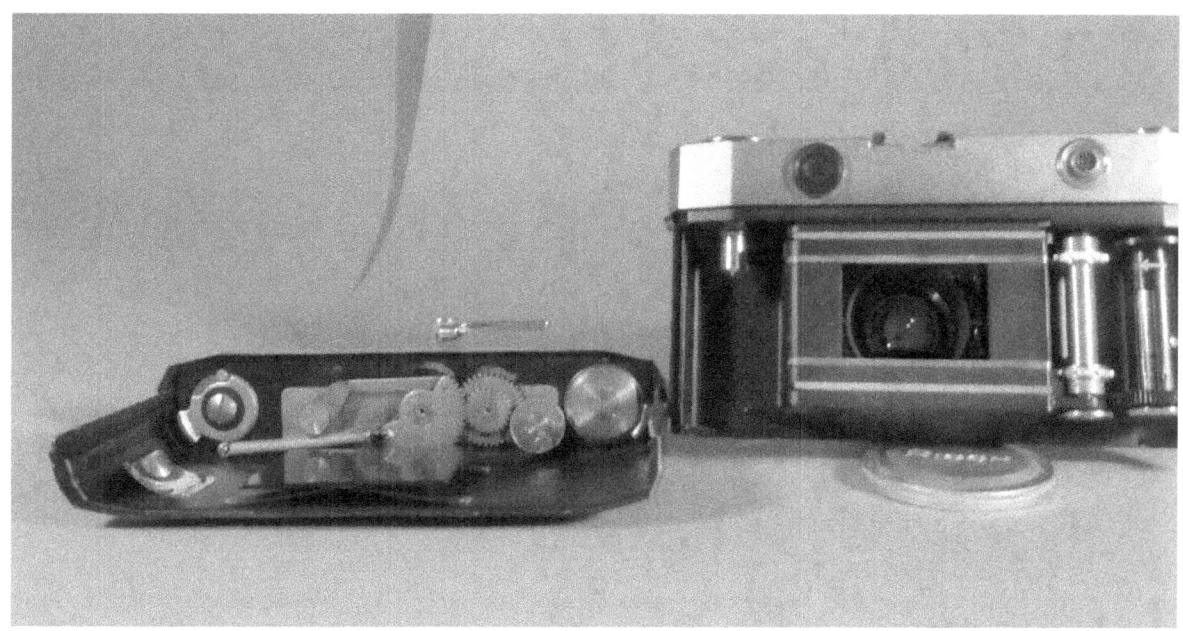

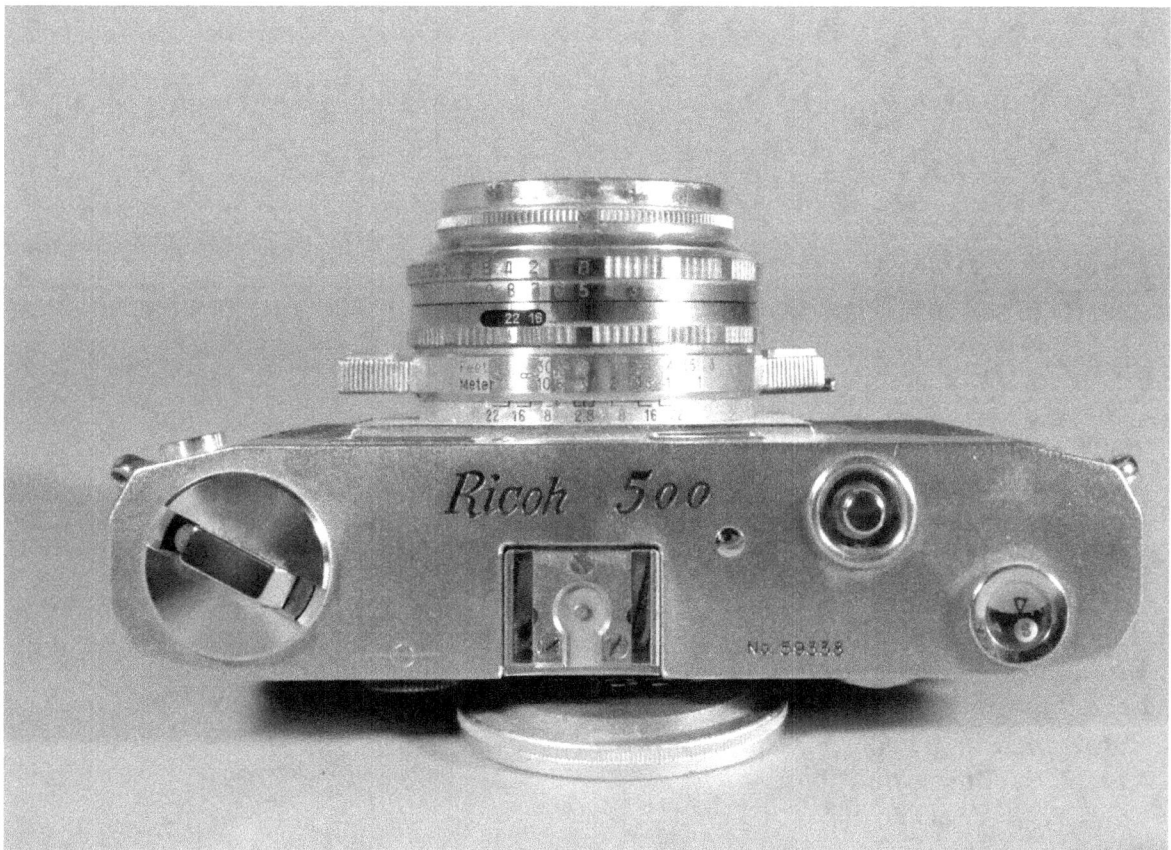

Button on right, front of camera is shutter release. Film counter is shown on right, back of camera.

Spartus

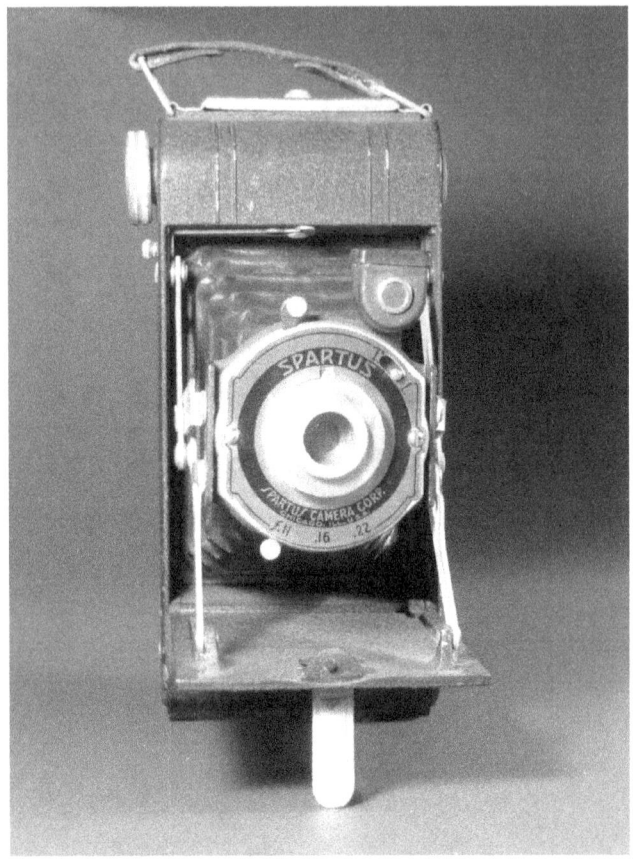

Name: Spartus
Type: Folding rollfilm.
Film Size: 120.
Year of manufacture:
Manufacturer: Spartus.
Country: USA.
Shutter settings: T, I.
Aperture settings: F/11 – F/22.
Exposure setting: Manual.
Lens: Zuiko F/1.7, 42MM.
Interchangeable lenses? No.
How do you focus? Fixed focus.
Viewfinder: Waist level.
Loading film: Open back, insert full roll, thread paper leader onto takeup spool.
Automatic film advance? No (manual).
Automatic film rewind? N/A.
Cable release socket: No.
Tripod socket: No.
Battery type: None.
Unique features:

Spartus

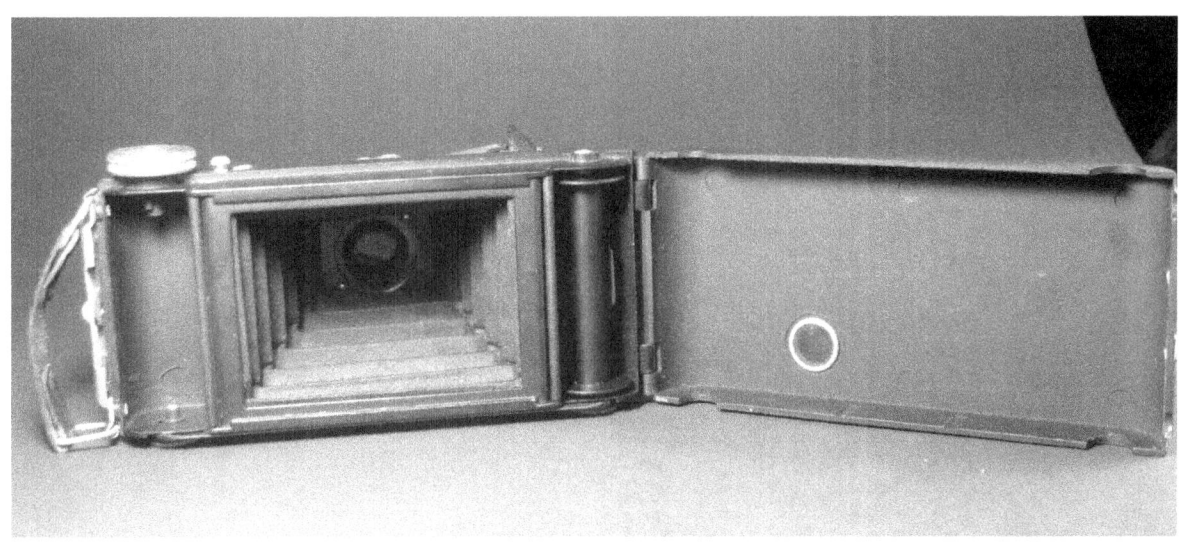

Voigtländer Brillant

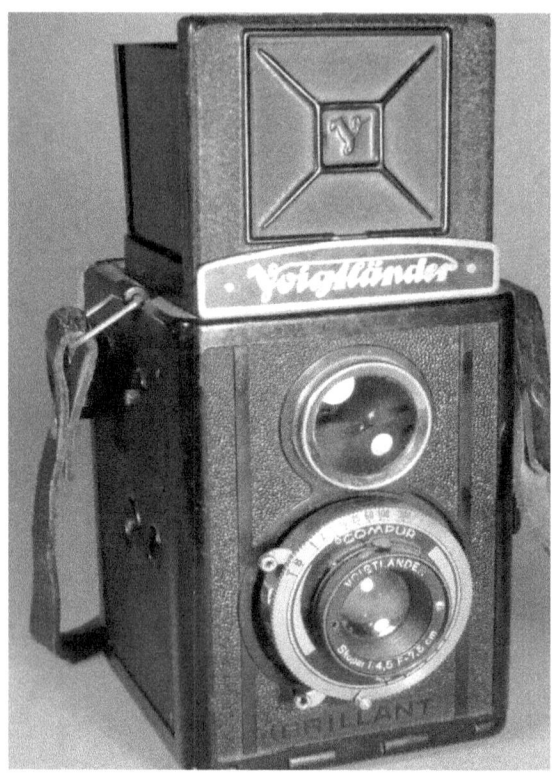

Name: Voigtländer Brillant, model possibly V6.
Type: Twin lens reflex, rollfilm.
Film Size: 120.
Year of manufacture: 1932.
Manufacturer: Voigtländer.
Country: Germany.
Shutter settings: Compur T, B, 1 second - 1/300.
Aperture settings: F/4.5 – 16.
Exposure setting: Manual.
Lens: Skopar 75MM, F/4.5.
Interchangeable lenses? No.
How do you focus? Distance scale on camera lens. Ground glass is fixed focus. You don't see if photo is in focus.
Viewfinder: Waist level.
Loading film: Open back, insert full roll, thread paper leader onto takeup spool.
Automatic film advance? No (manual).
Automatic film rewind? N/A.
Cable release socket: Yes.
Tripod socket: Yes.
Battery type: None.
Unique features:

Voigtländer Brillant

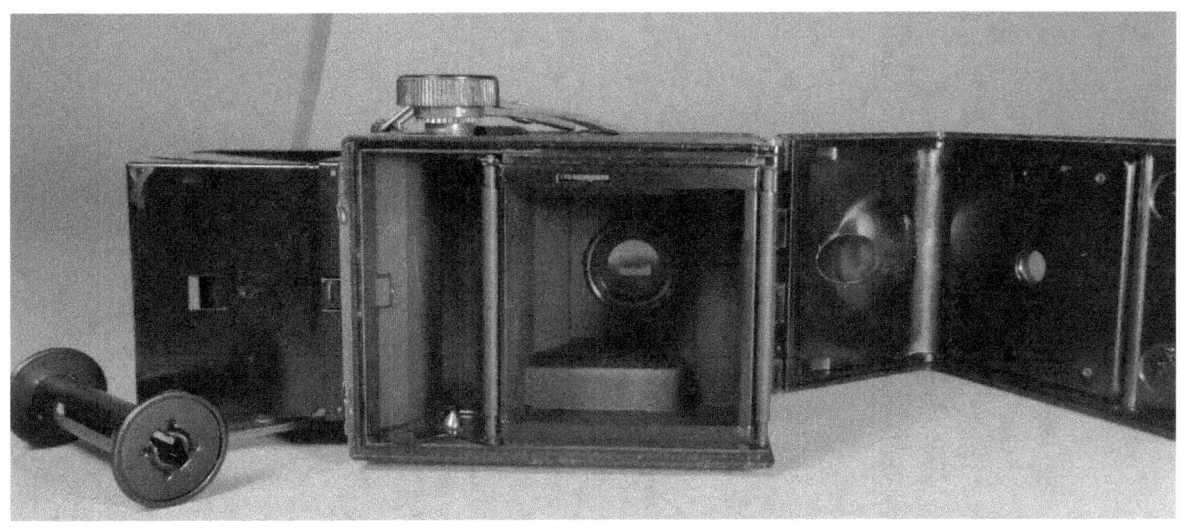

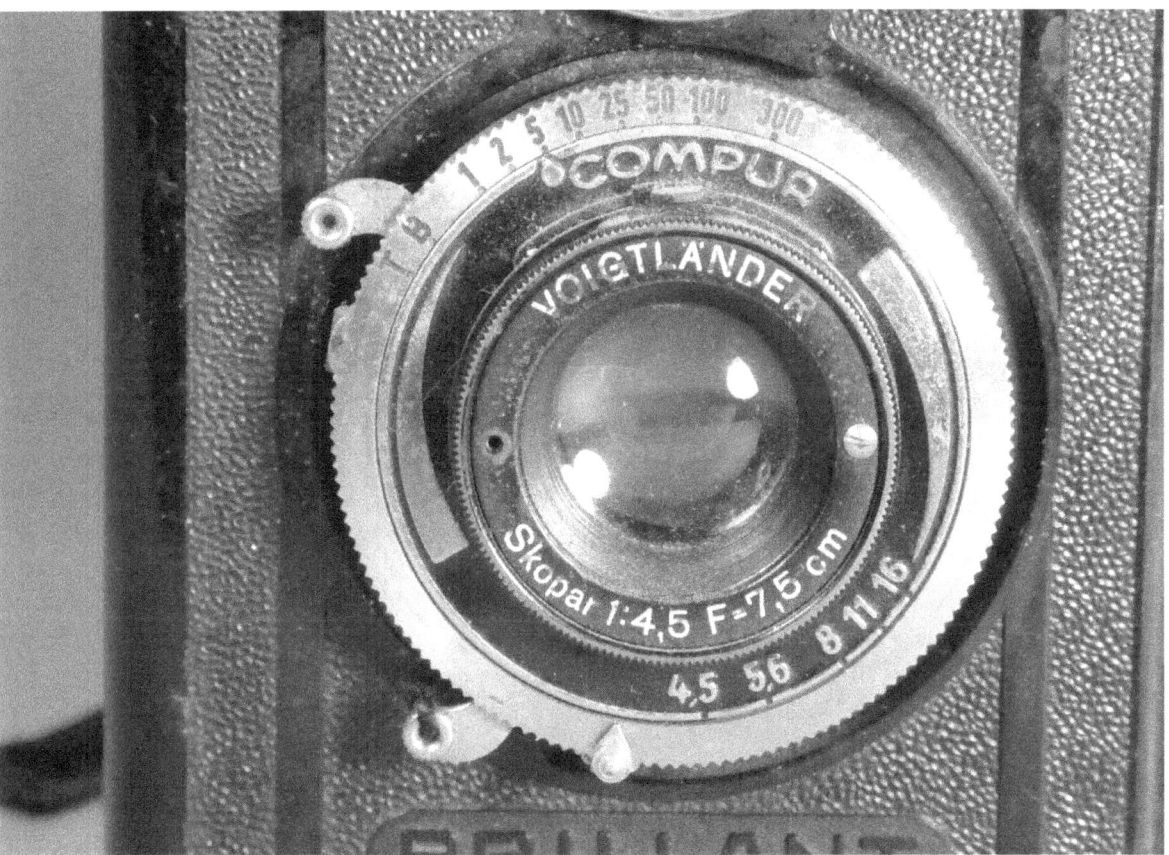

Welmy 35

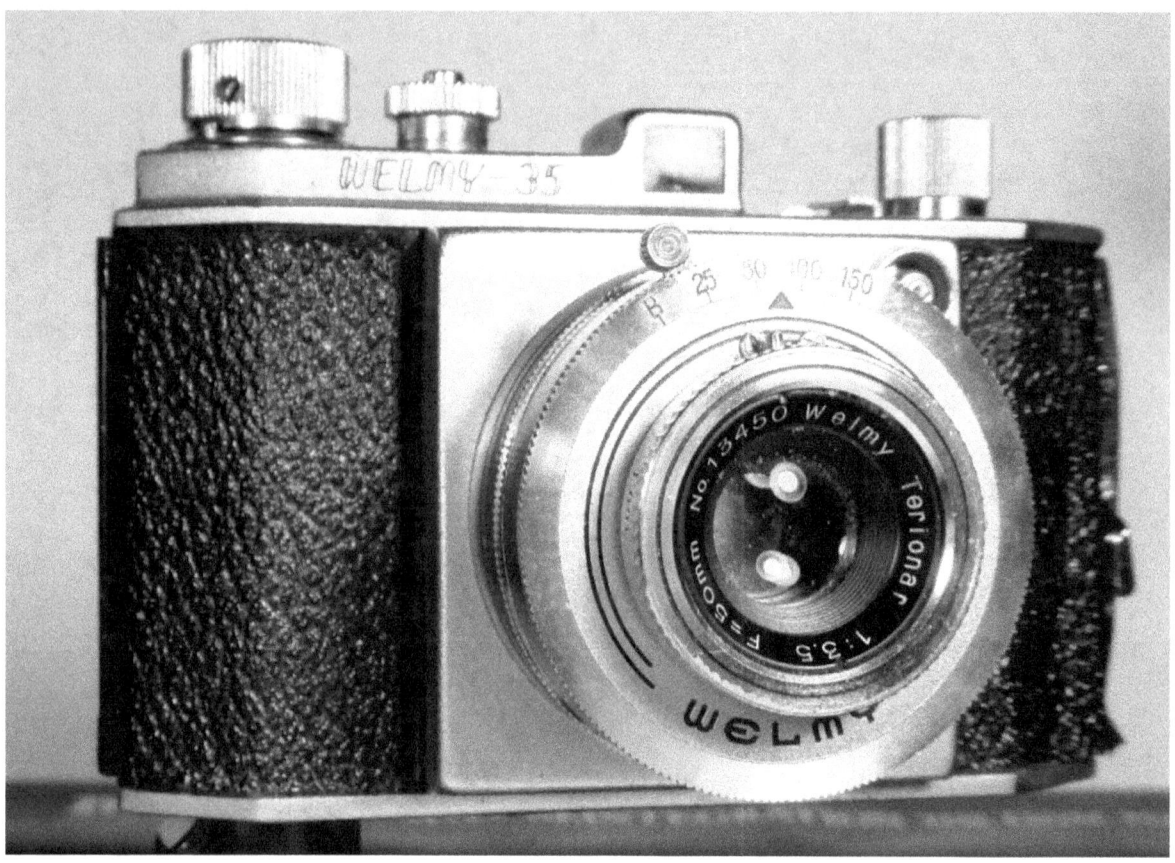

Name: Welmy 35.
Type: 35MM.
Film Size: 35MM.
Year of manufacture: Around 1955.
Manufacturer: Tasei Koki.
Country: Japan.
Shutter settings: B, 1/25, 1/50, 1/100, 1/150.
Aperture settings: F/3.5, 4, 5.6, 8, 11, 16.
Exposure setting: Manual.
Lens: Welmy Terionar F/3.5, 50MM.
Interchangeable lenses? No.
How do you focus? Estimate distance, turn front lens element.
Viewfinder: Eye level.
Loading film: Open back, load full cassette, thread into takeup reel.
Automatic film advance? No (manual).
Automatic film rewind? No (manual).
Cable release socket: No.
Tripod socket: Yes.
Battery type: None.
Unique features:

Welmy 35

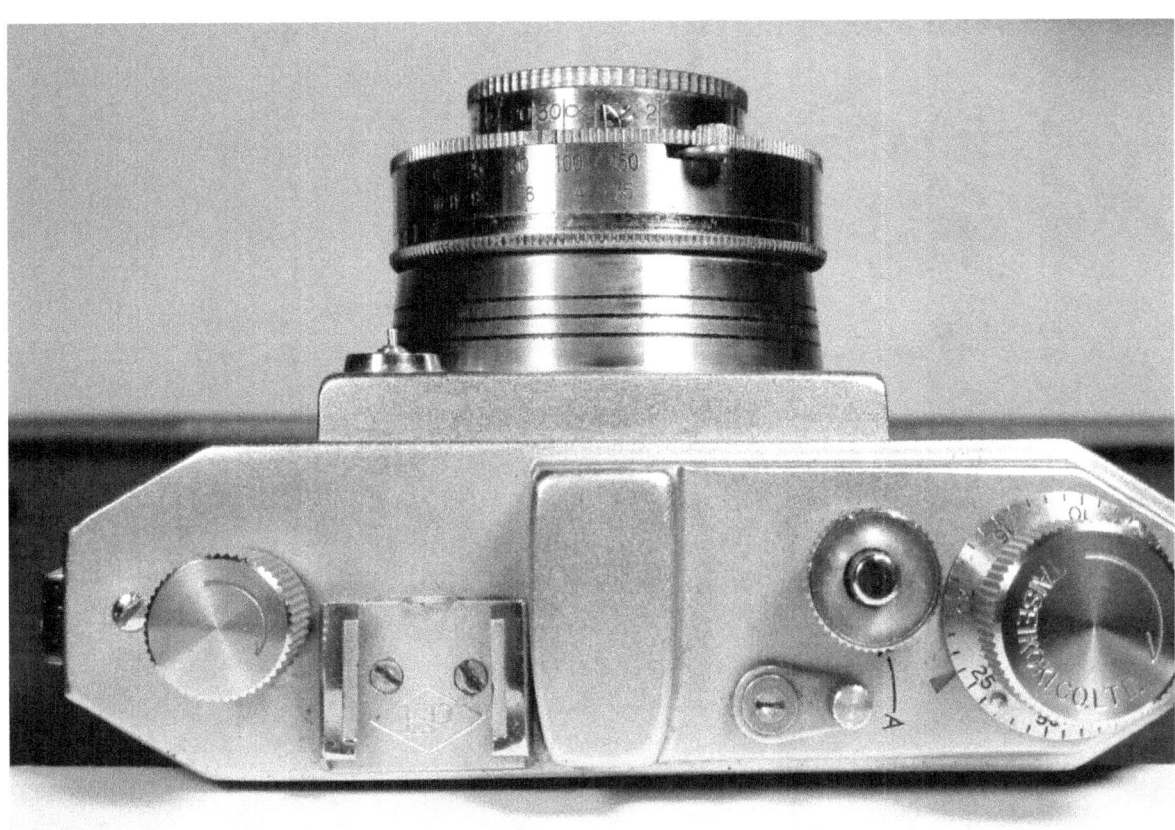

Lever on top of camera, near film advance dial, is used to select "A" film advance, and "R" rewind.

Yashica Mat-124G

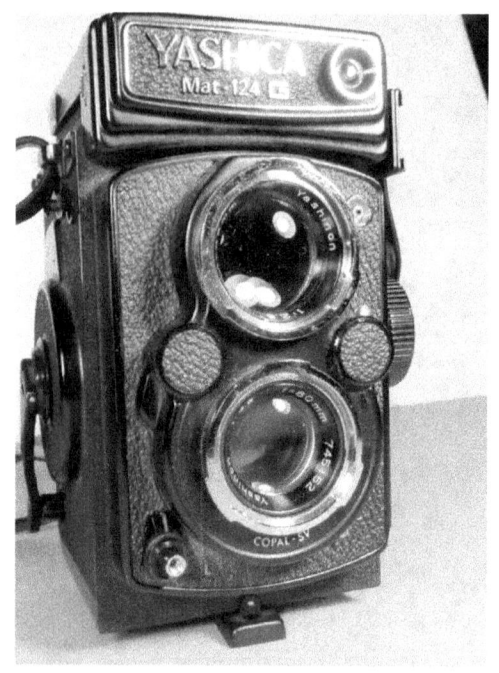 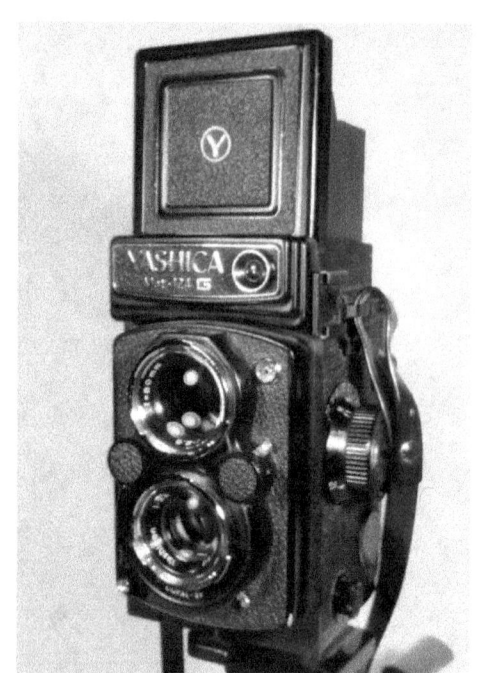

Name: Yashica Mat-124G.
Type: Twin lens reflex, rollfilm.
Film Size: 120 or 220.
Year of manufacture: Mid 1980s.
Manufacturer: Yashica.
Country: Japan.
Shutter settings: Copal-SV B, 1 second - 1/500.
Aperture settings: F/3.5 – 32
Exposure setting: Match needle with exposure meter. Shutter priority.
Lens: Yashinon 80MM, F/3.5.
Interchangeable lenses? No.
How do you focus? Through the lens, turn knob until image is in focus in viewfinder.
Viewfinder: Waist level, eye level sports finder.
Loading film: Open back, insert full roll, thread paper leader onto takeup spool.
Automatic film advance? No (manual).
Automatic film rewind? N/A.
Cable release socket: Yes.
Tripod socket: Yes.
Battery type: PX-13B or EPX-13 1.3 V mercury.
Unique features: Will take film sizes 120 and 220. You just slide the film pressure plate to choose film size.

Yashica Mat-124G

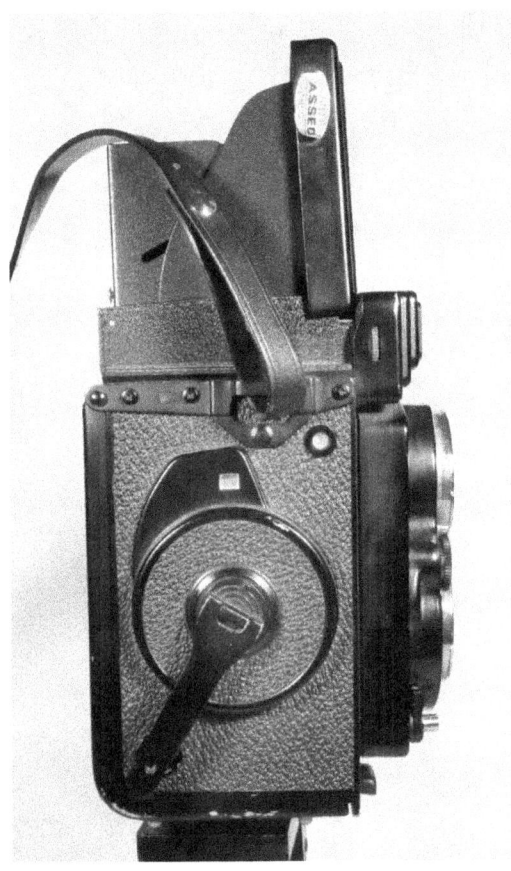

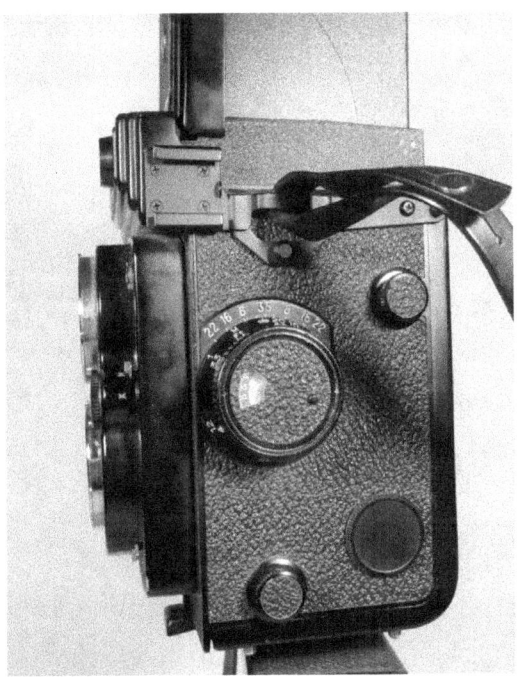

Focusing dial with depth of field scale.

Index

126 film, 42, 70
16MM film, 64, 66
616 film, 6, 54
620 film, 56
8MM magazine, 108
8MM, double 8, 26
A-116 film, 58
Advanced Photo System, 18, 30
Agfa Ansco Corp, 6
Agfa Apotar lens, 8
Anastigmat lens, 28, 56
Anaston lens, 46
APS, 18, 30
Auto Miranda lens, 76
Autofocus, 18, 68, 78, 80, 82, 86, 88, 90, 100
Box camera, 32, 36
Canon lens, 16
Carl Zeiss lens, 22
Cintar, 12, 14
Compur shutter, 114
Copal shutter, 118
Date back, 44, 100
Double 8, 26
Doublet lens, 54
Ektanar lens, 30, 38, 42, 48
Ektar lens, 44, 52
Exposure values, 104
Folding, 8, 48, 54, 56, 58, 102, 104, 112
Fujinon lens, 24
Hawk-Eye, 36
Ihagee, 22
Instant print, 102, 104

Index

Kinegon lens, 106
K-mount lens, 96, 98
Lumar lens, 10
Magicube, 42
Mamiya Sekor lens, 60
Mamiya-Kominar, 62
Minolta lens, 74
Movie camera, 26, 38, 40
Nikkor lens, 82
Point and Shoot, 44, 50, 80, 86, 88, 90, 94
Polaroid, 102, 104
Quantaray lens, 100
Rangefinder, 12, 14, 28, 46, 52, 60, 62, 70, 84, 110
Ricomat lens, 110
Rokkor lens, 64, 66, 70
Rollfilm cameras, 6, 10, 20, 32, 36, 54, 56, 58, 112, 114, 116, 118
Schneider-Kreuznach Reomar lens, 48
Sekor lens, 60
Skopar lens, 114
SLR, 16, 22, 72, 74, 76, 82, 92, 96, 98, 100, 106
Subminiature, 64, 66
Super 8, 38, 40
Tasei Koki, 116
Tokina lens, 72
Twin lens reflex, 10, 20, 34, 114, 118
VEB KameraWerke, 106
Velostigmat lens, 20
Welmy Terionar lens, 116
Wollensak Velostigmat lens, 26
Yashinon lens, 118
Zuiko lens, 84, 92, 94, 112